Math **Diagnosis** and **Intervention** S

Booklet D: Measurement, Geometry, Data and Probability in Gr

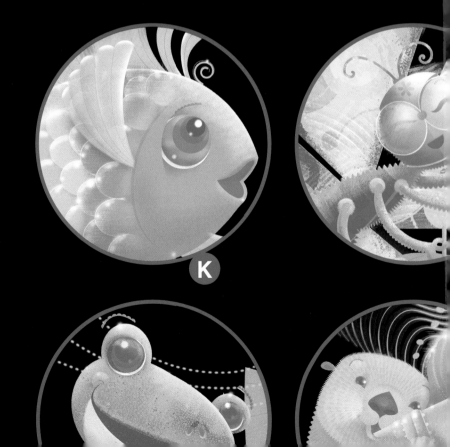

K

Better Serving Teens through School Library–Public Library Collaborations

Recent Titles in
Libraries Unlimited Professional Guides for Young Adult Librarians
C. Allen Nichols and Mary Anne Nichols, Series Editors

Serving Urban Teens
Paula Brehm-Heeger

The Teen-Centered Writing Club: Bringing Teens and Words Together
Constance Hardesty

More Than MySpace: Teens, Librarians, and Social Networking
Robyn Lupa, Editor

Visual Media for Teens: Creating and Using a Teen-Centered Film Collection
Jane Halsall and R. William Edminster

Teen-Centered Library Service: Putting Youth Participation into Practice
Diane P. Tuccillo

Booktalking with Teens
Kristine Mahood

Make Room for Teens!: Reflections on Developing Teen Spaces in Libraries
Michael G. Farrelly

Teens, Libraries, and Social Networking: What Librarians Need to Know
Denise E. Agosto and June Abbas, Editors

Starting from Scratch: Building a Teen Library Program
Sarah Ludwig

Serving Teen Parents: From Literacy Skills to Life Skills
Ellin Klor and Sarah Lapin

Teens Go Green!: Tips, Techniques, Tools, and Themes in YA Programming
Valerie Colston

Serving Latino Teens
Salvador Avila

BETTER SERVING TEENS THROUGH SCHOOL LIBRARY– PUBLIC LIBRARY COLLABORATIONS

Cherie P. Pandora and Stacey Hayman

Libraries Unlimited Professional Guides for Young
Adult Librarians Series
C. Allen Nichols and Mary Anne Nichols, Series Editors

LIBRARIES UNLIMITED

AN IMPRINT OF ABC-CLIO, LLC
Santa Barbara, California • Denver, Colorado • Oxford, England

Copyright 2013 by ABC-CLIO, LLC

Library of Congress Cataloging-in-Publication Data

Pandora, Cherie.
  Better serving teens through school library-public library collaborations / Cherie Pandora and Stacey Hayman.
      pages cm. — (Libraries unlimited professional guides for young adult librarians series)
  Includes index.
  ISBN 978-1-59884-970-7 (pbk.) — ISBN 978-1-59884-971-4 (ebook) 1. Libraries and teenagers—United States. 2. Young adults' libraries—United States.
3. School libraries—United States. I. Hayman, Stacey. II. Title.
  Z718.5.P36 2013
  027.62'6—dc23   2013018497

ISBN: 978-1-59884-970-7
EISBN: 978-1-59884-971-4

17 16 15 14 13   1 2 3 4 5

This book is also available on the World Wide Web as an eBook.
Visit www.abc-clio.com for details.

Libraries Unlimited
An Imprint of ABC-CLIO, LLC

ABC-CLIO, LLC
130 Cremona Drive, P.O. Box 1911
Santa Barbara, California 93116-1911

This book is printed on acid-free paper ∞

Manufactured in the United States of America

For Greg and Michael who taught me how to
see the world with new eyes and for my husband,
Jeff, who supports me in everything I do.

—Cherie

A first book requires a thank you to the first important
people in my life. In memory of my Mom and Dad;
she was a strong lady with a wonderful sense of humor
and he was the smart cookie who chose her.

—Stacey

CONTENTS

SERIES FOREWORD

We firmly believe that teens should be provided equal access to library services, and that those services should be equal to those offered to other library customers. This series supports that belief. One of the challenges we both faced when working as teen librarians was the practical difficulties surrounding our efforts to work with our local schools. We are very excited about *Better Serving Teens through School Library–Public Library Collaborations* as the newest addition to our series. Cherie Pandora and Stacey Hayman have provided information and real-life examples of how to overcome those challenges to better serve teens.

We are proud of our association with Libraries Unlimited/ABC-CLIO, which continues to prove itself as the premier publisher of books to help library staff serve teens. This series has succeeded because our authors know the needs of those library employees who work with young adults. Without exception, they have written useful and practical handbooks for library staff.

We hope you find this book, as well as our entire series, to be informative, providing you with valuable ideas as you serve teens and that this work will further inspire you to do great things to make teens welcome in your library. If you have an idea for a title that could be added to our series, or would like to submit a book proposal, please email us at bittner@ abc-clio.com. We'd love to hear from you.

Mary Anne Nichols
C. Allen Nichols

PREFACE

We are writing this book from two different viewpoints, with each of us commenting on the work of the other and adding examples from our own experiences. Our goal is to make this a practical tool full of suggestions useful to librarians, those fresh out of graduate school as well as those veteran librarians who mentor the newest members of our profession. The chapters don't need to be read in numerical order but can be browsed or selected as the reader's curiosity is peaked by a certain topic. We hope that you will enjoy referring back to this book over and over again. Stacey Hayman has worked at Rocky River Public Library (Ohio) for over 15 years, serving first as the teen librarian and now as a reference librarian. Cherie Pandora served as the high school librarian and library coordinator for Rocky River City Schools for 25 years until her retirement in 2010. We began our collaborative efforts decades ago and are confident that our experiences will be of help to you. Stacey starts some chapters, where her expertise is superior; and Cherie adds her thoughts, comments, and experiences. Cherie starts other chapters with Stacey doing likewise. As you begin reading the different chapters, we're pretty sure you'll be able to tell who began the chapter and who applied the finishing touches. Or maybe you won't. You'll just have to read on to see, won't you? Like any of our collaborations this has been a shared experience; as we continue to learn from each other and our colleagues, we wanted to make sure we were creating the best guidebook possible for our readers. We hope you enjoy reading this as much as we enjoyed writing it.

ACKNOWLEDGMENTS

I was mentored by some wonderful librarians, administrators, and professors when I began my career in the Parma City Schools—special thanks to Pat Hinkle, Janet Rowland, Ralph Grieco, and Dr. Mary Kay Biagini who taught me how to serve both students and teachers. To Nancy Levin who helped me to create the outline, proposal, and chapter headings that started this venture, thank you for your willingness to collaborate on any project! I cannot name all of the wonderful librarians and teachers who made my job at Rocky River High School a real joy, but I owe them a debt of gratitude and have tried to mentor others to honor their unforgettable assistance. To the Library La-Las, Book Club, and my sister, Karen, I offer great thanks for your ideas, opinions, and support for this project! To our editors, C. Allen Nichols, Mary Anne Nichols, and Barbara Ittner, thank you for your patience with us!

Cherie P. Pandora

It's wonderful to have people believing so strongly that you can do something, even when you're pretty sure they're wrong. In this case, it was I who was wrong! And so I'd like to send a big, huge shout-out of a THANK YOU to all the people in my life who told me it wasn't crazy to think I could write a book. (Would it be possible that you wonderful people might consider this acknowledgement as my formally written note of apology?) I'd also like to thank Cherie for asking me if I'd like to be her coauthor and to all our editors for keeping the faith.

Stacey Hayman

INTRODUCTION

WHAT WE CAN DO NOW!

Librarians who work with school-age children in all types of libraries share a long history of collaboration. They promote a love of books and reading and support each other's literacy programs. Public librarians visit schools in their communities regularly to issue library cards and to promote special programming. Included in these promotions are the public library's own extensive summer programming and summer reading activities, which include giveaways and prizes that celebrate reading of *any* kind. The easy camaraderie that results benefits all students and both institutions. 'Tweens are often proud to be known as avid readers, and show eagerness to take part in these out-of-school activities at their local library. Teen and school librarians dealing with 'tweens and teens need to rely on each other for support to accomplish their common goals—encouraging leisure reading, providing assistance with information-seeking and retrieval skills, and encouraging the use of appropriate databases. This collaboration strengthens the relationship, and allows them to support each other as resources in the field, ultimately benefitting patrons at both libraries.

Whether the public library calls their specialist in literature for adolescents a teen librarian or a young adult (YA) librarian, these professionals can be one of the greatest allies school librarians have in the process of selecting quality materials and encouraging reading. It is important for the librarians to make this connection, and reach out to their counterparts. Secondary school librarians can promote the inclusion of their public library colleagues into the school's summer reading selection process. As older students become inundated with increasing loads of homework, out-of-school activities, sports, and jobs, librarians and teachers need to work together to identify books that are most interesting to these patrons, and that "speak" to their needs to grab their attention.

Although our missions are different, school and public libraries share similar goals, similar budget difficulties, and, often, common patrons. School and public librarians are both trying to reach teen patrons to help them to grow both intellectually and emotionally. We want them to read (in multiple formats) and to succeed, to paraphrase an old American Library Association (ALA) slogan. If librarians did not coin the term "life-long learners," then we were among the early adopters who embraced it and worked to instill this love of learning in our young patrons. While the term has become a cliché, it is no less valid a goal. Former ALA president (2005–2006) and author Michael Gorman refers to this collaboration of librarians as the foundation on which all other librarianship exists; yet he also warns that budgetary problems will not soon disappear (Gorman 2005, 5).

Why not take advantage of our differences by identifying the strengths that each type of librarian brings to the collaboration? One of our goals could and should be to use these similarities, and differences, to the mutual benefit of both our shared customers *and* our distinct agencies. What better way to solve the dilemma of providing service at little cost than to work with a kindred soul at the nearby library? Let's work together to open the eyes of library directors and school administrators to the benefits that these partnerships provide.

Now more than ever, it's important that we create a symbiotic relationship—that cooperative relationship in which two groups work together for the benefit of both groups. Think of this project—of reaching out to another library and its librarians—as a means of gaining professional partners who will help you to provide more of everything for your patrons—more expertise, more resources, and more fun.

PURPOSE OF THIS BOOK

Our goal for this book is to help you, the librarian, regardless of the type of library in which you work, to successfully collaborate to maximize your program and better serve teens. The central questions this book answers are "How can we share our resources, our expertise, and our facilities to best serve our common patrons and our communities? How can we work together to benefit *all* of our patrons, as well as our bosses? How can we prepare students to better utilize those extra hours in the public library? How can we assist the public library staff by providing personnel or facilities to help them with *their* programs? How can public libraries determine what schools need in order to help fill gaps in school resources? How do we cross-promote these programs and ensure that the publicity gathered is positive? Finally, how do we make sure that such publicity reaches the eyes and ears of our directors, our administrators, our board of trustees, and our board of education?

For overworked librarians, this book provides practical ideas that can be used to initiate, or to add to, their existing repertoire of programs. Besides the many ideas and success stories, you'll also find anecdotes about the struggles and missteps we've made so that you can avoid them. You will also be forewarned about some of territorial attitudes you may encounter, so that you can attempt to avoid them altogether. Finally, you'll find guidelines and checklists that will help you deal with the differing calendars and work hours that can often challenge collaborations.

SCOPE

This book covers the who, why, what, and how of school–public library collaborations. It is intended as a starting point from which you can build. The chapters cover the following topics.

Chapter 1: What Is Collaboration, Why We Should Do It, and How to Get Started: How can we share our expertise? How do we convince another librarian to work with us? Can we assist our partner librarians in gathering appropriate materials for a school project or to promote their own programming? Some reasons for collaborating with our colleague librarians as well as some ideas for selling these projects to your directors and administrators are found here. If you are unsure where to start, you might want to look at the "Checklist for Successful Collaboration" that ends DelGuidice's (2009, 39) article. A short listing of the research on public school library collaboration is provided so that you have facts and research to bolster your case with your supervisors. If you worry about convincing your director or administrator of the benefits of this partnership you'll want to read the first page of the article coauthored by Krista Taracuk, former School Librarian at Thomas Worthington High School (OH) and Heidi Fletcher, Director of the Mount Sterling Public Library

(Ohio). Their article entitled "Building Partnerships" lists eight separate benefits that can be gained through such cooperative efforts (Taracuk and Fletcher 2009, 36).

Chapter 2: Professional Projects: Have you ever served on a committee together? As a start you can volunteer to serve on each other's strategic planning committee. If one of you works on a state or national committee, your counterpart may be the perfect person to serve as a sounding board or advisor for you. If you have a library advisory board we recommend that you ask your counterpart to serve as a member of this vital group. Besides bringing expertise this colleague can serve as an advocate for your project to your board and also back at their home library.

Chapter 3: Programs: One of the fun parts of the job will be discussed here—connecting our patrons with books and programs that are just plain enjoyable. These activities may include booktalks, summer reading promotions, and the marketing of reading and literacy as a fun activity. Sample topics for special joint programs are provided as well.

Chapter 4: Celebrate Reading!: Both types of libraries promote reading as a valuable leisure reading activity. Cross-signage, at both agencies, can help to promote summer reading and programs for each library. A timeline of special weeks that celebrate reading is included in Appendix A.

Chapter 5: Summer Reading: Summer reading is a wholly different process in each type of library. How can we improve the process? Here we include a best practice timeline, decision-making help, and suggestions for making changes to existing listings without "breaking the bank" of either library.

Chapter 6: Author Visits: A how-to guide that provides you with a list of all the decisions you need to make when planning an author's visit to your library. Cross-promotion and a checklist to help you plan a visit are included in this chapter. Sharing resources and promoting each other's projects is good for both libraries and both sets of patrons. It can also serve as a great way to publicize and promote your libraries to your boards and administrators.

Chapter 7: Poetry Slams: What do you do if you want to sponsor a poetry slam? We provide you with a list of resources, suggestions, and advice from a public library that has held poetry slams for over a decade. From the school perspective, we share the process, the pitfalls, and a list of suggestions, including what to do and what to avoid, when planning an open mike poetry slam at the school. We also provide suggestions for providing music for your event for little or no cost.

Chapter 8: Technology and Social Networking: To connect with our Millennial patrons, those between the ages of 13 and 29 (http://pewre

search.org/pubs/1437/millennials-profile), we need to understand these tools and provide programming that meets their interests and their needs. Whether our topic is the safe use of social networking sites, digital citizenship, or gaming, we need to learn and serve our teens via Web 2.0 tools while planning for Web 3.0 programming.

Chapter 9: Homework Help: Communication between school and public libraries can help students to maneuver through homework, problem assignments, and research papers. Suggestions are made as to how to showcase your work to parents and teachers as well as to students.

Chapter 10: Teen Advisory Boards: Book clubs and teen boards at either agency can be cross-promoted through displays at both libraries and public announcement (PA) notices in the schools. Blogs, wikis, and chat can be an additional means of communicating with and receiving suggestions from teens and 'tweens.

Chapter 11: Budget/Finance: Who pays for the collaborative programs that you devise? Some projects require no money. Some will require items that are not provided in your budget such as food or facility rental fees. Providing the public library with auditorium or classroom space at the local school can be provided at no cost *when* you collaborate.

Chapter 12: Grants: Both types of libraries have more needs, and wants, than they have operating money. Working together to create, and prioritize, a wish list of projects, collaborating on research and writing grants can help to solve the problem of too little money. Supporting each other through the writing of letters of support is one more way that we can help each other. This is often a "**no cost**" means of supporting each other's programs in order to create dynamic plans for teen patrons.

Chapter 13: Resource Sharing: Booktalks and/or team teaching classes are two ways to bring public librarians into the school. These activities not only provide students with twice as many resources but also they introduce nonlibrary users to a friendly face, a name, and a reason to step into the local library. Sharing ideas and suggestions for collection development can support the needs of our common patrons, the students, while also meeting the needs of their parents and teachers.

Chapter 14: Professional Development: Public libraries often provide wonderful FREE training on word processing, spreadsheets, presentation, and graphic design programs. Their training staff creates sessions to help adults to use the databases that are available to the public; perhaps they would provide a specialized workshop for your teaching staff. They are often the first to offer special programs on newer technologies such as eBooks, podcasting, and using the functions of handheld mobile devices. In turn schools can provide special training on their newest technologies, be they interactive whiteboards or classroom performance systems (also known simply as the "clickers") for participants to respond to questions from the trainer. Increased visibility can come to your library partnership through joint presentations at local or regional meetings and statewide conferences. If money for attendance at conferences is reduced in your buildings, then sharing your expertise via written articles, podcasts, and webinars can be helpful to other librarians.

Chapter 15: Reporting Your Success: Both types of librarians serve many bosses including boards, directors, superintendents, our student patrons, parents, and members of our communities. We must showcase our effectiveness via data, not just anecdotal evidence. We need to generate reports that promote our cause for additional funding and that provide data which our public relations departments can include in annual reports to the community.

Resources: Appendix A: Reading Calendar Month-by-Month provides a calendar of promotions that can be used to promote reading and literacy activities in either type of library. Appendix B contains a Listing of State and Provincial Library Associations for both public and school librarians. The Bibliography is full of web, book, and journal resources for your use.

Throughout the book you will find a number of forms that can be copied and used to help you as you plan and collaborate with other librarians. They are labeled with both the chapter number and the number of the item within that chapter, for example, Figure 2.1.

We have researched and gathered programs and partnership ideas from across the country, so that you don't have to do the research yourself. Each chapter includes a list of cited references, so you can easily locate the article or website that we have referenced. In addition, we've included suggestions for further reading.

FORMAT AND STYLE

For the sake of flow, we've chosen to use certain terms consistently throughout this book. To avoid the awkwardness of the "he/she" and "his/her" dilemma, we have chosen to use the plural form librarians to reference our colleagues. We use "teen librarian" and "YA librarian" interchangeably for public library settings and use the American Association of School Librarians' (AASL) preferred official term "school librarian" (rather than "media specialist") for professionals in a school setting.

In this book you'll find many references to the Search Institute's "40 Developmental Assets for Adolescents (ages 12–18)" (http://www.search-institute.org/system/files/40AssetsList.pdf). This can be used a guideline to create new programs, new lessons, and new displays. The nonprofit Search Institute's mission is to research what helps children to succeed. Compiling years of research, they list elements which, if present in the lives of adolescents, are shown to help them to avoid dangerous, damaging, or illegal behaviors. Their goal is to provide agencies that deal with adolescents with a means of creating positive and safe experiences for teenagers.

CLOSING

Dr. Carol Brown (2004, 7), associate professor at East Carolina University, says that the most important element to the success of your endeavor is not the budget or the size of your respective library staffs; it is your willingness to work together, to share duties, and to communicate! Here are real-world examples to help you to enrich the services that you already provide for your patrons. Please pick and choose those programs or ideas that can help you immediately. Leave the rest for implementation another day.

There are distinct differences between simply assisting each other and being full partners in collaborative projects and programs, but you need to begin with a simple project. Notice that the resources we've cited refer to one type of library or librarian but not to both groups. In most cases these reflect those articles that best explained the topic and can easily be adapted to fit the other type of library.

If you do not yet have a relationship with your counterpart at another library, make that your first step together; then, you can test just one of the ideas you find here. **Promote it! Publicize it!** When you are done you'll see the benefit of continuing and growing that collaborative relationship.

In most libraries, both school and public, there is only ONE librarian who deals with teens and YAs. No one else on staff does exactly what you do or works with a more wonderful, or more difficult, clientele. You are kindred spirits who need each other, in part so you have someone who understands your dilemmas as well as your victories, and who can help you to arrive at solutions. Tricia Suellentrop, deputy county librarian for Johnson County Libraries (Kansas City, Kansas), and Margaux Del-Guidice, library media specialist at Garden City High School (New York) remind us that sometimes the best way to serve our patrons is to physically **LEAVE OUR LIBRARY** to reach our teen audience (Suellentrop 2006, 39). We believe that outreach is not a frill but a necessity for teen librarians, regardless of the type of library in which they work (DelGuidice 2009, 38).

HOW TO USE THIS BOOK

Use this as a guidebook, but don't feel compelled to read it straight through like a novel. Instead, peruse the chapter headings to find programs that would best serve your teen audience. Feel free to jump around to the chapters that you need most **right now.** The first two sections offer general information. You'll learn what misconceptions have prevented librarians in the past from seeking the help of their colleagues from other libraries. You'll also find some hints for sharing your facilities with each other.

To further help you to decide where to start, check the overview of each chapter listed earlier in this chapter. Each chapter includes two different kinds of bonus segments. "Notes from the Field" provide you with success stories that you can replicate. "In Our Experience" segments point to dilemmas that can be addressed for the benefit of both school and public libraries.

REFERENCES

Brown, Carol. "America's Most Wanted: Teachers Who Collaborate." *Teacher Librarian* 32, no. 1 (2004): 13–18.

DelGuidice, Margaux. "Are You Overlooking a Valuable Resource? A Practical Guide to Collaborating with Your Greatest Ally: The Public Library." *Library Media Connection* 27, no. 6 (2009): 38–39.

Gorman, Michael. "The Indispensability of School Libraries (and School Librarians)." President's Message. *American Libraries* 36, no. 9 (2005): 5.

Search Institute. "40 Developmental Assets for Adolescents (ages 12–18)," http://www.search-institute.org/system/files/40AssetsList.pdf (cited February 22, 2012).

Suellentrop, Tricia. "Get Out of the Library!" *School Library Journal* 52, no. 9 (2006): 39.

Taracuk, Krista, and Heidi Fletcher. "Building Partnerships." *Ohio Media Spectrum* 61, no. 1 (2009): 36–42.

FURTHER READING

Keeter, Scott, and Paul Taylor. "The Millennials." PEW Research Center, http://pewresearch.org/pubs/1437/millennials-profile (cited February 22, 2012).

1

◇ ◇ ◇

WHAT IS COLLABORATION, WHY WE SHOULD DO IT, AND HOW TO GET STARTED

How do you make your counterpart librarian your BFF—best friend for-ever? What do you like best about the times when you get to sit and talk with your colleagues? Is it the chance to share stories, compare services, learn more about this other person who has a similar job but with a dif-ferent mission? Have you used these conversations to revise and renew your library program or counteract the isolation felt from being the <u>only</u> public teen librarian, or the <u>only</u> school librarian, in the building? Whether at a conference, a workshop, a class, or a strategic planning meeting most librarians love the chance to discuss their day-to-day problems with other librarians—those who TRULY understand what the job entails. After all, this is a situation where you can talk using the shorthand of technical terms and jargon without having to explain the nuances of these terms or your passion for your teen patrons. Colleagues can help us formulate new ideas, brainstorm, search for solutions, as well as offer support. And some-times they are simply someone to listen and act as our sounding board.

Can you name the librarian at the local high school and middle school? Is there a school librarian for each building or does just one person cover the entire district? What are the hours of operation at your local public library? Does your public library call its specialist a teen librarian or a young adult (YA) librarian? (DelGuidice 2009, 39). If so, do you know the phone number and email address of this librarian? Finding the answers to these questions is your first step to building a great relationship with your counterpart at the neighboring library.

REACHING OUT

If you have not yet met your counterpart, this is the year you should begin to build that relationship. Visiting your counterpart in their home library is essential to forming this relationship, and to better serving your teen patrons. It is also likely that this person will help to save your sanity. After all, who else deals as closely with the trials and tribulations of your favorite patrons?

Reaching out to your counterpart does not have to be a difficult process; you won't generally need to secure permission and proceed through administrative channels; after all, this is networking for the benefit of your teens! Start by checking the website of the library to search for the name of the teen or school librarian. If staff members are not identified by name on the website, ask the receptionist to connect you to the appropriate extension or voicemail. Your initial call can be a wonderful chance to introduce yourself, learn more about each other, exchange email addresses, and set up a face-to-face meeting. You can plan this initial meeting in a school building, in the teen room of the public library, or at a local coffeehouse. Meeting in one of the libraries may be more comfortable for both of you. While touring the library you will be able to view the layout, the resources provided for teens, and, most likely, some flyers for programs or special activities planned. After you get to know each other when it is time to start actual planning meetings consider moving your meeting outside of your libraries to minimize interruptions.

If you will share with us your kids, we'll share with you our resources.

—Nancy Levin,
Director Cleveland Heights-University
Heights Public Library, Ohio.

If your library and school district have no previous history of cooperative ventures, plan a group meeting of all librarians in the district—both school and public librarians. If you are in a small library or school district, instead set up a group meeting with school librarians from those schools that use the services of the same public library. For example, when Cherie Pandora took the job at Rocky River High School she was pleased to learn of the long history of library staff meetings. Librarians from each school met on a monthly basis during the school year with the children's librarian and the teen librarian from the public library. This is how the authors of this book, Stacey Hayman and Cherie Pandora, first met. Guest librarians from other departments of the public library, for example, Reference, Training, Special Collections, were invited to share information about new resources, databases, training sessions, and programs. Administrators and public relations specialists were invited from the school district when their presence was helpful to both groups.

DISCUSSION TOPICS

What did they discuss at these meetings? They discussed everything related to their respective libraries and their patrons. They shared calendars, classroom assignments, upcoming program dates, and promotional flyers. They discussed summer reading, special promotions, and testing and vacation schedules that would have an impact on the other library. They explained problems they encountered and sought solutions from their colleagues.

These meetings will help you to learn what types of materials are included in other libraries. For example, is there a graphic novel collection in the public library? Are multiple copies of the current best-selling teen novels available at the school library? Do teens have a large, dedicated space, or are they forced to work in a small space with a limited, or nonexistent, budget? What kind of support does your counterpart have from their fellow staff members and the administration? All these factors affect how much assistance can be given, or received. In addition, it is vitally important to you, and to your "reading regulars," those students who frequent BOTH the school and public libraries daily, needing more than one library to meet their needs whether it is to find a copy of the latest hot teen read or an extensive selection of materials for debate or Science Olympiad projects.

DEFINITION

What is collaboration? It is the practice of partnering with another agency to enhance services for all patrons. How does collaboration differ from cooperation? Cooperation, for our purposes, is a relationship based simply on sharing information; it does not necessarily denote actively working together on projects but focuses more on sharing information about programs, events, and problems (Jones, 2009, 194). Many school and public libraries already work together to some degree, but how can this working relationship be expanded—from simple cooperation to active collaboration?

As a school librarian, start by sending emails to neighboring libraries providing them with the school calendar and alerting them to the dates when school starts and ends, including Open House dates, and the dates of athletic contests and plays. Include a listing of special events, vacation schedules, testing dates, and days when students are not in school (e.g., for teacher in-service days or parent conference days) as these non-school days are liable to create a greater demand for the services of the public library. Provide teen and reference librarians at the public library with an annual listing of all teachers, departments, and grade levels for each school. This list will prove invaluable to them as they assist your students with research during nonschool hours (Jones 2009, 373).

As a public librarian, consider providing the dates that the library is closed for staff training and a listing of programs including Game Days, financial aid programs, technology training offered, or craft projects planned for YAs in the community. School librarians would welcome a roster of relevant public library employees, job titles, and extension numbers.

Sharing paper or electronic communication is a wonderful start, although it does not require that librarians from each institution actually meet. What it **does** accomplish is to start the communication process thus leading to the type of proactive working relationship that fosters true collaboration.

Notes from the Field

To all public libraries: Please, school librarians beg of you, do not plan a staff development day for the same day that students are out of school! In the past we have had an annual county-wide in-service day that provided high school students with a three-day weekend. Students were assigned longer writing assignments and projects to give them that extra day to prepare, and revise, their work. How disappointed students were to find that the library had chosen that day to close the library to patrons! This is, from many points of view, the perfect time to add a program for teens or middle school students as more students may have the chance to participate.

ASSIGNMENT ALERTS

Cooperative ventures should include sharing information regarding class assignments. Most public libraries have a standard form, often called an "Assignment Alert," which helps them to better serve their teen patrons during evening and weekend hours. Such forms usually request the name of the teacher and the course, the dates of the assignment, including the date the assignment is due, the topic to be researched, and the number of students who will be working on the project. Public librarians request a copy of the actual assignment, so that they can determine which of their resources will best assist students, and which, if any, resources students are *not* allowed to use. It is helpful to have this information ahead of time so that the reference and teen librarians have time to prepare. Too often the explanation of an assignment by a teen provides too little or misleading information, as the teen didn't fully understand what the teacher intended. Providing the public library with such forms (and a copy of the assignment), for major, multiday assignments is one way by which the school librarians can help their colleagues. Calling to discuss the fine points of the assignment is an added benefit as you can discuss the sources that students use at the school and the resources that the public library can supply to aid students.

Whether the public librarian prefers to receive this information via phone, fax, chat, or email, the information is sure to help both the librarians and the teens. With the possibility of up to 150 secondary students working on the same or similar projects, we want to get this information to our fellow librarians ASAP (As Soon As Possible)! We also want to avoid the problem that occurs when the first student through the door signs out all books on the topic or misrepresents the resources that can be used for the project.

For the school librarian, this means reminding teachers of the necessity of providing this information BEFORE assigning the materials to students. School librarians need the early notice just as much as the public librarians do! (If you do not have such a form you can adapt the form that we used. See Figure 1.1.)

Try to complete an assignment alert form for every class requiring research assistance. Be sure to include any databases, reference works, or other items that will be helpful, as well as any that the teacher has determined are not to be used. Remind students to bring their public library cards, or their bar code numbers, to school on library research days, so that they can search more efficiently and maximize the quality of the resources that they find in each type of libraries.

Teacher: _____ Today's Date: _____ Number of students: _____

Subject: _____ Assignment Due: _____

Date assignment was emailed/faxed to the public library/ libraries? ___/___/___

1. **Task Objectives:** (Please attach or email a copy of the assignment)

   Unit: _____

   What help will students need? _____

   Students will work: individually   small groups   whole class project

2. **Information Gathering:** (Please check all that apply)

Primary Sources	Specialized reference books	Books
Online catalog	Citing resources	Teacher provided web-sites
Online database	Webquests	Magazines or Journals
Distance Learning	Literary Critiques	Search engines
eBooks		

3. **ACCESS:** Which databases, web sites, and books can be used? Please attach any handouts, bibliographies or webographies given to students.

School Library—

Public Library—

Websites—

Figure 1.1: Assignment Alert Form

Source: Adapted from a form created by Nancy Jasany, former Librarian at North Royalton HS, OH.

From *Better Serving Teens through School Library–Public Library Collaborations* by Cherie P. Pandora and Stacey Hayman Santa Barbara, CA: Libraries Unlimited, Copyright © 2013.

4. **Teaching:** Handouts are needed on: _____

                         Instruction is needed in:_____

5. **Product:**   Worksheet   Paper   Webquest   Powerpoint Poster

Other (Please specify): _____

6. **Special requests and requirements:**

Is the student limited to one type of media?

How long or short will their end product be? Is there a page, or word, count that must be met?

Are there specific tools that the student has been instructed to use?

Are there specific resources that the student has been instructed <u>NOT</u> to use?

7. **Evaluation:** What should we do differently next year?

Figure 1.1: Assignment Alert Form (*Continued*)

From *Better Serving Teens through School Library–Public Library Collaborations* by Cherie P. Pandora and Stacey Hayman Santa Barbara, CA: Libraries Unlimited, Copyright © 2013.

Consider keeping these assignment forms in a notebook. Not only does this help you anticipate when all students would be working on the Gilded Age in history class, but it also allows you to help the student who lost the assignment. You will need to decide on a system that works best for your library. Schools may wish to organize assignment notebooks by department rather than the date started, as that is how students tend to reference their assignments. Public libraries may find it more useful to arrange their files by date, or by the name of the teacher making the assignment. Share paper copies for those assignments that came to you via email. Of course, not all teachers remember to send them this way. It may take time and extra patience on your part to keep reminding teachers about this important step in the process. A less convenient method, for school librarians working with teachers who continually forget to forward an assignment, is to photocopy a student's assignment sheet and fax or scan it to the public library.

Collaboration requires the building of a relationship based on mutual respect; and it necessitates an effort to share responsibilities (Katz 2009, 29). It requires true teamwork and a sense that the partnership will last long term beyond the length of a single program. The process of relationship building is interactive; it is more intense, more organized, more demanding, and more powerful than simple cooperation (Georges 2004, 35).

What then are the benefits? The benefits result in the best possible service to our common patrons, most often in the same community at no additional cost to our respective libraries. Phone calls, an email, a fax, a tweet, are all no-cost means of communicating, which can help you to stay in touch easily, and in a timely manner.

School and public librarians can not only support each other but also find ways to become advocates for each other. School librarians might advocate for the book discussion groups and the programs held at the public library. They recognize the importance of reference librarians to the continued success of readers and student researchers both after school and on weekends. They also recognize that the public library provides curriculum resources for teachers as well as research and technological expertise for students.

Public librarians often come to schools bearing gifts in the form of books that either support the curriculum or promote literacy and leisure reading. They understand that school librarians have greater, in-depth knowledge of the teens in their community, and will be the best source for knowing who might be interested in being a volunteer or joining a writing program. They may even alert the public librarian as to who might be on the troublesome side. Public librarians know that working with the schools can be an excellent way of securing an audience for a particular program by finding out which teacher(s) would be willing to offer extra credit for attendance.

Notes from the Field

Multnomah County Library system in Portland, Oregon, provides preselected groups of books that they call "Bucket of Books" to area schools. These collections not only contain books but also a pathfinder to assist in research, teacher resources, and a listing of websites appropriate to each topic (Catalano 2010, 4). View a listing of their book buckets or find out more about their program at http://www.multcolib.org/schoolcorps/bucket.html.

Once you have established a rapport and a means of continuing your communication via email, phone calls, and meetings, you can begin to create joint projects that enhance the status of each library. For a monthly guide listing ideas for collaboration, please refer to Figure 1.2. Do not let this listing limit your creativity! Each community has its own culture, needs, and problems. Working together can help you to promote both libraries to your patrons, communities, local agencies, and your taxpayers.

BENEFITS OF COLLABORATION
Expertise

Besides directly serving your patrons, collaboration can help you to improve the services of your own library. Librarians cannot be experts in every area under their responsibility. If you haven't yet had much contact with the librarian "next door," keep in mind the differences between the two types of libraries and their respective missions. Public librarians often have skills in working with patrons of all ages, as they often serve as reference librarians part-time. They are also well versed in the books, both fiction and nonfiction, that are popular with all age groups. School librarians are teachers who understand how teens and preteens learn (see Figure 1.3).

Artwork

Just as one librarian might be happy to leave the artwork, displays, and bulletin boards to those on staff who are more gifted in the visual arts, you can work to maximize your respective strengths as school and public librarians. This becomes a win-win situation.

August—Meet to discuss programs and themes chosen by each institution;
   Exchange contact information (via email or phone) for the teen librarian,
      each school librarian or relevant staff members (since not all schools
      will have a librarian);
   School librarian should collate and share this information as well as a list-
      ing of departments, teachers, and department chairs.
   Devise a method of continuously communicating public library programs
      of interest to teens, both for teacher awareness and for announcement
      to the student body.

September—Share calendars; include dates and titles of plays, and testing dates
   Invite the teen librarian to Meet the Teacher Night/Open House
   Celebrate Banned Books Week

October—Invite the teen librarian to speak briefly at faculty meeting;
   Invite teachers to sign up for library cards,
   Explain the benefits/policies of Teacher Loans
   Explain how Assignment Alerts help you to help students; distribute forms
   Make announcements for any book clubs for adults
   Consider creating a joint book club or joint activities for teen advisory clubs
   Celebrate Teen Read Week
   Invite the school librarian to a department meeting and to a library board
      of trustees meeting for introductions and for greater familiarity with
      the mission of the public library.

November—Parent conferences—may be a release day/non-school day for
      students
   Teacher Inservice day might be a great day to copresent on literacy, tech-
      nology. . . .
   Share holiday program, concert, and vacation dates
   Alert reference librarians to the guidance department deadline for college
      applications. (College research will be heavy in the preceding weeks.)

December—Share information about homework and research assigned over
      holiday break:
   Alert public library as needed;
   Discuss whether quiet areas are needed for students during finals weeks in
      January

Figure 1.2: Opportunities for Collaboration

From *Better Serving Teens through School Library–Public Library Collaborations* by Cherie P. Pandora and Stacey Hayman Santa Barbara, CA: Libraries Unlimited, Copyright © 2013.

January—Digital citizenship and Internet Safety programs for new semester
  Possible second school inservice day

February—Public Library Summer Reading Programs ideas finalized
  Possibly a second parent conference day

March—Staff Development—new technologies for coming year
  Work on *Read Across America* programs or projects
  Celebrate Teen Tech Week
  Alert public library of summer reading titles as soon as possible

April—Holiday breaks and dates of final projects
  Celebrate National Library Week and School Library Month

May—School summer reading materials should be finalized, ready to be
    posted online and sent directly to the teen librarian for display near
    required reading titles
  Present booktalks on summer reading titles and/or plan summer reading
    assemblies at middle schools; public librarians should take advantage
    of the opportunity and bring informational handouts and sign-up
    sheets for their summer reading program.
  Hold a summer reading book fair at the high school; allow the public
    library to have books for checkout, if possible.
  Provide the dates for finals; senior projects and senior project juries

June—Finals weeks (change in school attendance); end of school year

Figure 1.2: Opportunities for Collaboration (*Continued*)

From *Better Serving Teens through School Library–Public Library Collaborations* by Cherie P. Pandora and Stacey Hayman Santa Barbara, CA: Libraries Unlimited, Copyright © 2013.

Differences	School Libraries	Public Libraries
Mission	Teaching information, technology, and literacy skills	Cradle to Grave support and service
Audience	Built in, captive audience; may include mandated weekly visits	Voluntary visitors
Internet access	Parent may control at home, can deny access at school	Student access assured under Library Bill of Rights
Internet filtering	CIPA filtering mandated by law	Up to individual library system; may or may not filter
Web 2.0	Limited social networking	Policies may allow or encourage chat, IM, and social networking
Customer focus	Limited by age or grade with emphasis on curriculum	Cradle to Grave customer service
Funds for programming	May not exist	Departmental
Hours	School day and extended hours	Evening and weekend hours in addition to daytime hours

Figure 1.3: Differences Chart

Differences	School Libraries	Public Libraries
Materials selection	School age specific: Limited by age or grade level	Extensive collection; fewer limitations; more balanced
Calendar	9.5 months	12 months
Summer reading	May be mandated	Extensive, voluntary; all grade levels and adult reading encouraged
Staffing/departments	May be a one person show with few support staff; may no longer have a certified librarian	Tasks may be specialized tasks, e.g., cataloging and technical services, reference, teen/YA, children's, or librarians may cover their area and reference services as well
Graphics department	May have one in larger districts or individual schools	Many larger libraries will have a department

Figure 1.3: Differences Chart (*Continued*)

From *Better Serving Teens through School Library–Public Library Collaborations* by Cherie P. Pandora and Stacey Hayman Santa Barbara, CA: Libraries Unlimited, Copyright © 2013.

Strengths

Once you have begun collaborating with your counterpart, you will become comfortable in sharing your weaknesses and your strengths with them. Perhaps you have a talent that would enhance the work of your counterpart, and vice versa. Perhaps your strength is presenting lessons and your counterpart's strength is programming; how exciting to learn from someone who shows great talent in an area where you are less confident!

Sharing

Sharing your individual strengths, and weaknesses, might not be the first conversation you have, but don't be afraid to share. Teen librarians and school librarians can bond in many ways—by team-teaching a lesson on electronic databases, sharing bibliographies, or providing staff development instruction for faculty and staff. The benefits of collaboration become even more evident as students increasingly visit the public library during their teen years, access it remotely during their college years, and eventually, as the taxpayers who decide the fate of library levies (Catalano 2010, 5).

Saving Money

Your collaborative efforts may also save money for your libraries. Do you know if your libraries each purchase the same, or similar, databases? Do either of you pay a surcharge to provide remote access for your teens? Meeting and chatting with your counterpart can uncover these facts. For example, perhaps you are duplicating efforts in purchasing the same literary reference database. Would it benefit your teens to have two different, but complementary, databases dealing with literary topics? Perhaps you can coordinate purchases, either alternating the purchase or by purchasing two complementary literary databases. If both the databases provide free remote access, it will not matter to your patrons which library is the one that supplies the product to them. Hopefully your state has improved your buying power by providing volume discounts for public libraries that purchase databases as part of a consortium. While far fewer states have made similar provisions for school libraries, it is worth checking to see if there are educational discounts for K–12 databases. Should this not be the case, then pool your purchasing power with other libraries to further reduce your costs (DelGuidice 2009, 38).

Pooling money to provide additional speakers, authors, or special event programming is another way by which such collaboration can be used to stretch your budgets. Besides sharing speaker's fees, working as a team allows librarians to creatively solve a host of money issues. The public library usually has a marketing director who can provide valuable advice to school librarians about graphic design and newsletters. The school librarian, in return, can have the school print shop reproduce flyers and bookmarks for teen programs. Instructors, students, or staff can be tapped to assist with programming topics that relate to their cherished hobbies, for example, photography (refer to Chapter 6 for more specific information on working together to secure authors for your programs).

OBSTACLES TO COLLABORATION

Before discussing collaboration, let's first review some misconceptions from the library world. We sometimes hear that librarians working in public libraries are envious of school librarians, bemoaning the fact that they are lucky enough to have a captive audience to work with. Librarians in public libraries hear that school librarians envy the fact that they are encouraged, even required, to READ during the workday. This is a rumor public librarians wish were actually true, but their off-floor time is sadly limited to reading reviews to keep current in purchasing YA fiction and nonfiction materials. Their off-floor time is similar to the elusive planning period for school librarians—preparing for programs or meetings, and consulting with staff members. Do not let these rumors hinder you in your attempt to forge a relationship with your library colleague. School librarians realize that students receive invaluable help with homework, research, and book selection from staff at the public libraries during their evening and weekend hours. Librarians in public libraries expect that their colleagues in schools will teach students how to locate and use books and electronic databases. In addition, these librarians in the public sector have the advantage of seeing teens during weekends, school breaks, and throughout the entire summer. The fact is, school librarians and their public library counterparts were never competitors or adversaries, although sometimes their respective boards or directors may have acted as if this was so. One of their primary strengths has been their collective ability to work together regardless of, perhaps in spite of, the politics being played out in administrative offices.

What are the existing barriers to collaboration? You may encounter negative attitudes and people who throw bureaucratic roadblocks at your efforts as you strive to forge a great working relationship. With any luck you will not be faced with a librarian who sees you as competitor (Ritzo 2009, 83). If there are territorial issues between the libraries, or their managers, then you first need to allay the fears of your fellow librarian. Convince your colleagues and both sets of administrators that working together will not weaken the support for each library, but will instead strengthen community support for BOTH libraries. If you encounter these types of situations, you MUST communicate and connect with your counterpart to set aside the issues of territory and boundaries. Librarians better serve their communities when they work in tandem.

While teen and school librarians share the mission to serve YAs, the means of achieving these goals differ, and yet are complementary. School librarians serve as instructors and have a teaching role to play, while teen librarians create entertaining programs while still providing reference support for school work and much-needed recreational reading materials in both print and electronic formats. Jeff Katz (2009, 29), adjunct professor in the School of Library, Archival, and Information Studies at the University of British Columbia asserts that the failure to collaborate hinders service to favorite patrons. He encourages all librarians to provide a repository of services, not just to teens but to their teachers as well.

Another barrier is an unintended one, that is, not totally understanding the mission, responsibilities, and goals of our counterpart in our sister libraries. School and public librarians often take for granted their similarities, and forget that sometimes there are major differences in their missions and daily tasks. Meeting on a monthly basis can reduce some of these misunderstandings and allows you to learn to truly appreciate the demands on your fellow librarian. When you plan for your own staff development you likely attend only the conferences geared to your own type of library, and may forget that you would be a welcome addition to state or national conferences open to all librarians (Wepking 2009, 26). What might you learn if you attended the state or regional conference with your counterpart? If you can't attend a conference due to budgetary constraints, or a lack of professional release time, register for the webinar version of the conference or the electronic list that serves other types of libraries within your state. Understanding the issues, problems, and concerns of your friend and colleague helps you to be a better partner, and opens your eyes to alternate means of assisting your counterpart. Better yet, if possible, try to attend a local conference or workshop together. Sharing transportation to the event provides you not only important time to talk with your colleague (without patron interruptions) but also the opportunity to view the event through the eyes of your counterpart.

FACILITIES

As you begin to plan your first joint venture, determine the best venue for the event. Be aware that the best locale will change with the types of programs that you create. What facilities can be reserved for the program of your sister library? Oftentimes the size of the community room in the public library cannot accommodate large audiences, while the school librarian can easily arrange for their auditorium to be used for the public library's program. Conversely, the school auditorium does not have the cozy feel that the school might desire for a small meeting or a training session. In such a case, the community room, or even the story room, may be a perfect fit for the school's program. In either case, it is essential that librarians check the policies of their agency to ensure that facilities can be used without cost. Rental fees usually charged for the use of the school auditorium (generally the cost of custodial time) may be waived if the event ends before 10 P.M. and the space is requested by a staff member who will attend the meeting (see Chapter 6 for further information).

Public libraries have traditionally shown creativity in meeting the needs of teens by providing "homework centers" during the school year, and even special study areas during final weeks (Katz 2009, 30). School libraries are beginning to realize what amazing resources they can tap if they communicate with the teen librarians at their local public library, and involve them in the literacy and research activities of the school, for example, selection of summer reading materials. Public librarians are generally more than happy to provide additional resources if they know what schools are able and unable to purchase on their more limited budgets (see Chapter 9 for more information about homework help centers).

The key elements to a great working relationship are flexibility, respect, and an open mind. Working together can provide both the libraries with new groups of library advocates—students who are prepared to use school libraries, who will return to the public libraries on many occasions for their needs, and who will fondly remember both during the times when tax levies are placed on the ballot.

REFERENCES

Catalano, Lee, Catherine Carroll, Kiva Liljequist, and Susan Smallsreed. "It's as Simple as a Phone Call." *OLA* (*Oregon Library Association*) *Quarterly* 15, no. 4 (2010): 4–7.

DelGuidice, Margaux. "Are You Overlooking a Valuable Resource? A Practical Guide to Collaborating with Your Greatest Ally: The Public Library." *Library Media Connection* 27, no. 6 (2009): 38–39.

Georges, Fitzgerald. "Information Literacy, Collaboration, and Killer Apps: New Challenges for Media Specialists." *Library Media Connection* 23, no. 2 (2004): 34–35.

Jones, Patrick, Michele Gorman, and Tricia Suellentrop. *Connecting Young Adults and Libraries: How-to-Do-It Manual.* 4th ed. New York: Neal-Schuman Publishers, 2009.

Katz, Jeff. "A Common Purpose: Public/School Library Cooperation and Collaboration." *Public Libraries* 48, no. 3 (2009): 28–31.

Levin, Nancy. Phone interview by Cherie Pandora. January 13, 2012. Cleveland Heights, OH.

Multnomah County Library. "Bucket of Books," http://www.multcolib.org/schoolcorps/bucket.html (cited February 27, 2012).

Ritzo, Christopher, Chaebong Nam, and Bertram (Chip) Bruce. "Building a Strong Web: Connecting Information Spaces in Schools and Communities." *Library Trends* 58, no. 1 (2009): 82–94.

Wepking, Mary. "From Communication to Cooperation to Collaboration: School and Public Librarians as Partners for Student Success." *Library Media Connections* 28, no. 3 (2009): 24–26.

FURTHER READING

AASL/ALSC/YALSA, "School/Public Library Cooperative Activities," http://wikis.ala.org/readwriteconnect/index.php/AASL/ALSC/YALSA_School/Public_Library_Cooperation (cited February 27, 2012).

ALA, "School/Public Library Partnerships Bibliography," http://wikis.ala.org/readwriteconnect/index.php/School/Public_Library_Partnerships_Bibliography (cited February 27, 2012).

ALSC Association for Library Service to Children, "School/Public Library Cooperative Activities," http://www.ala.org/ala/mgrps/divs/alsc/externalrelationships/coopacts/schoolplcoopprogs.cfm (cited February 27, 2012). (In spite of the title, there are activities that deal with middle school students and high school students, e.g., Assignment Alert program and book discussion.)

Collett, Amy. "Practical Tips to Help the Collaborative Process Work More Effectively in the School Library Media Program." *Library Media Connection* 26, no. 4 (2008): 20.

Fresno County Public Library, "Read Watch Listen," http://www.fresnolibrary.org/teen/hc/schools/html (cited February 27, 2012).

Murvosh, Marta. "Partners in Success." *School Library Journal* 59, no. 1 (2013): 22–28.

Vincelette, Pete, and Priscilla Queen. "School and Public Library Collaboration." *School Library Monthly* 28, no. 4 (2010): 14–16.

YALSA Professional Development Center. Professional Development Topics, "School and Public Library Cooperation," http://www.ala.org/ala/mgrps/divs/yalsa/profdev/schoolpublic.cfm (cited February 27, 2012).

2

◇ ◇ ◇

PROFESSIONAL PROJECTS

Collaborating on professional projects gives you a chance to stretch your wings beyond the four walls of the library where you work. These projects can be kept simple, such as reaching out to the Parent-Teacher Association (PTA) or Friends of the Library for financial support. Perhaps your goal is to cosponsor a speaker to help teens select and pay for a college education in pursuit of their dream career. Think also on a grander scale, such as serving together on the *Voice of Youth Advocates'* (*VOYA*) Nonfiction Honor List Selection Committee, reviewing and critiquing nonfiction books to create a listing of outstanding titles. This process is addressed in detail later in this chapter. Your work together can also be something that is primarily for your library's own benefit, whether that means joining a state committee to fight for freedom of speech or starting a blog in which you gain followers based on the clever programming you share with your colleagues.

GET ACQUAINTED MEETINGS

A low key, but great way to expand your repertoire is to hold monthly library meetings (Brown 2004, 15). These meetings should include the public library's youth service librarians and school librarians for multiple grade levels so that everyone can discuss upcoming programs, activities, and research assignments; such meetings provide wonderful opportunities for brainstorming and cross-collaborative support.

Notes from the Field

Director of Library Services, Shaker Heights (Ohio), Kathy Fredrick's (2012) advice is to "learn the name of your counterparts at the public library and then to talk to them early and often. You need to be in the loop and to keep them in the loop."

Knowing what's next in both institutions is the best chance we have for success in our respective projects. Minutes should be sent to all participants as well as to the directors and administrators of all buildings. Sharing this information with your management team is another way to keep your bosses on board with current and future projects; it also helps to promote the benefits of collaboration to the board of education & the board of trustees. Monthly meetings allow us to discuss our common patrons, including which students are succeeding and which students need help or are being disruptive in either the public or school setting. It is often surprising for both sides to hear of completely differing behaviors from the same students. Working together and sharing what is seen in alternate settings can provide clues as to whether a teen is simply experiencing normal feelings of rebellion, or if there might be a serious issue that needs to be addressed. Just like the kids, adults enjoy a treat after a hard day of work. When it's your turn to host the meeting, don't forget to provide a snack or the refreshment of your choice!

LOCAL COMMITTEE WORK

Involving your library counterpart in the important committee work of your organization can be an asset for both of you. Suggest that your school library counterpart become a part of your public library's strategic planning process. This is an excellent opportunity for school librarians to learn about the workings of the public library, and vice versa; it also provides a means for you to advocate for your colleague and for your shared vision (Wilson 2005, 34). There may be other school committees that would benefit from the expertise of your public library colleague; realize also that it is possible to have someone attend one or two meetings to provide feedback without having to commit to a monthly meeting schedule. For example, having a reference librarian serving on the school district's technology task force could solve compatibility issues that plague students when they work on assignments at both libraries. A teen services librarian from a public library would be a wonderful asset to any school's Summer Reading Selection Committee. (See Chapter 5 for specific ideas.) A school librarian can be a big help to public librarians planning their own summer reading program. Many districts have curriculum advisory committees that are comprised of community members and parents; what a wonderful opportunity this would be for a reference librarian to share, and demonstrate, databases that support the curricular needs of the YAs in the community!

SPECIAL COMMITTEE WORK

There are a variety of opportunities for big or small projects centered around reading and evaluating materials sponsored by professional organizations like Young Adult Library Services Association (YALSA) and teen-focused journals like *VOYA* or *School Library Journal* (*SLJ*). When Stacey was presented with the chance to be committee chair for *VOYA*'s Nonfiction Honor List, she knew she was interested, but the decision to volunteer required more than just showing an interest. Taking into consideration the significant time commitment required, both at the library and at home, she had to decide if she could make that commitment before even thinking about obtaining the consent of the library's administration. The personal benefit of this growth experience, the library's benefit of thousands of dollars of free print materials, positive publicity within the city, and the benefit of strengthening relationships with school librarians representing nearby cities all outweighed the extra time that would eventually be dedicated to this project and permission was sought.

Once the project was approved, the actual process was fairly straightforward. Stacey contacted Cherie and another school librarian, Donna Zmrazek. Cherie represented Rocky River High School and Zmrazek represented elementary schools in Berea, Ohio. Each suggested another person to round out the first year of the committee, namely Bay High School librarian Sheila Benedum (Bay Village, Ohio) and Middle School teacher Margie Coffey, also representing Berea City Schools. Choosing to decline for the second year, Coffey's spot was filled by Priscilla Spano-Wiles, a middle and high school librarian from North Olmsted, Ohio. All of these school systems are within a 30-minute drive to the public library where Stacey works but represent a wide variety of socioeconomic groups. The geographic closeness and strong mix of communities made this more than an opportunity to discuss the submitted titles; it also became a way to better understand the surrounding school systems. Sharing honest opinions of what books work and why, how students representing the different schools responded to the books, and even taking time to brainstorm teen topics unrelated to the Nonfiction Honor List, helped promote this group from a wonderful networking opportunity into a team of fellow advocates who could be called upon for feedback long after the project was finished. This group represented a great deal of experience, the continuing curiosity of great librarians, as well as a healthy respect for both YAs and quality reading materials. The members of the group were in place long before the actual work began, and it began with the selected books shipped directly from the publisher to Stacey at her library. (This is a good time to remind librarians, especially messy, craft-loving librarians, that it is a very good idea to always treat the maintenance department with extra kindness and respect! They may be less annoyed when bits of glitter, or heavy boxes of books, keep popping up.)

When the caravan of boxes began to arrive in September, Stacey started the process of unpacking the books, checking the contents against the shipping list, recording the title, author, ISBN, and publisher in a spreadsheet and sorting the books into separate, but complete and exact collections for each member, as well as a full collection for *VOYA* to award as a prize package. Committee members were then contacted and arranged over convenient timings to pick up their books, an ongoing process. Starting and keeping these detailed records from the start made it possible for each member of the group to track their own notes, student feedback, and note which titles were borrowed by interested teachers. The spreadsheet also became a resource for tracking the total value of titles received and became an important document to share with managers, principals, and school and library boards. Once those at the top could see an actual dollar amount, this information also became an easy set of facts to share with the communities involved.

The first face-to-face meeting was scheduled in February, after the submission deadline passed; and the group had a chance to look over the titles for obvious noncontenders (too young, too old, wrong publishing year). Before anything was taken off the list, even the obvious noncontenders, there was always an opportunity to persuade the group if one person felt strongly, for or against, a title. Stacey created a members-only wiki with a master list that could be referenced, so members could easily review the current standing of each title and read comments from other committee members in between actual meetings. Committee members also asked teens at their respective schools and at the public library to look over the books and make honest comments, both positive and negative. Teen feedback provided another opportunity for the adults involved to discuss the similarities and differences they experience in working within their own environments. There were only five in-person meetings, with email and the wiki helping to keep everyone informed. Discussions of books were lively as we chose the best of the year's books for middle school teens. The final list of 30 titles was selected from the close to 200 titles submitted by publishers. Short descriptions were included with the bibliographic information and teen comments on the winning titles were added; an introduction to our group's approach to the experience, and committee biographies, rounded out the finished article that was published in the August issue of *VOYA*. As a reward, each librarian was able to keep each and every book submitted for their system, a real boon for those on a tight budget. Items that were too young or too old for their own libraries were passed on to other libraries. We estimated that each librarian received the equivalent of $3,000 worth of books each year for their efforts.

LETTERS OF SUPPORT

One way by which you can help your colleagues, and they can help you, is to offer to write a letter of support. When the public library applies for a Customer Service Award or an award for teen services, volunteer to write a letter! Explain how the public library helped your students to be successful, and provide as many examples as you can. Likewise, when the school library seeks grant funding (an annual process for some schools), librarians at the public library can write an official letter of support indicating the value of the project to the entire community. Grants often include partnership requirements. Partnering with the public library now can lead to future offers of assistance long before you could even think to ask for such a letter.

In Our Experience

Faculty Workshops

One of the best ways to entice teachers to use public library resources is to simply show them what is available. By attending a faculty meeting early in the school year, or volunteering to make a presentation at a fall faculty in-service, teen librarians can reach many faculty members.

Demonstrating those databases that are purchased for teens should help teachers to promote your resources. You may even find that teachers include your resources in their assignments! Working together with the school librarian helps the administration, as well as the teaching staff, to see the value that you add to their curriculum (Georges 2004, 34).

TEENS AS COMMUNITY VOLUNTEERS

If you have a more elaborate idea for collaboration, such as creating a platform for teens to volunteer with the local food bank or serve meals to those in need, you have a great opportunity to build support within your library and community. Consider all aspects of the project before advertising it to teens. Be sure to secure approval from your director and/or principal, and devise policies as objectively as possible. For instance, create clearly written guidelines that outline who will be accepted for this opportunity and how they will be selected. Find out which service groups operate in the school. Some groups, such as Key Club and National Honor Society, require service hours of their students; they are always searching for a worthwhile project. If the food bank is in an area with a substantial immigrant population, consider also reaching out to the foreign language teachers in the schools as additional partners.

In Our Experience

Our American Field Service (AFS) and Spanish Clubs spent time tutoring and helping students in the barrio. Our students enjoyed working with younger students and helping them with their homework; in return they practiced their Spanish language skills with native speakers and learned the satisfaction of reading to and working with children. In December students held a successful book drive at the high school to ensure that students would have books to share once their homework was done. Chaperones are always needed for this and other field trip ventures. Why not invite a teen librarian to accompany you? If your public library contains foreign language publications, these resources may be useful to volunteer students for learning or for sharing with the children in the project.

Don't overlook planning how teens will be transported to different locations. Due to insurance and liability issues, your policy needs to be in writing. Check the policies for both libraries. Many organizations actually forbid employees from transporting teens. Lawyers for both public and school libraries should be consulted, if there is not already a carefully detailed policy in place to protect individuals from lawsuits. Your project may continue to expand as more teens, and more adults willing to supervise, become interested. The best aspect of this project might be the chance it provides teens to share in a feeling of responsibility for the world around them, as well as for both the school and public libraries to continue as anchoring establishments for the city, town, or village they already serve. Often seen as ambassadors for the teen population, teen and school librarians will likely enjoy the chance to step out of the library and work with teens at their best. While the specifics are flexible, allow this project to inspire you to find new ways to advocate for your teens. Such projects generate good public relations for both teens and libraries, allowing for feel-good moments all around.

REGIONAL COLLABORATIONS

You can also start small by joining a regional committee (Vaillancourt 2000, 84). Throughout the state of Ohio, there are smaller, geographically organized groups of public libraries; and within those regional consortiums, there are many committees that need volunteers. After being a member of the Cleveland Area Metropolitan Library System (CAMLS) Young Adult learning group for a year or so, Stacey was asked to serve a term as the committee chair. Meetings were arranged by the staff at CAMLS. However, guidelines required that she select and present topics for discussion at the meetings. The most popular meetings centered on best practices—sharing ideas that people had tried, or wanted to try, explaining what worked or did not work. Suggestions on how to modify programs for diverse populations were invaluable. This is a great chance to bring creative ideas or specific concerns of your school library partner to a broader audience. The bigger the group, the better the chance there might be useful feedback on just about any situation. Once your fellow public teen librarians see how much insider school information on teens and teachers you can access, others are sure to follow in your footsteps. School librarians will want to try this same method in their own regional meetings. Once your fellow school librarians see how much support in terms of materials and technological access you receive from your public library, others are sure to follow in your footsteps. After working on a committee at the regional level, if you find the experience rewarding, you might want to explore what opportunities your state organization provides for further growth. These experiences provide you with the chance to make new friends and connections that will be an asset to your current, and any future, positions. (Please refer to Appendix B to start searching for suitable opportunities.)

IDEAS FOR COLLABORATION

YALSA (Young Adult Library Services Association) offers librarians many ways to step outside their comfort zones. You'll find a number of simple ideas on how to effectively speak up on behalf of librarianship on their Advocacy page (http://www.ala.org/yalsa/advocacy). These ideas can be especially helpful when either library is facing staff or budget cuts or needs to convince the community that additional operating funds are needed. Become your counterpart's advocate; don't be afraid to promote them and their mission to your library's managers. Just select the subtopic that is most interesting to you on their Get Involved with YALSA page (http://www.ala.org/yalsa/getinvolved/getinvolved); there is something here to intrigue everyone. Each school and teen librarian should consider selecting a few of the topics that sound like they could be a good fit for your community as well as your different interests and strengths. Sit down with your counterpart to discuss the possibilities and consider if any of these options might provide you another unique opportunity to collaborate. Of course, only one librarian will be required to be on record as volunteering for a committee or for undertaking a specific task, but if you consult your counterpart first your job has just been made that much easier and that much more rewarding. Reviewing these sites together gives you an idea of the amount of time and level of commitment involved in volunteering.

For teen librarians wanting something less conventional than a group that reads and evaluates a huge stack of books, there is a long list of discussion and interest groups at http://www.ala.org/yalsa/working withyalsa/discussion. These groups were not created, nor are they run by YALSA; instead they were started, and continue to exist, through the interest and efforts of current, working teen librarians. Perhaps you and your school counterpart have already created an outstanding project of your own and you'd like to offer the idea to others; this could be a great forum to share your experiences. This could also be a good opportunity for you both to ask fellow librarians near and far how they have attempted, succeeded, or failed, on a particular topic. Ask their advice. Ask what they learned and how they would modify their programs if they offered them again. Gamers, those working with at-risk teens, techies, and librarians who want to fight for intellectual freedom, can find like-minded people in one of these off-shoots of a much larger organization.

Notes from the Field

Want a great project that will bring 100 teens and numerous teachers into your library and help you make connections with both groups? Youth Services Librarian Kate McCartney, Library Media Specialist Carmen Riddle, and school Library Aide Connie Froehlich joined forces to maximize students' understanding and use of mobile devices. Consider it a Mobile Devices Petting Zoo. Students were encouraged to bring their smartphones, iPads, Kindles, and Nooks to Marysville High School. If you time your program to take place in early December, participants have the chance to explore different devices to see what they'd like to purchase at holiday time (Riddle 2012).

MOBILE DEVICES PETTING ZOO

Start the day with the teen librarian giving a short presentation each class period, demonstrating how to download books and music for free from the public library website. Provide a variety of phones, tablets, and eReaders from the collection of both libraries. Allow students to visit from their study halls and to bring their own handheld devices to school; be sure to market the program to teachers as well. Both librarians should help students to create accounts to request books from the public library website. Encourage students to try different devices to see what they like best. Allow time for the teen librarian to converse with teachers during their conference periods, to promote the resources the public library has for their department. Spend the remaining time in an open forum where students can ask questions and have a chance for some hands-on practice with their device or others' you've provided.

These open forums will likely create a snowball effect when each student who attended shares their new found skills with their friends, who shared with other friends, and so on (Riddle 2012). Costs should be minimal, basically the cost of lunch for the youth services librarian and a few door prizes for drawings during the day. Know that you might be creating demand for a similar workshop later in the school year.

The benefits of such collaboration are many; teens and teachers will understand how to make their mobile devices more productive, not just as a toy or tool for entertainment (Karabush and Pleviak 2011, 52). The day also allows the teen librarian to get to know more students and interact with both students and teachers.

If your public library can't afford mobile devices, you have a wonderful opportunity to put your grant-writing knowledge to good use (see Chapter 12). A grant that shows the benefits to both the public and school libraries has a better chance of being awarded, since the return on the investment is that much greater. In fact, one of our first collaboration projects was writing a Drew Carey Ohio Library Foundation Grant application; sadly it was unsuccessful, but working together taught us a great deal. The grant was aimed at bringing our public library's electronic resources together with teachers, and eventually would have allowed us to install computer labs in both libraries. Ensuing grants and budgets helped us achieve some of the same goals we described in the grant application. The experience we gained working closely as a team toward one common goal for both organizations continues to be a positive memory and absolutely worth the time.

As you get to know your library counterpart, you'll discover each other's strengths and interests. Allow this information to help direct projects you select, the leadership of specific projects, and which ideas to pass over as neither of you have the skills or desire to accomplish. Hopefully, this chapter has provided you with some ideas and a wide variety of choices; but there is always something new to try. Just remember you don't have to do it alone when you begin your next professional project.

REFERENCES

Brown, Carol. "America's Most Wanted: Teachers Who Collaborate." *Teacher Librarian* 32, no. 1 (2004): 13–18.

Fredrick, Kathy. Personal interview with Cherie Pandora. March 21, 2012. Shaker Heights, OH.

Georges, Fitzgerald. "Information Literacy, Collaboration, and 'Killer Apps': New Challenges for Media Specialists." *Library Media Connection* 23, no. 2 (2004): 34–35.

Karabush, Cynthia and Pam Pleviak. "Talk Me Off the Ledge: Surviving Solo Librarianship." *Knowledge Quest* 40, no. 2 (2011): 48–53.

Riddle, Carmen. Phone interview by Cherie Pandora. March 28, 2012. Marysville, OH.

Vaillancourt, Renée. *Bare Bones Youth Adult Services: Tips for Public Library Generalists.* Chicago, IL: ALA, 2000.

Wilson, Stu. "Saint Paul's Strategic Plan." *Library Journal* 130, no. 1 (2005): 34–37.

FURTHER READING

Hart, Roger A. *Children's Participation: From Tokenism to Citizenship.* Florence: UNICEF, 1992, 8.

Mulder, Natalie. "Encouraging Community Service in the Public Library." *Young Adult Library Services* 10, no. 1 (2011): 25–27.

Oliver, Jo. "A Practical Partnership: Library, Museum and Family History Society Cooperation in Camden NSW." *Aplis* 24, no. 4 (2011): 167–71.

Rutherford, Dawn. "Building Strong Community Partnerships: Sno-Isle Libraries and the Teen project." *Young Adult Library Services* 9, no. 1 (2010): 23–25.

3

PROGRAMS

Programming for teens can often feel like a thankless task. After all, their parents aren't with them to suggest a "thank you" for an enjoyable time. And too often the very teens who have requested an event are too busy to attend. Of course, teens are reluctant to become enthusiastic participants in anything educational, including library activities. But take heart! You can still win them over! By working together, and getting the right blend of timing and incentives, you can offer programs when there aren't as many competing activities from other sources, balancing as many entertaining options as potentially educational programs.

Finding balance with programming poses an ongoing challenge, often made more difficult by a lack of funding, competing offers from other organizations, levels of library staffing, resources available, and the constantly changing faces of the teen patrons who participate. As most of these elements are out of your control, school and public librarians need to work with the elements they *can* control, their own creativity, and getting help from the people around them.

SPECIAL EVENT PROGRAMMING

Some months of the year lend themselves to special programming that recognizes religious holidays; national holidays, that is, Martin Luther

King Day, Presidents' Day, Independence Day; or month-long celebrations such as Black History Month, Women's History Month, Poetry Month; and so on. Besides these annual events there are many categories of programs that you can tap to interest your teen audience. You can create craft events, film nights, puzzle or board game nights, book discussion groups, gaming tournaments, how-to demonstrations, or health and wellness programs. You can reach teens with special interest programming that meets their needs, such as babysitting clinics, anime or manga sessions, and gaming nights (Ott 2006, 279–282). Also, consider creating multiple book discussion groups divided by age, grade, gender, or genre. For example, one year our high school allowed seniors to choose two novels for their summer reading. This activity was promoted by the school and public libraries. The culminating activity was a book discussion facilitated by a librarian or teacher and attended by all students who read the book; multiple discussion groups met in the public library to discuss books that varied from current topics to survival to nonfiction to science fiction and fantasy. Numerous choices were available at both the public library and the school library for these discussion groups. *Nineteen Minutes* by Jodi Picoult, *Speak* by Laurie Halse Anderson, *Hot Zone* by Richard Preston, and *The Hitchhiker's Guide to the Galaxy* by Douglas Adams were only a few of the titles read and discussed that year. (Additional details on how these styles of book discussions were conducted can be found in Chapter 5.)

Gaming tournaments can be based on whatever most interests your students. They can be chess, board games, computer system games, or a game show type format based on popular television shows. Your collaboration can take a few different directions when it comes to implementing a tournament. If the public librarian is taking the lead, choosing the type of tournament, and hosting the actual event, then the school librarian can be brought in to provide more materials, more potential teen participants, and to further promote the event throughout the school. The school librarian could suggest what might be most popular based on what she sees and hears on a daily basis, or based on a teacher's current academic focus. If the school librarian has taken the lead, the public librarian can provide materials, potential prizes, such as reduced fines for the winner(s), and she can volunteer to attend the event as another adult to make the tournament run smoothly.

Likewise a how-to demonstration can be given on any topic you or your teens desire. The public librarian might engage a speaker to demonstrate how to design a web page, or offer a program on cartooning, cooking, photo editing, or creating an oral family history. These demonstrations can be scheduled to coincide with what the school librarian has indicated is on, or will be on, the academic calendar at the different times of the year. Or a demonstration can be suggested to cover topics that the schools are unable to address due to time or budget constraints. Health and wellness offerings can deal with medical and safety issues for students as well as their families; programs based on fitness, avoiding dating violence, and anti-bullying programs can provide the foundation for discussion in many venues and will allow you to partner not only with the school but also with local agencies that serve teens as well.

Another option is to contact your local American Society for the Prevention of Cruelty to Animals (ASPCA) to request an informational program about caring for your dog or cat. If your library allows, ask the ASPCA to bring animals that can be adopted on the spot. Charge teens from the library and the school with the task of spreading word of this event in local pet stores, coffee shops, and at afterschool events. Allow your volunteers to offer creative solutions on how to encourage on-the-spot adoptions; can they suggest incentives or create a short guide on how to care for your new family member? Ask if there might be extra credit offered in class for teens who have winning suggestions. Even if there isn't an adoption, or the possibility of adoption, teens will learn about pet care, volunteer opportunities at their local shelter, and vocational ideas for teens who love working with animals. (Yes, when our public library did this program there was at least one cat adoption that day, and it wasn't Stacey!)

Notes from the Field

Hampton Bays Public Library goes even further with their animal programs. They have an active Animal Lovers Club that created an Animal Shelter Binder after a visit to the local shelter. They create fliers for each cat or dog that can be adopted, complete with pictures and information, and keep the binder at the circulation desk. They conduct drives throughout the year, during which they accept food, blanket, and toys for the animals. Twice a year the library sponsors a Pet Sitting 101 course led by the librarian who is also a veterinary technician (Owens 2011, 340).

If you and your counterpart are inspired by Hampton Bays Public Library, you can start a similar program but why not try a broader approach? Create a career exploration program with help from the school's guidance counselors, school librarian, and a representative from a local college or vocational school. Include a science teacher to discuss animal physiology. Allow the teens who are working on the Animal Shelter

Binder to make it part of their art class, with photography, poster designing, or even web designing. The public library could be used as the site of regularly scheduled adopt-a-thons, with the teen volunteers growing into greater responsibility for the event over time. This program could become a multispeaker event, spread over many days or weeks.

INFLUENTIAL TEENS

If you aren't sure which programs would work for your students, survey them at school as well as at the public library to gauge their interests. If you have a Teen Advisory Board (TAB)—many public libraries and schools do—then these are the leaders who can help you to determine which programs will work and which may not be as popular. Create a list of possible topics with your counterpart, and ask for advice from your TAB. When the list has been reduced to a manageable size, post the survey results on the Teen page, the websites for both public and school libraries, and send out an email blast from school and public libraries to your teen mailing list. If you have a YA newsletter, be sure that the results are included, and be sure to include teen program information in the library's complete list of programs being offered as well. The school librarian can talk with the advisor for the school newspaper to create awareness of this new group and its activities. No matter which location the event is held at—school or public library—alert the school newspaper reporters each time a new event is scheduled and let the buzz begin. Reporters can interview members of your teen advisory board or the teen librarian. Each avenue touches a different group, and should help to boost awareness, and hopefully, attendance at your program (Honnold 2003, 170, 174).

Don't forget to run your ideas past your most avid teen readers as well. Some will not be "joiners" who are interested in being a part of a formal book club or advisory group, but they may still introduce you to topics that interest them and other teens as well. Identify and reach out to those teens who are not frequent users of the library. You may find some YA patrons who are more comfortable chatting with you online or giving you their opinion without a face-to-face meeting. Search for a way to include them in your decision-making process as well through online teen surveys, Twitter or Facebook accounts, or other forms of social media. A goldmine of willing teens might be just around the corner, or down the street, sitting in the school's library. Ask the school librarian if you can stop in when they are sure to have students in the library to explain what you're interested in trying and see if these teens will share their thoughts in return. Try leaving paper surveys for teens to fill out during the day, over a set period of time. You can collect the surveys from your counterpart one to two weeks later.

FINDING PROGRAMMING IDEAS

Many websites, journal articles, and books offer great programming ideas. Using these resources can save you a great deal of time and missteps, showing examples of what to avoid as well as learning what worked in other libraries. Some favorites are the guide created by former Wadsworth (OH) Public Library's Reference Manager Valerie Ott, *Teen Programs with Punch: A Month-by-Month Guide* (2006) and RoseMary Honnold's (19–23) programming calendars, and the programs suggested by her related to each Dewey category found in *101+ Teen Programs that Work* (Honnold 2003, 185–186). As editor-in-chief of *VOYA*, Honnold also created the web page "See YA Around: Library Programming for Teens" (http://www.cplrmh.com/). In their book *Connecting Young Adults and Libraries: A How-to-Do-It Manual* (2009), YA authors Patrick Jones, Michele Gorman, and Tricia Suellentrop provide you with the tools to plan and organize your joint program, including a "School Planning Form" to help you to start your collaboration. Most programming falls into one of two categories: passive or active. Whichever you do, you can collaborate.

PASSIVE PROGRAMMING

Passive programs can be defined as events that a librarian sets up, allowing teens to participate with little or no supervision, dropping in at their own convenience. These programs are easy to create and even easier to run; they have a great return in participation versus the time and money they take to plan. Passive programs seem to be popular on a cyclical basis; but why not keep it in your list of things to try? Maybe it's time for this style of programming to become popular again. Passive programming is inexpensive, easy to plan and execute, and teens are often as happy to have something productive to do on their own in their free time as they are to plan around your regularly scheduled programming. Passive programs are more inclusive to teens with busy lives and also appeal to teens trapped in the library waiting for a parent to pick them up after school. What's not to like about passive programs?

An example of passive programming is the Internet Scavenger Hunt, which can be done either inside the library, or from home. This type of program can be a good mix of educational and entertaining programming. The scavenger hunt might be a list of questions found on the library's website with clues to what information or which resources the teens are meant to find. Each clue builds on the next, with a final answer that can be dropped off or emailed to the librarian sponsoring the contest. It is also extremely easy to make this a cross-library event. The first clue can be provided by either organization and can direct teens directly to the other organization's website; from there it's extremely easy to come up with a series of databases, websites, or online activities that both the librarians find useful. The ultimate goal of the search can also be used as a method of promoting secondary events at either—or both—locations. This activity works best if the search and end result are fairly narrow and easy to discover, so that teens can successfully learn about one topic or idea without much guidance. For example, the first clue can come from a recent lesson at the school library that focused on effective Internet searching and might be, "What search engine will find you the largest number of returns from a group of other search engines? Hint: The name of this search engine might be something like: man's best friend." From there, the teens can learn more about how Dogpile.com works, from the definition of metasearching to the adventures of Arfie, Dogpile.com's mascot. The second clue might lead teens to the public library's website with the clue, "Ask Arfie to help you find locations in your area that offer teens a free class in resume writing." When teens find the public library's teen resume writing program, make sure they can also easily find directions for registration. Continue to draw teens' attention onward until everyone is satisfied that plenty of fun and learning have been accomplished.

More examples of passive programming to get you started are given here.

Counting

A good way to attract teens' attention is by asking them to count food in containers. Is it February? Why not celebrate National Chocolate Month by asking teens to estimate the number of individually wrapped chocolates in the sealed jar? This program can be run concurrently in both the public and school libraries, with the same or different types of candies. It would be a fun learning challenge if both containers had the exact same amount of candy but the shape of the container (short and wide vs. tall and slim) was the variant. Or it could just be a great incentive to draw a larger than usual number of teens into your space, and then take advantage of their presence to discuss other programs or secure feedback on other programming ideas. The teens that come into the library will be able to clearly see the three dimensions of the container, a decided advantage for them and a bonus opportunity for the teen librarian to interact with them, but you can also post a photo on the Internet for teens who can't visit the library. Entries can be accepted by telephone, email to the teen librarian, or in-person slips of paper submitted by a set deadline. The number of candies is then counted and a winner selected. If there is more than one participant with the right, or nearly right, answer, a random draw selects the winner. The prize? The large container of candy!

Pop Culture Trivia Quizzes

Easy to make, these "time wasters" give teens something to think about, and something productive to do while they're "hanging out" in the library. Grab some trivia about current celebrities or topics from teen-friendly places such as MTV, *Entertainment Weekly, People, Rolling Stone,* Yahoo, and *VOYA's* "Pop Culture Quiz." Librarians can take turns creating one quiz to distribute in both libraries at the same time, allowing teens to start looking for answers in one location but finishing in the other. Clearly mark the start and finish dates for the quiz, and identify the prizes being offered. Prizes can range from a free book to a food treat to a free pass to spend time in the school library to extra help researching a school paper to a library fine waiver. If you're truly ambitious, you could post a running "scoreboard" listing teens who've answered the most quiz questions correctly (offer to use nicknames for anonymity). Award a grand prize for overall points at the end of a specified time period, ranging anywhere from a month, through summer break, or as long as an entire school year. As you are in constant contact with your counterpart, it will be easy to decide ahead of time how you'll be dividing up the responsibilities. If you created the quiz, would it make more sense to track the answers and award the prize or would be it better to divide the task by asking your counterpart to take over after you've posted the quiz? If you choose to have an online component for teens, find reputable, trustworthy sites ahead of time and make a text, telephone number, or email address readily available for teens seeking assistance.

ACTIVE PROGRAMMING

Have you ever considered how many people you know? Are you aware that all these people have "hidden talents" that they might be willing to share? This can be one of the best revelations you ever have as a teen or school librarian, that your coworkers and the staff of a variety of stores where you already purchased programming supplies, all have talents and hobbies they are willing to teach to teens—most often at no charge. The following are some examples of active programming.

Craft Clubs

The Knitting and Crochet Club came about, thanks to a craft store employee who was willing to share her needle crafting abilities with the library teens for free. The library purchased the supplies, needles, and yarn; but there are low-end options that won't break the bank if you choose to try this program. The craft store was in a nearby town and was the locale where we purchased most of the library's craft supplies; however, this particular employee wasn't motivated by anything except her interest in teaching others about the hobby she enjoyed. Teens were able to complete simple scarves by the time the lessons were over. This can be an ongoing program for the library, such as a knitting and crochet club; or it can be held for a limited time with an end goal, such as creating a scarf. Select any craft that appeals to your teens; any craft that someone is willing to teach: scrapbooking, woodworking, watercolors, print making, the list is endless. One of our high school art teachers is a gifted scrapbooker who would be a good resource for a teen program. Supplies for scrapbooking can be obtained inexpensively from discarded magazines or shabby picture books weeded from the collection, and the glue, scissors, and foundation paper can come from the library's general supply closet. Don't think this type of program only benefits the public library. It's fun for teens to see their teachers, including their school librarians, outside of their familiar setting. A volunteer from the school, teaching a craft in the public library, can provide a chance for teens and adults to interact in a new way, with different goals and might yield some good surprises for everyone. Don't forget to survey your local businesses. Would a garden store sponsor a community garden at the library? Would a mechanic show teens how to care for their car? Also check the local vocational school for teachers, or advanced students, who can speak about car maintenance.

Babysitting Clinics

One of the most popular programs at our library has traditionally been the Babysitting Clinic; but the program itself continues to change and evolve each time a new teen librarian takes charge. Some changes that were made were recruiting a Red Cross volunteer to demonstrate but not certify teens in lifesaving techniques; a city firefighter and police-man to speak on how, when, and why to contact them for help; and a library patron who was a nurse to share child development information, including activities appropriate for each age group. Teens were required to attend all sessions, there were too many people with too much to say for one day, and complete a "homework" assignment detailing what they would do in a fictional babysitting experience. If all tasks were completed, they were presented with a certificate to share with potential clients.

Does your local high school have a parenting class? If so, the school librarian might contact the teacher as a possible speaker. The parenting class teacher could lead you to additional speakers and resources, used in the past. Her students could be a ready-made audience for your program or could serve as your assistants or hosts and hostesses for the event.

In Our Experience

Do be careful about becoming "the" babysitter resource for your com-munity. In our library, I began my hosting of this particular program by keeping a list of teens who completed all tasks related to the babysitting clinic and were interested in being contacted for jobs. Parents would call me and I would call the teens. Not actually knowing the parents who were calling left me in an awkward position and feeling uncomfortable, so this part of the program was ended. If you're considering being a conduit between teens who complete the clinic and parents looking for sitters, discuss the idea with your management team, and consider it in accordance with your individual library's policies and the community in which you work.

Creative Writing

Local nonprofit organizations are another great resource. There is a writing group near our city and when Stacey contacted them to see if there were any writing contests for teens, she wound up with something even better. The head of the organization was not just willing, but was interested in sharing tips, tricks, and tools for successful writers at the public library. All for free! Teens were invited to bring writing samples and the chance to form their own writing group at the library. This pro-gram was not as popular as Stacey had anticipated, but for the few teen writers who embraced the experience, it was worth the effort. The teens who participated had direct conversations with a published writer, and were lucky enough to be provided with inside tips on how to be published themselves. It also gave these teens a chance to begin "networking" in a field where good contacts count for a lot, even if they didn't know that's what they were doing. This shouldn't discourage you from undertaking a creative writing program of your own, instead be sure that your programs are advertised in all nearby schools.

Ask your school librarian for help contacting the English or language arts teacher to see if extra credit might be offered, or for help partnering with the teacher to build your small program into something larger. Often there are creative writing or poetry clubs at schools and these teens may be interested in participating if they hear about this opportunity. This could even be the beginning of a joint public/school library newsletter written by, and for, teens who attended the creative writing program. Don't forget to ask your expert volunteer who's teaching the program for ideas you can promote ahead of time at both the school and in the public library.

Why not try alternating your passive and active programming, so that you can offer the most opportunities to teens, both inside and outside of your library's walls? This will keep you from totally depleting the public service desk staff while still providing teens something interesting to occupy their time. Keep a record of the programs you've sponsored, the speakers you've used and the dates. (See the programming log in Figure 3.1.) The columns allow you to easily sort your programs by year or month, even by time frame.

In Our Experience

Every disappointment can become a chance to reimagine your original idea into something new, something that might be even better! Don't be afraid to try the same program again later that year, or in a few years. Just because the teens one year don't have the writing bug, it doesn't mean that the next year won't be full of aspiring writers. If you like the idea behind a program, keep trying and tweaking it until you find a way to make it work for everyone!

INTERNET SAFETY PROGRAMS

In Our Experience

In February 2010, our local school district wished to create in-school programs for students dealing with Internet safety (also known as digital citizenship). In a "Ripped from the Headlines" moment, the district's focus was to create an awareness of the dangers of the practice of "sexting," sending inappropriate pictures via phone, or computer, or posting them on social network sites. Nearby cities had arrested some juveniles and were determining what crimes may have been committed through the act of forwarding these pictures throughout their online networks. Talk of labeling these 15-year olds as sexual offenders who would need to register their whereabouts for the remainder of their lives had received regional coverage on television new stations, talk radio, and in newspapers. Parents and adults who work with teens were very concerned when they learned about sexting and the potential consequences.

The high school decided to create an awareness program for students followed by an evening program for parents. A committee was appointed, consisting of the chair of the guidance department, the school's social worker, the school librarian, her assistant, and the police liaison to the school. This patrolman also happens to be a member of our state's Internet Crimes Against Children (ICAC) task force. The main task of the school librarian was to create lists of useful sites for parents. These lists would be included in the resource packets distributed at the evening program. The librarian immediately contacted both the teen librarian and the manager of children's services at her local library. Together the four library staff members gathered websites and resources, removed duplicate entries, and revised the materials to fit the packet. The program was deemed a success as approximately 60 parents and community members attended the event. None of the librarians spoke at the session; their task instead was to organize the event, provide space, promote the occasion, and to gather, then share information and additional resources. Future programs dealt with similar topics but were updated to reflect changes in the law.

Notes from the Field

Look for chances to meet with parents and community members during a school's Meet the Teacher night or Open House. One Open House evening our school scheduled a financial aid counselor who spoke to parents about securing financial aid for college. Since this is normally a well-attended program, we invited our public library's teen librarian to set up a booth in the back of the auditorium. As parents left, she distributed bookmarks listing resources housed at the library and showcased books on financing a college education. The reverse side of the bookmark now contains lists of test-taking databases, their websites and passwords, or an advertisement for your own SAT/ACT practice test program.

MARKETING YOUR PROGRAMS

Part of the difficulty in creating programming comes from determining exactly what will grab the interest and attention of your teen audience, and getting them to attend. Here again, collaborating helps. Create online

You may prefer a spreadsheet format so that minutes can easily be calculated for reports. The year is placed in a separate column so that you can sort your programs by year.

Year	Date	Title	Description, include age or grade level	Time Frame	Contacts	Phone and Email	Supplies needed and costs	Evaluation
2010	2.10	Internet Safety	For parents: keeping your children safe, cyberbullying, sexting	120 min	City police officer, school librarian and assistant, school social worker and Head of the Guidance department		Speakers were free; community members	Internet Crimes against Children task force (ICAC) officer is a must. Packets for parents must include materials from both school and public libraries. Reception after should have table displays of materials

Figure 3.1: Programming Log

From *Better Serving Teens through School Library–Public Library Collaborations* by Cherie P. Pandora and Stacey Hayman Santa Barbara, CA: Libraries Unlimited, Copyright © 2013.

surveys with your counterpart to gather ideas from your teens and promote them at both libraries; brainstorm with your student workers, your student book club participants, your student advisory board, and your voracious readers. Perhaps you can plan a joint social event that allows the TABs from school and public libraries to meet and evaluate programming ideas. Check library literature and listservs for ideas from colleagues; use social network channels for additional lists of dos and don'ts. Once you have made your tentative list, search for ways in which you can market and advertise the programs of your sister library through your own resources. Special programming announcements can be placed in a banner on your website's home page. Call in the details to your local weekly newspapers for inclusion on their event calendars. School librarians can create short public service announcements (PSAs) for their morning video announcements, and add the information to their electronic signs, as well as to online, and cable, bulletin boards. The information can also be added to the online newsletters and bulletins that are sent to parents, PTA members, community members, and Friends of the Library groups. If the event is scheduled a few months ahead, try to get your information into the director's message, a superintendent's newsletter, or a publication from the board of trustees and/or the school's board of education.

Once the programs have been set, get the word out through as many avenues as possible. If your library is lucky enough to have a marketing director or public relations person, your job will likely be a little easier. The person in this role has many contacts and has a better chance of securing publicity via articles in local newspapers and community bulletin boards, both electronic and physical boards. Besides placing advertisements on your home web page and the teen pages, hang posters and distribute flyers in those places where your teens congregate. While this means the school library and the school in general, it also means coffee houses, recreation centers, and local retailers, or anywhere else your teens like to spend time. If your program involves music, be sure that you reach the multiple music stores in both your town and neighboring towns. Students who travel to the music store for lessons, valve oil, sheet music, or guitar picks are likely to see your posters there. The same holds true for your gamers; place posters about your game night in the stores where they buy and sell back their computer and video games.

In her book *Bite-Sized Marketing*, Nancy Dowd (2010, 9) explains that most of us have a system for external marketing but we also need to remember to market our programs, with our own staff. Dowd refers to what she calls "WOMM—Word-of-Mouth-Marketing." She believes that you need to target the 10% of folks who are the most influential. We call them "power parents"; she calls them "influencers." Whatever you want to call them, they will help you to reach the other 90% of your target audience (ibid., 9). Your library staff includes folks also willing to be advocates for your teens. Many of them are coaches, community leaders, or scout leaders; many more will be parents. They can spread the word through channels that you may not otherwise reach. Oftentimes they can get the word out to neighboring communities as well.

CROSS-PROMOTION

The programs you create in your library are often designed to appeal to students from multiple communities and multiple schools. In addition to the local public school, your public library draws students from parochial, private, and independent schools from within your community's borders and from outside the city limits. You are also likely to bring in students and parents from surrounding cities and school districts that simply enjoy your library. Be sure to market your program to all these agencies.

BUDGETING

Depending on what your program is, you may be able to secure corporate sponsors to help with the costs of your events. Hopefully your PR or marketing person has a precrafted template for sponsorship; but don't panic if you have to work on creating your own letter. Try searching the Internet for "sponsorship request letter" and you'll find samples and suggestions to use, and reuse as you need to modify the wording to request financial support of your various programs. Brainstorm with your counterpart to find sponsors who may be able to supply prizes, gift cards, or cash to help with the cost of printing posters. For example, if your program deals with a sports topic, contact local sporting good stores, recreation centers, and the appropriate community organizations that sponsor these sports. You may want to send word to multiple schools' athletic directors and athletic trainers so they can forward it to the appropriate coaches. It would be a great show of solidarity for both librarians to sign the letter. Clearly indicate who should be contacted with questions or offers of sponsorship to prevent confusion. If you secure sponsorship, be sure to include your sponsor's company name (and logo, if there is one) prominently on all flyers, posters, and on your electronic notices of the program. (If you are considering writing a grant you'll want to read Chapter 12.)

EVALUATING PROGRAMS

Keep a record of *every* program that you attempt, whether successful or not. Having a notebook (paper or electronic) that contains your programming log will help you to recreate or modify programs, should you choose to do it again. As mentioned earlier in this chapter, sometimes a program falls flat one year but, is wildly successful the next as your teen population changes, children move up to the teen area, or related news items surface and build awareness around a topic. Keeping such a notebook allows you to describe the program, record your attendance and the age level of the students who attended, and include a list of supplies needed and the costs incurred (Honnold 2003, 179–180). Be sure to include feedback from the teens themselves, as well as the comments of the staff members and any speakers involved. Having the words of the teens themselves is the best evaluation for your programming efforts! You can also use teen comments to build those parts of the program that got the most positive feedback, allowing you to go from a successful program to a wildly outstanding program! Besides helping you to remember your programs from year to year, this notebook is very handy for writing the quarterly or annual reports that you must submit to your manager or director.

Now that you feel inspired to try something new, or to tweak a previously less than successful program, don't forget the three most important lessons we've learned over the years:

1. Even the biggest program flops were worth trying at least once, because you never know what will be a surprise hit,
2. If you love a program, it will translate into an excitement teens will pick up on and feel too, and
3. Use all the available resources you have, which should naturally include your teen services counterpart!

REFERENCES

Dowd, Nancy, Mary Evangeliste, and Jonathan Silberman. *Bite-Sized Marketing: Realistic Solutions for the Overworked Librarian.* Chicago, IL: ALA, 2010.

Honnold, RoseMary. *101+ Teen Programs That Work.* New York: Neal-Schuman Publishers, 2003.

Jones, Patrick, Michele Gorman, and Tricia Suellentrop. *Connecting Young Adults and Libraries: A How-to-Do-It Manual.* 4th ed. New York: Neal-Schuman Publishers, 2009.

Ott, Valerie A. *Teen Programs With Punch: A Month-by-Month Guide.* Westport, CT: Libraries Unlimited, 2006.

Owens, Theresa, and Jackie Dunn. "Super Projects for Super Teens!" *VOYA* 34, no. 4 (2011): 340.

FURTHER READING

Hampton Bays Public. Library. HBay Teen Services. "Blog," http://hbayya.blog spot.com/ (cited February 29, 2012).
Vittek, Robyn E. "The People in Your Neighborhood: Using Local Collaboration to Advocate for Teen Patrons." *Young Adult Library Services* 9, no. 1 (2010): 13–14.

Programming Idea Websites

Looking for more places to connect with librarians who work with the teen population? Here are a few places to begin your search:

American Library Association, "Programming Librarian," http://www.program minglibrarian.org/library/programs.html (cited February 29, 2012).
Honnold, RoseMary. "See YA Around: Library Programming for Teens," http:// www.cplrmh.com/ (cited February 29, 2012).
IPL2, Internet Public Library. "Clubs and Organizations (Programming Ideas)," http://www.ipl.org/IPLBrowse/GetSubject?vid=10&cid=2&tid=2630&pa rent=0 (cited February 29, 2012).
YALSA. "2011 Teen Tech Week Mini Grants," http://ala.org/ala/mgrps/divs/ yalsa/teentechweek/ttw11/grants/mg11.cfm (cited February 29, 2012).
YALSA. "Calendar of Teen Programming Ideas," http://wikis.ala.org/yalsa/index .php/Calendar_of_Teen_Programming_Ideas (cited February 29, 2012).

4

◇ ◇ ◇

CELEBRATE READING!

As stereotypical as it may sound, most librarians like to read in their spare time. Our joy, and our challenge, is figuring out how to pass that love of reading to the next generation. Today, more than ever before, there are so many more ways of successfully putting teens together with the written word. In this chapter, school and teen librarians can explore some of these new creative outlets for excited, as well as reluctant, readers, and learn how to maximize their impact through collaboration.

First, stop thinking that reading is defined as picking up a book and consuming the whole thing from cover to cover. Instead, broaden the definition to include comic books, graphic novels, popular blogs, magazines, even a series of facts and figures such as those you find in almanacs, or a book of sports statistics.

Working with teens who may not yet love to read can be challenging, but don't despair. In this chapter you'll find some strong resources and activities to begin turning those kids around, from reluctant into enthusiastic readers. You'll also find resources that will help you continue to challenge your more enthusiastic readers to keep trying new challenges. You'll also discover how your counterpart can help you in this worthy endeavor!

When it comes to reading promotion, there are so many different chances to collaborate with your counterpart, it's almost dizzying. We suggest that as you read down the list ask yourself these two questions:

1. If I find this interesting or inspirational and I'm willing to bear the brunt of the work, how can I get my counterpart involved in the pay off?
2. If I think this idea is better in my counterpart's venue and I'm willing to suggest it, how can I be of assistance?

For example, if a teen librarian in the public library has a video camera available, and an interested teen book discussion group, they might consider getting the teens thinking about a book that's been discussed and challenge the teens to create a book trailer promoting their selected title. Share the finished book trailer with the school librarian, who can suggest teachers who might be willing to show the trailer in their classroom. Show the trailer in the school's library, as well as on both librarians' social media networks. Or, to work the other direction, it could be that the teen librarian at the public library is fascinated by the possibilities presented by the BookUp or another reading program, but knows the school librarian is much more likely to be able to enroll the right students and volunteer instructors. Offering materials, physical space, program incentives as needed, and all the encouragement possible might be just what the school librarian needs to try something similar. Try reading over the list with your counterpart present, and let the brainstorming begin.

RESOURCES FOR PROGRAM PLANNING
BookUp

The National Book Foundation created the BookUp Program (http://www.nationalbook.org/bookup.html#.T2-hp_Vc6So) aimed at middle school students. BookUp states that they chose to focus on the middle school years after research that indicated this is the time when young people are at the greatest risk of losing the reading habit. The program is staffed by authors who are also educators; and it is currently only offered at five sites in New York City and, as of September 2010, in Brazos Valley, Texas. Held once a week after school for a period of 24 weeks during the regular school year, this program encourages teens to participate in activities that demonstrate how reading can be fun and interactive in unexpected ways. There is hope that eventually this program can be adapted to afterschool programs throughout the country, inspiring teens every-where to become lifelong readers. For sample activities to try in your own library, check out the suggestions on BookUp's website (http://www.nationalbook.org/bookupnyc.html#.T58Grtl1bAw).

GUYS READ

New ways to connect boys with books is always a topic of interest. The first official National Ambassador of Young People's Literature, author Jon Scieszka, created a nonprofit, literacy initiative based website called GUYS READ as a one-stop resource where you can find facts, figures, ideas to try, books to read, and links to further resources you can try. Maybe the public and school librarians would like to combine a core group of guys to start a GUYS READ Field Office (http://guysread.com/program/) with the tips provided. Remember, the main thrust of this site is an all-out effort to get guys reading (http://guysread.com/about/).

National Ambassador of Young People's Literature

The Center for the Book within the Library of Congress, the Children's Book Council (CBC), and the CBC's foundation, Every Child a Reader, are responsible for creating the National Ambassador of Young People's Literature program. Begun in 2008, this program highlights the impor-tance of encouraging young people to read by selecting well-known and well-loved authors who use their ambassadorship to promote a spe-cific platform aimed at encouraging the habit of reading. Walter Dean Myers is the third, and current, author honored with the title; Kather-ine Paterson was the second author to be so honored following the ini-tial ambassador, Jon Scieszka. School librarians might want to consider using materials from the public library, including books and databases, to supplement student research on past and present honorees, or to sug-gest future honorees.

The Exquisite Corpse Adventure

The Center for the Book offers numerous everyday tools to help you reach out to teens with interactive websites, suggested lesson plans, and author webcasts for kids to watch (http://read.gov/educators/). Share The Center's "The Exquisite Corpse Adventure" (http://read.gov/exquisite-corpse/) to get your teens started on their own progressive storytelling experiment. Provide an action-filled beginning for the story and let the teens, and their imaginations, run wild to keep the story going. Think of this as a wiki for storytelling where dozens of teen authors collaborate to write a story. Before adding a new section, each teen has to read what's come before; and they won't be able to resist finding out how the next author changed the storyline they left hanging. Print up the end result so it can be shared with the greatest audience possible.

Figment Write Yourself In

Teens who like to write and teens who like to read are often the very same teen. Figment Write Yourself In (http://figment.com/) is a website for teens that enjoy reading, writing, and sharing their thoughts about the written word. The site requires that users be 13 or older for individual sign-ups. There is also an option for an adult working with teens to create a group account (http://figment.com/signup/educators) to use the "virtual writing workshop" lessons offered. Teens can read professional reviews as well as see what other teens think about different books. Either the public or school librarian can provide access to this site and encourage students to begin participating. As with any project you will want to discuss such ideas and decide who takes the lead so that you can offer support without duplicating efforts. In addition, teens can enter contests with their writing or artwork, and win books and other prizes through random chance drawings. Some publishers also offer teens the opportunity to read and review books through their websites. A brief list includes:

- Random House (http://www.randomhouse.com/teens/)
- HarperTeen (http://www.harperteen.com/)
- Harlequin™ Teen offers the Harlequin™ Teen Panel (https://www.harlequinteenpanel.com/PORTAL/default.aspx)
- Disney Hyperion (http://disney.go.com/books/index)
- Teenreads.com (http://www.teenreads.com/) for all the news about new titles, writing opportunities, and even the chance to win free books.

BOOK TRAILERS

Video book trailers, growing in popularity all the time, are a great way to engage the interest of teens. Short clips featuring the author, or highlighting some portion of the plot, are being produced, primarily by publishers, to generate interest in books for all ages and all types of books. Most book trailers can be found safely on publisher websites, and tend to be less than five minutes long. An interactive book trailer for the popular book series *Gone* by Michael Grant was recently created (http://www .harperteen.com/feature/gone/), offering hours of interactive entertainment. It encourages readers to promote their favorite books by creating original book trailers that can be shared on your website or blog. Creating book trailers could be a project for the public library's TAB members, or a project for school librarians to adapt and use with English and language arts teachers. Wherever it is created, it is something that can be shared and cross-promoted with your counterpart.

VIRTUAL AUTHOR TOURS

Teens might be interested in participating in a virtual author tour by following a favorite author as they "guest post" on a succession of different blogs. This takes the effort of at least one teen dedicated to a specific author or an adult who is willing to read a larger number of blogs that center either on teen literature or favorite authors of their own. There is often a call for questions in advance of the "tour," and there's nothing more empowering for a teen than the feeling that a published author is paying direct attention to them. As this is a more independent experience, the school and public librarians might want to work together in keeping teens up-to-date with a list of sources about the authors they can find on a virtual tour.

Another way to connect readers with an author is through Skype. As detailed in the *School Library Journal* article "Met Any Good Authors Lately" by Kate Messner (http://www.schoollibraryjournal.com/arti cle/CA6673572.html) using videoconferencing can bring authors, near and far, directly into your classroom. Check author websites, blogs, Facebook pages, or publishers' websites to find authors willing to speak for a fee you can manage or, even better, for free. Keeping in touch on a regular basis will help narrow the search for authors to those who will complement upcoming public library programs or a current language arts unit.

CHALLENGES AND CENSORSHIP

Appeal to the activists in your crowd and encourage teens to stand up for everyone's right to read without restrictions. Have your teens create displays of materials that have been banned or challenged with information on how or why some adults have questioned whether teens should be reading those particular titles. To get the teens started, have them look at Challenges to Library Materials (http://www.ala.org/advocacy/banned/challengeslibrarymaterials) and Censorship in Schools (http://www.ala.org/advocacy/intfreedom/censorshipfirstamendmentissues/censorshipschools) for inspiration. You can tie this activity in with September's Banned Books Week or create your own special week to celebrate intellectual freedom. (See Appendix A for additional ideas). Ask teens to select a challenged book to read and share how they would defend their book against the reason(s) given for removal from the school or public library shelves. If they enjoy the process of reading and defending one of the books from a challenged book list, keep the process going. Each reading will sharpen their critical thinking skills just that little bit more and soon you'll have teens ready to participate in debating the merits of any book. You can then stage an actual debate for the public to witness, in multiple venues, allowing teens to share their new found passion with other teens and adults.

MOCK AWARDS

Perhaps your teens are already skilled at discerning which books have the qualities that might be worthy of a Newbery Award. Why not start a Mock Newbery or Michael L. Printz Award process? Even better, why not devise an entirely new book award from beginning to end? You and your teens will have fun creating the name of the award, deciding the criteria required for a title or author to be eligible, setting in place a time frame that would start with the selection of eligible titles up until the time that the winning book would be announced. Teens can design an actual award, and, if possible, contact the winning author to share the good news. Librarians working together can make sure this new award is advertised, announced, and displayed prominently in both locations. Who knows, maybe someday we will all be celebrating the bestowing of this newly created Book Award.

BOOKTALKS

An oldie but a goodie, booktalks have long been used by librarians as a way to spark interest in new or topical books. This is a great time to practice those public speaking skills, and enlist a friendly coworker or counterpart, if possible. The basic outline of a booktalk is as follows: select new, high-demand titles or books on a particular topic supporting a curriculum unit; scan the books and reviews as thoroughly as possible; write key information to share verbally; produce a written list for the teacher or students; and present your titles to as many classrooms or small groups as you can manage. As you work together, you'll want to double check your lists to prevent duplication and make some time to practice your presentation. Be excited about the books but never, not even if you've been swept away by your audience's positive reactions, never give away the ending of a book. Give them a reason to come in and check the book out, or maybe a different, equally interesting book, while they wait their turn for the booktalk title. This is a great way to reach the greatest variety of teens as your talks can be about anything and can lead to individual readers' advisory sessions.

DISPLAYS

Don't forget the power of simple displays; market your titles to stir up enthusiasm for your programs. Pulling out books on a theme, fiction or nonfiction, will allow easily distracted teens to look over a manageable selection of titles. Call this the "booksellers effect." Libraries of all types have emulated display styles found in popular brick and mortar bookstores to make their libraries more inviting to patrons. You'll often find best sellers and popular magazines close to the circulation desk, just like the candy aisle near the checkout lanes in a grocery store; the placement of these materials is designed to encourage impulsive decisions—in this case for patrons to take out additional items on a last minute whim. Displays are fun to design and can tap into the artistic talents of your teens. Allow your TAB the chance to brainstorm ideas for display cases, ask them to craft the visuals and select the books for your kiosks and shelves. Brainstorm with your counterpart to coordinate themes at public and school libraries; consider including titles from each collection in each display. From a thematic group of four or five titles, to a row of books, you can go as big or as small as you have the space and time to pull items on a topic. Use the Reading Month-by-Month list of ideas in Appendix A for timely inspiration, or ask teachers about upcoming lesson topics to support the curriculum. Once in a while you might want to challenge the teens, and yourself, to see if anyone can guess the common theme of what is on display.

In Our Experience

Would you be willing to create displays for each gender to see if they attracted more readers? Rocky River High School library has done so in the past. Cherie created special displays on hairstyling and fashion for girls (at their request) near prom time and often created displays of sports materials for boys. What interests your patrons? Why not challenge your patrons' perspective? How about car or bike repair for girls? What about cooking for boys?

BOOK CLUBS

Some teens are interested in discussing books primarily for the social aspect, but will also enjoy learning more about the author or digging deeper into ideas presented in the story. Consider making your book club into a cosponsored group by either alternating locations, leaders, or providing the materials between you and your counterpart. The average book club experience can be fairly easy and straightforward to organize. Share possible titles for selection, make sure enough copies are secured for interested teens, set a time and place, encourage teens to bring questions to supplement your ideas, and prepare for an interesting hour.

For those teens who are regular readers and devour books faster than you can suggest new titles, you may want to start a different type of book club. You can customize the club to meet the needs of these teens. Perhaps you have fantasy fans who would like their own book group; why not try a specialized group? Are your teens service oriented? Collaborate with the high school's service learning teacher and locate some books that deal with volunteerism (Kunzel and Hardesty 2006, 53–56). Are they potential leaders who need a shot of confidence? Why not read the stories of people who have made a difference in the world. Ask teens to suggest lists of their heroes and add some inspiring role models that will speak to teen interests (ibid., 42–46). Remember that a book discussion group can meet to read and discuss one book; it need not be a yearlong project.

READING PROMOTIONS FOR BOYS

As author Scieszka (2012) asserts on his website GUYS READ (http://www.guysread.com/), mentioned previously, libraries need more ways to encourage reading among young male patrons. Approach this as another opportunity to have a conversation with your counterpart, talk about what works or does not seem to work when the teens are in your location.

Some libraries have had success with book clubs just for boys, particularly with the middle school age group. Do your young men enjoy stories about fantasy or science fiction? Which book series fly off the shelves? Promote their favorite genres with special displays and continue to request their suggestions for books, programs, and displays. Ask if they are interested in a book club based solely on their favorite types of books. If your male readers are do-it-yourself types, then stock how-to titles on anime drawing, game creation, or snowboarding, whatever topic is most interesting to them. Observe what the teen boys are looking at when they're in the library. Ask middle school librarians which books and magazines are most popular with their boys who read. Are they checking out sports, computer or gaming magazines, horror, humor, or graphic novels? If you let boys select the materials for a book club you may even create a new group of readers (Brozo 2010, 187–188). Brozo mentions a teacher who created a rack of books in his classroom to encourage his male students to read; he labeled it the "Guys Rack" (ibid., 93). The bookshelf contained books on topics that his boys liked to read but girls were encouraged to choose from these books as well.

For public and school librarians, the idea of encouraging teens to read, for pleasure or for education, seems so obvious that you may take it for granted that teens will approach you when they want a book. Think again! Teens need to see us as readers, as nonjudgmental and enthusiastic providers of the written word. Teens need to witness how willing we are to accept all the different ways they like to read, to process the information, and to share their own opinions about what they've read. As you begin to expand your idea of what it means to read, the variety of formats, the opportunities to mix books with new media, you will find a greater understanding of how to market books to teens, books that they might have never known that they really want to read. Be ready, willing, and able to move outside the expected and you'll find more ways to celebrate reading every day. Remember, there are plenty of people and organizations willing to share ideas and resources to help make a difference.

REFERENCES

American Library Association. "Censorship in Schools," http://www.ala.org/advocacy/intfreedom/censorshipfirstamendmentissues/censorshipschools (cited October 3, 2012).

American Library Association. "Challenges to Library Materials," http://www.ala.org/advocacy/banned/challengeslibrarymaterials (cited October 3, 2012).

Brozo. William G. *To be a Boy, to be a Reader: Engaging Teen and Preteen Boys in Active Literacy.* Newark, DE: International Reading Association, 2010.

The Center for the Book. "Educators and Parents," http://read.gov/educators (cited October 3, 2012).

The Center for the Book. "Exquisite Corpse," http://read.gov/exquisite-corpse/ (cited October 3, 2012).

Figment. "Write Yourself In," http://figment.com/ (cited October 3, 2012).

HarperTeen. "Gone: Gone Series," http://www.harperteen.com/feature/gone/ (cited October 3, 2012).

Kunzel, Bonnie, and Constance Hardesty. *The Teen-Centered Book Club: Readers into Leaders.* Westport, CT: Libraries Unlimited, 2006.

Messner, Kate. "Met Any Good Authors Lately?" *School Library Journal* 55, no. 8 (2009): 36. (http://www.schoollibraryjournal.com/article/CA6673572.html).

National Book Foundation. "BookUp," http://www.nationalbook.org/bookup.html#.T2-hp_Vc6So (cited October 3, 2012).

Scieszka, John. "Guys Read," http://www.guysread.com (cited October 3, 2012).

FURTHER READING

Agosto, Denise E., and Sandra Hughes-Hassell. *Urban Teens in the Library: Research and Practice.* Chicago, IL: ALA, 2010, 41, 160–62.

Alessio, Amy J., and Kimberly A. Patton. *A Year of Programs for Teens 2.* Chicago, IL: ALA, 2011, 74–75, 66–67, 118–19.

Anderson, Sheila B. Extreme *Teens: Library Services to Nontraditional Young Adults.* Westport, CT: Libraries Unlimited, 2005.

Krashen, Stephen D. *The Power of Reading: Insights From the Research.* Westport, CT: Libraries Unlimited, 2004.

Lodge, Sally. "Spotlighting YA." *Publishers Weekly* 258, no. 40 (2011): 24.

5

$\diamond$ $\diamond$ $\diamond$

SUMMER READING

Having the freedom to read for FUN is, well, a librarian's dream! To leisurely sit under a tree or sway in a hammock, sipping lemonade in the sun, reading a book from an endless list of novels to be enjoyed when there is time. What JOY! Unfortunately, many of our "'tweens" and teenagers view summer reading as just one more mandatory assignment and a monumental chore! Why is there no excitement? How can you bring back the joy of reading? And perhaps most importantly, *who* can help us to win over students and bring them back to reading? The answer to this last question can be found in collaboration between school and teen librarians.

To understand why working together on summer reading projects is so important, look to: "The Dominican Study: Public Library Summer Reading Programs Closing the Reading Gap." This effort by the Graduate School of Library and Information Science at Dominican University in River Forest, Illinois, studied the benefits of summer reading programs for students. During the period 2006–2009 in 11 sites across the United States, this group examined the summer reading loss of 367 students nearing the end of third grade and entering the fourth grade in the fall. Students completed pretests and posttests and surveys; their community and school librarians, teachers, and parents were also surveyed. The study found that students participating in public library summer reading programs showed better progress on standardized tests as well as better reading skills than those who had not participated. Surveys of the children also showed that students participating in these programs enjoyed reading as an activity, while parents reported that their children also read more books and spent more time actively reading during the summer ("Dominican Study," 2010). While the age group they studied was quite young, their results would likely also prove true for our preteen and teenage patrons.

Secondary teachers often bemoan the loss of skills over the summer. They are forced to spend precious weeks at the beginning of each school year reteaching grammar, writing, and reading comprehension techniques to make up for this erosion of skills. Librarians need to ensure that the summer reading programs are well managed and include materials that appeal to students, and in the case of schools, relate in some manner to curricular goals. Even when summer reading programs are in place, the results aren't always fantastic. Too many summer reading programs are poorly managed and executed. Let's take a closer look.

HOW IT TOO OFTEN WORKS

Many English Language Arts teachers are currently required to review the previous year's summer reading lists. The curriculum director, assistant superintendent, or dean of instruction generally advises them that all new selections must be accompanied by the proper form detailing the rationale for inclusion with a listing of *any* controversial subjects or language that can be found in the text (see Figure 5.1). Discussion of these books with other teachers or with school and public librarians prior to selection is nonexistent. Department chairs set a deadline for the classroom teachers, which may be as short as three weeks. School and teen librarians are not invited to participate in any part of the process. In many cases, teachers do not have the time or have not taken the time to reread the books, let alone to view them through the eyes of teenage students. The same list is often retained from year to year, because this saves teachers and administrators a great deal of time, and reduces the risk of selecting a book that is deemed "inappropriate." There is also an assumption that if the previous year's books have caused no uproar from parents and the community then the list MUST be a good one. Even if new books are added to the list they are "the usual suspects" from classical English and American literature—generally published 50 years ago or more. No contemporary YA titles are allowed; and very few titles from non-European authors are considered. If a YA title is added to the list, it must be a safe, older title that is no longer considered controversial. No one ever thinks to contact the school librarian or the teen librarian at the public library for advice on titles or on locating reviews!

Title _____

Author _____

Grade Level and/or Age level _____

Cost? _____

Circle one answer for each below:

    Fiction or Nonfiction?

    Available in hardback, paperback, or both?

Quality: What makes you recommend this book?

Popularity: Why would students enjoy this book?

Educational purpose: Topics and themes for discussion:

Figure 5.1: Summer Reading Suggestions with Rationale

From *Better Serving Teens through School Library–Public Library Collaborations* by Cherie P. Pandora and Stacey Hayman Santa Barbara, CA: Libraries Unlimited, Copyright © 2013.

Each fall, students write essays about their summer reading or take a prefabricated quiz from one of the reading programs. There is no discussion of the books read, just a grade entered into the grade book to satisfy the district's requirement. The result? A tepid reading list, bored students, and mediocre essays. Students often don't even bother to read the books; instead they gather all their information from generic online reviewing sources. School librarians (though often not a part of the selection process) receive phone calls from parents complaining that a book on the list is out-of-print or available only in hardcover, vastly increasing the parent's costs. The public library staff deals with frustrated parents who find that there are too few copies of the book available, that their children can't relate to the books, or that the library doesn't have copies of the book with the "correct ISBN."

Unfortunately, this process is typical for the selection of summer reading materials in many schools. Teen librarians—check with your counterpart to see how their school's selection process works; inquire if you can assist them by suggesting and selecting titles, or verifying the availability of titles already selected. Cherie would be hard pressed to number the times the librarians in the Children's and Teen Department saved the school's English teachers embarrassment by warning that a selected book was out-of-print!

HOW IT COULD WORK

The newly formed summer reading committee welcomes the school librarian and the teen librarian from the public library to participate in the selection process. Ideally, your committee will be 10–12 in number with the department chair and two representatives from the English Language Arts department, the librarians listed above, two students, two parents, a school administrator, and a representative from the library board of trustees.

Via email or collaborative online tools, committee members receive the timeline for selection; forms needed to propose new selections; and suggested dates for the three or four meetings needed to discuss the books. Book suggestions are welcomed and used to create a "long list" of book candidates. Student representatives are invited to join the committee. Committee members receive copies of the previous year's summer reading list, which includes descriptive and evaluative annotations taken from a published review, or one written by you or a colleague.

Librarians then recommend titles from the list, check to see if titles under consideration are out-of-print, and locate reviews for those titles that are considered controversial. Librarians gather copies of the books to be shared and discussed at these meetings. Voting by members of the committee results in a "short list" of four or five titles. Committee members are required to read each book and are invited to campaign for the titles that they wish to see included on the final list.

The most avid readers on the staff become a part of the process, regardless of the content area they teach or their job title. This process allows for buy-in from all staff members, including support staff. Adult and YA novels as well as nonfiction titles are considered. The committee discusses numerous titles for each grade and eventually selects one book for each grade level along with additional elective titles. Students, teachers, librarians, and administrators then read the novels appropriate to their grade level and refer to them, in class discussions, throughout the year.

The summer reading list is open to multiple formats, so students can choose the medium that best suits their dominant learning style. This is a wonderful benefit for students, because it provides numerous ways to reach the same goal! Students are allowed to read a book in the traditional manner, or use auditory tools or computer methods to read the material. Some formats include, but are not limited to the following: audiobooks, eBooks, Playaways, and MP3 files designed to reach students who learn best through the auditory medium or who need accommodations due to vision problems. (For more information on various learning styles visit http://www.teachervision.fen.com/intelligence/teaching-methods/2204.html.)

Adding factual material to the reading list brings science and history teachers and subject specialist librarians into the process, and provides students with a great advantage. Sample reading categories include science, history, multicultural studies, service oriented, business, and current read categories.

Sample Titles:

Science:	*The Hot Zone* by Richard Preston
	Genome by Matt Ridley
Multicultural works:	*Three Cups of Tea* by Greg Mortenson
	The Kite Runner by Khaled Hosseini (novel)
History:	*Fallen Angels* by Walter Dean Myers
	The Looming Tower by Lawrence Wright

STUDENT ASSESSMENTS

To find out whether your efforts achieved their goals, you have many options beyond the typical book report or essay. Discussion groups, podcasts, videos, dramatic readings, or almost any other project used in the classroom can be used as a summer reading assessment. While written assessments or reflections are the norm, consider having students meet in small discussion groups to discuss the books, their reactions to the themes and characters, and what they learned through reading this work. Discussion groups, led by teachers, librarians, guidance counselors, the social worker, or members of the support staff can be highly effective if student groups are limited to 10 or fewer students per group (see Figure 5.2). This offers a great venue for the library staff to take part in the process and to work with students and teachers in new ways. Adding a teen librarian to a discussion group at school will wonderfully complement the process and bring in additional expertise.

In Our Experience

Our students loved the book discussions and were happy that they had no assigned written report for the books they chose to read 'for fun.' For the first time we had students *who willingly read **more** books than required from the list.* Staff feedback showed that students _had_ read the books they chose and _wanted_ to talk about their reactions to the books.

Cherie Pandora, Rocky River High School.

SPECIAL TIPS AND SOLUTIONS

You would think that summer reading programs would work like clockwork. Public libraries have been promoting summer reading for decades. Schools have a vested interest in promoting literacy, but not all schools require summer reading. Still there are many obstacles and barriers that have to be overcome to create, promote, and sustain a successful program. As a public librarian, you might find that there is no longer a school librarian who works with the teenage group. In these cases, you can assist your teen patrons by working directly with the English Language Arts department chair or with individual teachers. If a summer reading list isn't sent from the school, call, email, or better yet, visit the school in person. Contact the public, private, and religious schools in your area and order materials according to the size of the student body and proximity of each school to the public library. If instead, you are a school librarian and find that there is no teen librarian at your local library, you

Discussion Leader _____

Book Title _____

Student names	Contributed to discussion?	Did he/she read the book?
1.		
2.		
3.		
4.		
5.		
6.		

Topics and questions for further discussion:

_____

_____

_____

_____

Figure 5.2: Student Discussion Feedback

From *Better Serving Teens through School Library–Public Library Collaborations* by Cherie P. Pandora and Stacey Hayman Santa Barbara, CA: Libraries Unlimited, Copyright © 2013.

need to find some teen-friendly advocates in other departments. Librarians in the children's room often work with middle school students and can help you with these preteens and younger teens. Reference librarians may be helpful for they see what teen patrons enjoy reading and which periodicals circulate to teens.

Unfunded Mandates

One problem with summer reading lists is that schools tend to work on a schedule that neglects the needs of the public library. Schools concentrate solely on the needs of teachers and students when selecting or revising their lists; they pay little attention to the costs in time and labor that it requires for public libraries to support these initiatives. School summer reading lists essentially present an unfunded mandate for public libraries. The reality is that most public library directors do not have the luxury to create a separate line item budget solely to support the summer reading lists of local schools. Instead, they rely on their departmental budgets to support the acquisition of these titles and provide for storage when these items are no longer in demand. A wholesale changeover in a school's reading list choices (e.g., from classic literature to YA fiction) could cost a public library *thousands* of dollars. Such changeover can decimate a library's fiction budget if monies must be reallocated to cover these unexpected costs.

Unforeseeable disasters can also strain the budget of the public library. Stacey's library suffered a ceiling leak in the storage area that housed hundreds of summer reading books; repurchasing summer reading books was a tremendous drain on the budget of our colleagues in the teen department.

Timeline Problems

Timelines for school reading lists can be problematic when they do not take into account the many steps needed for librarians at the public library to order, process, catalog, and prepare the books for students. On the other hand, your project will run more smoothly if the school librarian advocates for public librarians, and secures a timeline that allows a minimum of 8–10 weeks between the final decision on titles and the end of the school year. Consider March 30 as the latest date to provide public librarians with such information (see Figure 5.3).

1. Summer—Contact your counterpart at the public library and exchange email addresses, phone numbers, and other pertinent information.

2. Seek advice from the appropriate librarians at the public library, for example, YA/teen or children's. Gather their feedback on the summer reading process, on demands for each title and student frustrations. Solicit their suggestions for the next year, including the amount of lead time they would like in order to be prepared for the arrival of student readers.

3. Fall—School librarian offers to serve on Summer Reading Committee and to help create the list, borrow the books, gather reviews, and assist with marketing the titles.

4. Inform English department of the extent of support from the public library. (Be sure to check with librarians first before offering their services.) Librarians may offer to review choices, suggest titles and/or sit in on meetings where books are discussed.

5. As titles are suggested, check to be sure that titles are still in print and that title's and author's names are spelled correctly (Really!). Try to convince the Summer Reading Committee to change only a <u>few</u> books each year.

6. Pull book reviews for any titles that you think may not be age appropriate OR that may be challenged. Be Prepared! Archive these reviews to ensure that your teachers and administrators are prepared for any challenges.

7. Offer to lead a book discussion group or two if your school uses this model. Suggest other methods that can be used for student assessments such as podcasts, videos, and wiki or blog entries.

Figure 5.3: Best Practices Timeline for School Librarians

From *Better Serving Teens through School Library–Public Library Collaborations* by Cherie P. Pandora and Stacey Hayman Santa Barbara, CA: Libraries Unlimited, Copyright © 2013.

In Our Experience

Public Library Perspective—TIMING

Yes, parents have been known to bring their children to the public library in early June, or even May, to take out reading books before the school year is over. It is not unusual for parents to bring their children to the library the day after school ends, expecting that the public library will have all the summer reading books ordered, on the shelf, and ready for them.

Format of the Lists

Many schools provide students with a booklet, and/or a web page, of acceptable reads allowing students to choose the books they want to read from a lengthy list of options. Other schools identify two or three novels that are required reading for each grade level, often specifying additional or different titles for honors, Advanced Placement, and remedial English courses. For example, 10th graders might be reading *Fahrenheit 451* by Ray Bradbury and *A Separate Peace* by John Knowles, while 10th-grade honors students read *Lord of the Flies* (William Golding) and *A Tale of Two Cities* (Charles Dickens). Students may also have specialized reading from Advanced Placement science or history classes. In yet other schools all students in a specific grade level or even an entire building are required to read the same book; further choices are then made from a listing of reading choices. Teachers at each grade level then determine the method of assessment—a dramatic reading, an essay, a book jacket, a podcast, or another project that allows students to showcase what they have learned from their reading.

Notes from the Field

For an excellent example of online lists see those that Holly Bunt, library director of Western Reserve Academy (Hudson, Ohio), has posted on the school's website http://www.wra .net/page.cfm?p=618.

Annotate It!

To help students and parents, be sure that booklists and websites include author's names and summaries of each title. Teachers may not be aware, or maybe won't admit it, but often students select books based on the title or the cover, knowing nothing of the storyline. Students, and even parents, often request the shortest books on the list, which isn't always the quickest read or the best choice for the reader. To keep kids from regretting their choice, summarize the titles, print the list, laminate it, and make it available near the books that have been displayed in one general area for easy selection.

Public librarians can make the summer reading list more accessible at their libraries by making takeaway copies of the list, placing a binder or laminated copy near the school-assigned summer reading display, and posting the lists on their websites. This list should indicate grade level, school requiring the title, and a brief summary to help teens make their choice. Teen librarians are an invaluable asset in ensuring that the booklists contain books that are age appropriate; it is demoralizing for a seventh-grade student to be sent to the children's department to locate a book that really should be on an elementary school's list.

Notes from the Field

Public Library Perspective—Serving More than One School

A public library or library system may serve numerous communities, and more than one school district. Most serve multiple communities, many school districts and additional independent, private, and parochial schools as well. Serving so many schools multiplies the demands on their collection, technical services staff, and budget.

ISBN

Teachers often require that all students have the same version of each book and insist on one ISBN per title; their reasoning is that it is easier to review a book with the class if they are all, literally, on the same page. Booksellers love this as it makes for multiple sales, and simplifies the ordering process. The school librarian must be the advocate who explains that the public library cannot possibly replace all previous titles each year to meet this requirement. Of course, it would be helpful if at least the lists specified that teachers want students to read the unabridged versions of each novel. This will help the booksellers if parents decide to purchase the books. School librarians also need to advocate for those families who cannot afford to purchase summer reading books and who *MUST* borrow them from the public library. Teachers understand once the financial problem is explained to them; most principals/headmasters maintain a fund to assist needy students, especially those who meet federal guidelines for free or reduced lunches.

MARKETING

Get titles to other libraries and bookstores as early as possible. Make sure that librarians in the public library and bookstore representative receive advance notice of summer reading lists. You need to keep your counterparts in the loop throughout the process, informing them as each title is added, deleted, or the list is finalized. You don't want to keep them waiting until the end of the process.

Creating the list can be time consuming, particularly in the first year, as you determine which desktop publishing program works best for your library's web page. Email makes it much easier to gather details within the school's district, such as the number of student copies that need to be made for each building. Determine ahead of time which school secretary receives the lists at each building and which department at each public library and bookstore receives them.

Of the three public libraries to whom Cherie sent lists, one required that she send all materials to their technical services staff, while the others preferred that she send materials directly to the teen librarian. It takes only a few phone calls or emails to ensure that you get materials to the right person. If you have an in-house print shop, rely on the expertise of this staff member to clean up any school logos with their best graphics programs. Proof each listing and ensure that your list is easy to read, clear, and in a form that can be changed into a PDF format for posting on the web. It is best to then have all grade level lists printed at the same time. (NOTE: Remember that passwords for databases *cannot* be posted to public websites.)

Once your reading lists are finalized, consider sending five print copies to each library so that lists can be distributed to the reference, children's, and teen departments. An additional five copies could be sent to local bookstores and electronic versions are sent to both libraries and bookstores so that they can be uploaded to their own websites. Cherie sent her district's lists to three different library systems and five local bookstores (see Figure 5.4). Having these lists available at the public library provides a great service to teen patrons, both the students and their parents. It

	Phone	Intermediate School			Middle School			High School	High School	
		Grade 3	Grade 4	Grade 5	Grade 6	Grade 7	Grade 8	Grades 10–11	Grades 12	Folded
	EXT	Green	Pink	Yellow	Salmon	Ivory	Goldenrod	Blue	Peach	in 3rds
		back/back	back/back	back/back	back/back	back/back	(1 pg)	back/back	back/back	
Board of Education Receptionist		20	20	20	20	20	20	20		X
Board of Education Secretary		12	12	12	12	12	12	12		X
Primary School Secretary		202								X
Primary School Office		50								X

Figure 5.4: Sample Distribution List

From *Better Serving Teens through School Library–Public Library Collaborations* by Cherie P. Pandora and Stacey Hayman Santa Barbara, CA: Libraries Unlimited, Copyright © 2013.

		Intermediate School				Middle School		High School	High School	
	Phone	Grade 3	Grade 4	Grade 5	Grade 6	Grade 7	Grade 8	Grades 10–11	Grades 12	Folded
	EXT	Green	Pink	Yellow	Salmon	Ivory	Goldenrod	Blue	Peach	in 3rds
		back/back	back/back	back/back	back/back	back/back	(1 pg)	back/back	back/back	
High School—Office								50		X
High School Secretary—10–12								500	250	X
Libraries and book-stores		45	45	45	45	45	45	45	45	
Intermediate School Secretary			176	208	200					X
Intermediate School—Office		50	50	50	50					X

Figure 5.4: Sample Distribution List (*Continued*)

From *Better Serving Teens through School Library–Public Library Collaborations* by Cherie P. Pandora and Stacey Hayman Santa Barbara, CA: Libraries Unlimited, Copyright © 2013.

	Intermediate School			Middle School			High School	High School	Folded
	Grade 3	Grade 4	Grade 5	Grade 6	Grade 7	Grade 8	Grades 10–11	Grades 12	Folded
Phone	Green	Pink	Yellow	Salmon	Ivory	Goldenrod	Blue	Peach	in 3rds
EXT	back/back	back/back	back/back	back/back	back/back	(1 pg)	back/back	back/back	X
Middle School—Secretary					250	250	250		
Middle School—Office				0	0	0	0		
Total	379	303	335	327	327	327	877	295	

Grade level colors are maintained from year to year
Lists are folded into thirds to fit into report card envelopes
Secretaries receive lists to be distributed to students
Office means that copies are intended for NEW students

Figure 5.4: Sample Distribution List (*Continued*)

From *Better Serving Teens through School Library–Public Library Collaborations* by Cherie P. Pandora and Stacey Hayman Santa Barbara, CA: Libraries Unlimited, Copyright © 2013.

encourages parents to make the public library a frequent stop for school-age children and teens during the summer. Just as parents visit discount houses to gather student's supplies later in the summer we want them to visit the public library for their child's summer reading needs.

Consider including your summer reading lists on the front page of your district's web page—to make it visible for your patrons and easy for your partner libraries and book vendors to locate the list. Both the middle school and high school in our district also highlight the summer reading lists on their home pages. Be sure that your information is easily visible and not "lost" behind many layers of web design.

BOOK FAIRS

Summer reading programs can be further enhanced with an in-school book fair arranged with a local bookstore as well as your public library. Not only does this allow your students to purchase their books from the vendor, it also allows the public library to showcase itself and promote their own summer programs at an adjacent table. Provide the teen librarian with another chance to interact with your common patrons and to sign up those who are either new to town or who do not yet have their own library cards. If you aren't sure where to start as you compile lists of great reading materials, or great authors, for your 'tweens and teens, sample some of the listings in the References section that follows. We are sure that you will find some old, as well as some new, favorites.

Summer reading is a time-honored tradition that public libraries use to promote literacy through the summer months. Schools have joined the process viewing a formal listing of summer reading selections as a means to enhance and retain student literacy skills during the long days of vacation. The selection process in schools is greatly enhanced by the inclusion of school and teen librarians in the process to help with the selection, annotation, and ordering of materials. If group discussions take place as an assessment measure their expertise is invaluable for both students and faculty.

REFERENCES

Dominican University. "The Dominican Study: Public Library Summer Reading Programs: Closing the Reading Gap," http://www.dom.edu/gslis/down loads/DOM_IMLS_finalReport.pdf; executive summary, http://www.dom .edu/gslis/downloads/DOM_IMLS_executiveSummary.pdf (cited February 29, 2012).

Western Reserve Academy. "Summer Reading," http://www.wra.net/page.cfm? p=618 (cited February 29, 2012).

FURTHER READING

ALAN (Assembly on Literature for Adolescents). "ALAN Awards," http://com munity.alan-ya.org/ALANYA/ALAN/ALANAwards/ (cited February 29, 2012).

The New York Times. "Best Sellers," http://www.nytimes.com/pages/books/ bestseller/ (cited February 29, 2012).

TeacherVision. "Multiple Intelligences Chart," http://www.teachervision.fen.com/ intelligence/teaching-methods/2204.html?for_printing=1&detoured=1 (cited February 29, 2012).

VOYA. "NonFiction Honor List 2010," http://www.voya.com/wp-content/ uploads/2011/06/nonfiction_honorlist.pdf (cited February 29, 2012).

VOYA. "Top Shelf Fiction for Middle School Readers 2010," http://www.voya .com/wp-content/uploads/2011/06/top_shelf_fiction.pdf (cited February 29, 2012).

YALSA. "The Michael L. Printz Award for Excellence in Young Adult Literature," http://www.ala.org/ala/mgrps/divs/yalsa/booklistsawards/printza ward/Printz.cfm (cited February 29, 2012).

YALSA. "YALSA Award for Excellence in Nonfiction for Young Adults," http:// www.ala.org/yalsa/nonfiction/ (cited February 29, 2012).

6

AUTHOR VISITS

Do you want to ignite your teens with fervor for reading? Of course you do! Have you considered bringing in some inspiration in the form of an actual author? Author visits provide an excellent opportunity to collaborate with your neighboring librarian. Besides allowing you to share costs and workload, this is the perfect way to start or build your collaborative relationship. What fun it will be to bring authors into a library to interact with the readers who have enjoyed their books! Just picture it, teens and authors in one room—interacting, questions and answers flowing freely. While there are many details to work out when planning an author visit; it is twice as much fun and half as much work to plan this project with your counterpart at a sister library.

Start with a meeting between librarians from public and school libraries. Here you can both make suggestions as to which authors to invite, the type of programming that you want to provide and, if you have one, the extent of your budget.

FUNDING

If you don't have money in the operating budget for authors, then you need to decide how you will secure the necessary funding. Luckily, not all funds must come from a single source. It is possible that your school would be willing to use curriculum, Title 1, or other federal monies to help underwrite this event, since it promotes literacy and reading. Seed money may also come from a Friends of the Library group or other community agencies. You can also request grant money from the school's Parent Teacher Organization (PTO)/PTA or the educational foundation, if you have one. If the books you select feature themes dealing with Internet safety, teen drinking or drug abuse, suicide prevention, or other "hot" topics; chances are, there is a local agency who works to prevent these problems. Check to see if there is a local chapter of those national organizations who work to help troubled teens. Students Against Destructive Decisions (SADD), Teen Institute, and Drug Abuse Resistance Education (DARE) are just a few of the antidrug organizations who may be happy to work with you. Besides suggesting local agencies, the school's social worker or guidance counselors can provide you with the name and phone number of their personal contact at each agency. As you start your research, be sure to keep the administrators of both libraries, and any sponsors, apprised of your progress, either through email or scheduled face-to-face meetings.

SPONSORS

Successfully recruiting another organization or agency to take part in your author visit hinges on two things: the agency's mission and the level of involvement requested. Additional sponsors may be other schools, other public libraries, museums, special libraries (law, medical, corporate), bookstores, or social service agencies. The closer the agency's mission aligns with your theme, the more likely it is they will join you. For example, if your presenter will speak on digital citizenship, Internet safety, or cyberbullying, then your local police force may agree to copresent or provide materials for your program. Officers can often provide information on the Internet Crimes Against Children (ICAC) task force that identifies and arrests Internet predators.

The scope of involvement requested will be the second deciding factor. Your first inclination may be to simply ask for a monetary contribution; however, do not limit your vision to requests for cash. Tertiary sponsors may be able to contribute their valuable expertise or other services. They can provide refreshments, cover the printing costs of your promotional materials, or provide volunteers to help with some of the leg work involved in the event. Partners can also direct you to informational websites or to online resources such as public service announcements (PSAs) that can be presented to students.

Another benefit of partnering is that you are able to make a long list of potential sponsors and then divide the work. Hopefully you each already have contacts at some of the organizations on your list and they may already be prepared to assist in your efforts.

GRANTS

If grants need to be written, you will need to identify a grant source, learn the funding cycle, and plan your dates accordingly. (See Chapter 12 for additional information.) If the local educational foundation grant is due in October, approval may not be announced until December, with monies released in mid-January. The earliest that your author visit can take place then will be the spring of the following year.

Securing the support of the administrators of both agencies is a must at this point. Don't forget to talk with the financial agents of each institution (the treasurer of the public library, and usually the assistant superintendent or treasurer at the school). Be sure to ask if your public library is designated by the IRS as a 501 (c)(3) or equivalent organization. Many grants are only given to agencies with this nonprofit status, and most schools do not qualify.

Your financial officer can advise you on what is permissible by your state law. In some states, items such as food may not be legally paid for with funds from a school's operating budget; however, an administrator may have discretionary funds that CAN be used for this purpose. If your libraries cannot pay for food from existing budgets, then you may need to search for donations from local restaurants or catering companies, or look for an additional small grant to cover the costs.

SELECTING YOUR AUTHOR

First and foremost, review any information you have that can provide the history of author visits to your school, public library, or even local bookstores. Do not limit your definition of author to those who write fiction. Successful programs can be built around poets, writers of nonfiction books, articles, or even blogs. Working with your partner librarian start a wish list of authors you would like to invite, making sure to include authors residing within your state or in nearby states. Devise a survey that can be given to your teens electronically on the websites of both libraries, and scatter paper copies in the school library and the teen area of the public library. Ask teens which authors are their favorites and use this list as your starting point for discussion. If you wish, provide a list of potential authors for teens to choose from your own list and leave space for them to add their own suggestions. This will ensure that those authors listed are still living and available for a visit. You may be able to connect with your dream author if he or she has a commitment that is close by; but often local authors are more affordable.

However, since this is a brainstorming effort, you can be as wild as possible in your choices. Check the websites belonging to the authors on your list to see if their schedules and costs are listed. (Don't be discouraged if they are not listed.) Once the author has agreed to a date and times, discuss the possibility of visits with nearby schools and libraries the day before or after your presentations. If other schools or libraries can schedule a presentation or workshop on adjacent days, you can divide transportation, meal, and housing costs, if needed. You may wish to post a query on the listservs of the state library associations asking if anyone has an author scheduled or is interested in scheduling an author.

WHOM DO YOU CONTACT?

Once you've decided to schedule an author visit and have received formal approval, research the author's website to determine if contact can be made directly, or if it must be made through an agent or publishing house. Many programming decisions may be dictated by the requirements of each author. Some authors are willing to do large group meetings in auditoriums or gyms, while others prefer only to do workshops with smaller groups of teens. It is important that the person making contact with the author checks to see which type of programs the author is willing to do for the agreed-upon fee. Keep thorough notes on your conversations and, for continuity's sake, designate *one* librarian as the author's contact. You don't want to overwhelm, or annoy, the author with a deluge of contacts from various staffers. If policies dictate that one person from each agency must deal with the author, be sure to meet and communicate regularly with your partner! Create a list of duties, including the financial responsibility for the various jobs; designate the responsible party for each task; then formulate, share, and plan the questions you wish to ask the author so that you can avoid any repetition or duplicate questions. It may be useful to make contact via conference call, Skype, or webcam, if the author is amenable to that.

Most authors have standard contracts that will be sent to you, spelling out their wants and needs. Review this information together and share this information with the treasurers of both libraries. After the initial contact is made, a written record of all conversations should by created. Send one copy to the author for verification via email or fax, whichever format the author prefers. Keep copies of all contracts and conversations in your file. This written record will help you in your planning, reduce the chance of misunderstandings, and serve as a guideline for future author visits. Figure 6.1 will help you to prepare for your next author's visit.

	Project	Details	Assigned
1	Check author's website	Need information on costs, types of programming, and specific requirements	
2	Check calendars of both libraries, schools, and community calendars	Search for conflicts as well as events that can complement your program	
3	Confirm budget for author visit and how the costs will be divided	Ensure that all costs will be covered—meals, hotel, mileage, transportation	
4	Initial consultation with the author	Discuss dates and types of programs he/she will do	
5	Complete building use forms	Ensure no cost	
6	Call author to confirm dates, times, types of programs, and whether an autograph session can be held	Finalize requests and restrictions from the author. Will the author agree to be videotaped or be interviewed by the school or local press?	
7	Check with other local schools and libraries about sharing transportation costs or fees		
8	Reserve hotel room		
9	Arrange for meals		
10	Decide if you need to charge admission to cover costs. If, and only if, the author approves this ahead of time	This may result in a rental fee for school facilities and may reduce the size of your audience	
11	Contact the publisher or local bookstores	You'll want copies of his/her book to sell at the event.	
12	Prepare flyers and posters		
13	Contact local/regional media		
14	Assign driver for author		
15	File receipts with treasurer		
16	Write thank you notes	To the author and any partners who shared the costs	

Figure 6.1: Author Visit Roles and Tasks

From *Better Serving Teens through School Library–Public Library Collaborations* by Cherie P. Pandora and Stacey Hayman Santa Barbara, CA: Libraries Unlimited, Copyright © 2013.

FACILITIES

After learning what types of programming the author consents to do, determine the size of the rooms you need. Do you need a series of classrooms, or a smaller, more intimate space such as a conference room or storytime room? Would it be more appropriate to have an auditorium for a large group assembly or an evening or weekend program? Once these decisions are made you can determine which agency has the best facilities for the event. For example, if both libraries have auditoriums, which one would best serve your purpose? If the auditorium you wish to use is located in the school, then the school librarian must complete the building use form and plan to attend so that rental fees are waived. If the best place to meet is in the public library then the teen librarian should be the one to complete the proper forms. Due to budget cuts, many schools now charge outside agencies a rental fee (usually the cost of the custodian for the duration of the event). Note that charging an admission fee virtually guarantees that a rental fee will be charged by a school. As a community service most public libraries offer free use of their facilities by nonprofit groups, so this is generally not an issue.

MEALS

Once you've settled on a time frame for the visit, decide the meals you need to provide for your author. Find out if the author has any allergies or dietary restrictions that need to be taken into account. If the author must stay overnight, it is advisable to have at least one librarian serve as driver and meal companion. Besides caring for the needs of the author, this allows for some wonderfully candid conversations. If you like, invite other staff members to suggest questions that you can ask the author on their behalf. You may also want to organize a meal where staff or other participants can meet the author outside of your main event.

If planning a breakfast or luncheon for a large group at a school, check first with the school's food services department. Many schools have excellent food services departments that go well beyond the scope of cafeteria food. Be aware, however, that most food service departments work a very early shift; they may leave after the last lunch hour at 1:00 or 1:30 P.M. Therefore, it would be impossible to use their services for a dinner meal without adding overtime staffing costs to your bottom line. If a school, or nearby school, has a culinary arts program, consider having these students cater your event. Whether they can do this depends on their schedule, as some serve only a few days per week; however, the restaurant that they run in their school building might serve as a nice venue for your event.

For a dinner event, the library hosting the evening program may be the logical site for the buffet. You will need to check library policies to see if there are any limitations on serving food in the facility. Next, check with locally owned restaurants and catering companies, as they are more likely to answer you quickly because they need not get an approval from a corporate office. They may also be more likely to help you as a community project or for the PR value. If they cannot donate the food, they may be willing to offer you a discount. Always ask! Designate one staff member to do the research on these food options, and create a spreadsheet with their data. It will provide you with valuable information for this and future events. Remember, pizza is not the only inexpensive option; many restaurants offer selections of pastas, entree salads, vegetarian, or chicken dishes at a reasonable, often discounted, price. (Figure 6.2 provides a sample menu ordered from the local pizza parlor and, yes, they did discount their prices!)

The easiest way to solve the question of alcoholic beverages is to hold your dinner in a venue that prohibits them. This will save you from any awkward conversations with your authors. Schools and public libraries are unlikely to allow the serving of alcoholic beverages and many operating budgets for public entities prohibit paying for alcoholic beverages. If you prefer to take your author to a local restaurant where alcohol is served, give some thought as to how you will deal with this issue. Any drinks should be paid for separately, so that they do not appear on any receipts that must be approved by boards, trustees, or the state.

TRAVEL

Most libraries cannot afford to fly in an author from a remote state. Your transportation costs will, therefore, be limited to mileage reimbursement, parking, tolls, and meals eaten on the road. Booking an author within your state or a nearby state minimizes your costs, and makes it an easier trip for your author as well. You will need to provide the author with a form to complete that records the number of miles traveled; receipts will be required for any tolls or meals consumed while traveling. (See Figure 6.3 for a sample author expenses form.)

HOUSING

If the author you select is local and within driving distance, you may not need to concern yourself with securing a hotel; the author may simply

Author's dinner Sample menu/distribution of funds	Quantity	Public Library	High School Library
Garden Salad and dressing NO pepperoni in the salad	1/2 pan		$20.00
Penne Pasta Meatballs on the side	1/2 pan		$24.95
Chicken Pasta Florentine	1/2 pan	$27.95	
Rolls and butter	For 15 people	$7.50	
Delivery charge			$1.50
Total $81.90		$35.45	$46.56
Tip for delivery person		Paid	
Deliver to high school cafeteria at 5:30 P.M. Address: Phone contact:			

Figure 6.2: Sample Menu

From *Better Serving Teens through School Library–Public Library Collaborations* by Cherie P. Pandora and Stacey Hayman Santa Barbara, CA: Libraries Unlimited, Copyright © 2013.

Author's dinner Sample menu/distribution of funds	Quantity	Public Library	High School Library
Bill to: Address: Phone contact:	Paid: / /2011 PO #: Check #:		
Catering company: Address: Phone contact			

Figure 6.2: Sample Menu (*Continued*)

Miles _____ × 0.50 cents   = $_____

Our treasurers require receipts for the following items:

Tolls: = $_____

Meals: = $_____

Parking: = $_____

Please turn in this form prior to departure.

Our sincere thanks for visiting our libraries!

Figure 6.3: Author Expenses

be able to drive home after the program, or after your dinner. Should you need to find a hotel, the requirements are location, location, location. Amenities such as free parking, free Internet access, and an in-house coffee maker will be greatly appreciated by your author, and your treasurer. Unless your author requests it, you need not find a hotel with a complimentary breakfast; you will likely prefer to take the authors to breakfast to get to know them better prior to the first event of the day.

PROGRAM FORMAT OPTIONS

There are many options to consider when creating presentations to best serve the needs of your teen patrons. Spend some time conferring with each other before approaching your TABs. Ask them how they would like to interact with an author. A combination of large and small groups may meet the needs of your TABs and your reading regulars while a large group meeting may provide the numbers and the punch (per person cost) that treasurers and trustees like to see. Create a list of program options from these discussions and present them to your author. Some authors like to reach the largest number of students possible and don't mind presenting to the entire school or several large groups of teens. Other authors prefer to interact more directly with smaller groups of students. Some of the programming options that you might consider include:

1. School-wide presentations with the entire student body in attendance
2. A series of assemblies—either large or small, by grade level or content area
3. Workshops—interactive work with students; perhaps the author will help students to write poetry or to create thesis statements
4. Question and answer programs
5. Workshops for staff

Another option, particularly if you have a generous board, donor, or grant, is to create an "Author-in-Residence" program. Director of Libraries Dorcas Hand from Annunciation Orthodox School in Houston, Texas, tried many options for author presentations over the years, but felt that one-day presentations were not as effective as she would like. She chose authors who had been teachers at one time and who had books that appealed to her middle school students. She created a week-long series of master classes based on the "History as Story" model. An introductory assembly was held in the auditorium, after which individual classes met for an hour with the author to WRITE. Over the years, her students have written poetry, stories, or photojournalism projects. In recent years, some of the teachers in her schools created a writing project that required a research element. Students came into class with their research; they worked with the author to make their introductory paragraphs more dramatic. Hand (2006, 40–43) found that selecting one grade level and one project provided the optimum level of interaction. An added advantage of this approach is that students find it harder to plagiarize materials.

VIRTUAL AUTHOR VISITS

Technology today provides options such as videoconferencing or webinars for those libraries that don't have the budget or administrative support for a "live" author visit. With just a computer, a webcam (and some support from your technology department), you can connect with authors via Skype, Apple iChat, Google Video and Voice, or a number of other programs. Former middle school English teacher and blogger Kate Messner (2009, 37) has done both in-person and video-linked author visits for school book clubs. She found that both shared similar amounts of interaction between author and participants. She was surprised at the amount of discussion that took place and the ability of students to adapt to the technological format. While book signings aren't possible with the video format, Messner had her students design bookplates, and sent them to the author prior to the videoconference so that books could be signed and returned to the school. She also suggests a conversation with the author to determine who places the call to begin the visit. She has students prepare their questions in advance, and alerts them to the possibility that the audio or video could be lost during the program.

Messner created a list of authors willing to talk to students FREE of charge during a 20-minute Skype visit. She notes that some authors will provide longer visits for a fee. Like all savvy users of technology she recommends testing equipment BEFORE the big event and reminds librarians to test the equipment not just at home, but on-site as well, since filters and firewalls at either library could cause problems that aren't encountered on your home computer (ibid., 37).

If you're planning a virtual author visit, be sure to discuss your intentions ahead of time with your technical support team; this ensures that there are no big surprises that keep the program from running efficiently. You can find a full step-by-step checklist, as well as links to websites in the August 1, 2009, issue of *SLJ* (Messner 2009, 37–38).

BOOKS

Most author visits naturally result in a renewed interest in the author's works. Be sure that both libraries have multiple copies of the author's works available to students in the days prior to and immediately after the event. This may be the perfect time to partner with additional public libraries. If your state has an interlibrary loan system that allows librarians to shuttle books around the state then you may be able to enlist additional librarians, and secure additional books, for your event. As a benefit for your audience, it is appropriate to have books for sale at the event. You might choose to purchase a limited number of works ahead of time, have them autographed, and sell them yourself after the presentation; however, this approach results in a lot of extra work for your library staff. It can also lead to the problem of having too few books or too many of one title, since it is difficult to gauge what people will buy. In many cases, autographed books (signed ahead of time by the author) cannot be returned to the publisher or bookstore. Cross-check this with your vendor *before* making such purchases.

An easier solution is to bring in another partner, the community representative of your local bookseller. This bookseller can order books at no cost to you, and will run the sales for you after the author's presentation. If your event is open to the public, the store's marketing department will likely be happy to display your posters and promote your project in their store, increasing the chance that you'll reach another group of potential audience members. If you are privileged to have multiple booksellers in your community, deliver your posters to each one, but invite only one bookseller to your event. If you have an ongoing relationship with each bookseller, let them know that you will rotate the vendor you invite to future events.

In Our Experience

In February 2008, Nancy Levin, then deputy director of Rocky River Public Library, suggested to Rocky River High School Librarian Cherie Pandora that they collaborate and invite Arab-American author Dunya Mikhail to visit Cleveland to share her poetry and speak about her book, *The War Works Hard*. She provided workshops for high school students on the first day while the night event was open to the entire community, and invitations were sent to local schools and public libraries. Mikhail began by reading her poetry, and talked about her life in Iran, and the reasons she left her native land. She was our guest at a small-catered dinner at the school with teachers, librarians, and administrators. The following day Mikhail visited Cleveland State University speaking to Arabic language students in the Arabic Studies Cultural Crossings program. What would we do differently (WWWDD) next time? We would add students to the dinner so that they could continue discussions started during the workshops. Their omission was strictly a matter of funding.

Notes from the Field

What do hybrid author visits look like? Consider the experience of Library Media Specialist Joanna H. McNally. What began as an idea for her student book club became not just a success, but a phenomenon. In fact, math and science teachers laughingly told her that they had to ask students to stop reading in class and put their books away. Why? After 200 Charles F. Brush High School students purchased the book *Th1rteen R3asons Why* in preparation for author Jay Asher's visit to their school, they were hooked on reading.

McNally created an author visit that was a hybrid of face-to-face and video interaction. She was not content to simply have the author visit her South Euclid-Lyndhurst (Ohio) district, but wanted to include as many schools and students as possible. Mr. Asher visited Brush High School in the morning and Independence High School in the afternoon; he interacted with students from another seven schools scattered throughout Ohio who participated via distance learning.

Benefits to Students

The hybrid visit allowed many more students to participate and interact with the author than the standard in-person visit would have allowed. Twenty students in her school earned extra credit in their classes through the satisfactory completion of their projects while others read the book "just for fun."

Benefits to Schools and Libraries

Costs were distributed among 11 schools. Schools participating via distance learning paid $100 while those visiting the host high school paid $200. All remaining costs were paid by Brush and Independence High Schools. Having gone through this experience with great success, McNally (2012) commented "[I]t is so powerful to have an author come [to your school]."

As wonderfully successful as this program turned out to be, we hope all involved would now consider involving the public libraries nearby. How many more teen lives would have been touched? The teen librarian could have also had programs sponsored by local hospitals on stress management or how to participate in teen suicide prevention hotlines. Don't forget how much greater the impact is when you work together.

MARKETING

If your event is open to the public, create posters and flyers to advertise the event and a program for your audience that evening. Work with the staff at both libraries to determine which resources you can tap. Check the author's website for a photo you can use. You will need permission from your author, and possibly from the publisher, to use it for your flyers and posters. It is also appropriate to send a draft of all marketing materials to the author for approval before printing. Flyers can simply be smaller versions of the poster. Another approach is to have students design posters, and post them in both libraries and at various community events. Be sure to include in large print the journalistic four Ws—WHO, WHAT, WHEN, and WHERE, preferably in a list or bulleted format rather than in paragraph style. Also, the poster and flyer should display the author's name in a larger, attention-getting font. Add a photo of the author and a copy of the book jacket cover, or covers, above the author's name, if the publisher has granted you permission to do so. If the work(s) have won awards, include that information as well. Lastly, don't forget to include the HOW—credit your sponsors and funding agents at the bottom of the poster along with the logos for each agency. Flyers that will be used for placement around the school or public library can be in black and white and copied on the library's copy machine. You can also make one or two large posters for placement in the schools and the public library. Be sure that the author gets a copy of each marketing piece.

Programs for the evening event need to be short and can easily be done in black and white. You can create a simple program using an 8.5 × 11 inch sheet of paper folded in half. Be sure to list librarians, their libraries, as well as all sponsors. Include logos of all event sponsors with their web addresses on the last page. In the centerfold page, print a background statement on the author and list their relevant websites. If appropriate, include a picture or a list of the author's works. These elements should be part of your discussion with the author, and you should send a draft to the author a few weeks prior to the event so that there is time to correct any errors.

One of you can act as emcee to welcome the crowd, explain the structure and time frame for the evening, and provide information about book sales and signings. The other can introduce the speaker and recognize sponsors. Acknowledging administrators and board members in attendance is a sign of respect and is a good move politically.

In Our Experience

Always expect the unexpected! When it comes to author events, something unexpected always happens. A major snowstorm can result in fears that the project will be canceled; an unexpected guest may be added to the dinner at the last moment. For a Rocky River event, the author was asked to come in earlier than planned because of weather. She came in the night prior to the event, rather than the morning of the workshops, since snowstorms were predicted for her home state; and we didn't want her to travel in dangerous conditions. Although it was our decision to have her come in earlier, it did result in a second day's housing and meals, which weren't in the original budget. Luckily the storm did not close schools that day. The storm did, however, reduce the number of attendees at the evening presentation. We were pleased that 40 hardy souls braved the blizzard, and were happy to see that we had both community members as well as librarians from other schools and systems in attendance.

To add passion to your reading programs and ignite the interest of your teens, consider inviting an author to visit. On-site author visits are a wonderful experience for readers and are made more affordable by working together to share the work and the costs. Teen librarians and school librarians can start the process and partner with additional libraries or colleges to share travel costs and author fees. Email and listservs are helpful tools for connecting with local libraries that might want to cosponsor the visit. The advent of Web 2.0 interactivity and inexpensive web cameras now makes it possible to have authors visit electronically if you cannot afford to sponsor an in-person visit. Whichever method suits your needs best, know that your collaborative relationship will be strengthened through your work on this project, your teens will share a wonderful experience, and your libraries will both benefit from the publicity surrounding the event.

REFERENCES

"Activities: History as Story," http://www2.ed.gov/pubs/parents/History/Story.html (cited February 22, 2012).

Asher, Jay. "Th1rteen R3asons Why," http://www.thirteenreasonswhy.com/ (cited February 22, 2012).

"Award-Winning Poet Visits Rocky River High School," Westlife (March 5, 2008): 14B. Drug Abuse Resistance Education. "DARE," http://www.dare.com/home/default.asp (cited February 22, 2012).

Hand, Dorcas. "Adolescent Literacies: Reading, Thinking, Writing." Knowledge Quest 35, no. 1 (2006): 40–43.

McNally, Joanna. Personal interview with Cherie Pandora, February 9, 2012. Cleveland, OH.

Messner, Kate. "Kate's Book Blog. Authors Who Skype with Classes and Book Clubs," http://kmessner.livejournal.com/106020.html (cited February 22, 2012).

Messner, Kate. "Met Any Good Authors Lately?" *School Library Journal* 55, no. 8 (2009): 36–38. http://www.schoollibraryjournal.com/article/CA6673572.html (cited February 22, 2012).

Mikhail, Dunya. *The War Works Hard.* New York: New Directions Publishing Corp., 2005.

Students Against Destructive Decisions. "Welcome to SADD," http://www.sadd.org/ (cited February 22, 2012).

FURTHER READING

Henrico County Public Library. "Teen Stuff. Quick Picks," http://www.henricolibrary.org/teens/b&a_quickpicks.html (cited February 22, 2012).

NATI (National Association of Teen Institutes). "Teen Institute," http://www.teeninstitute.org/NEW%20SITE/site/ (cited February 22, 2012).

National Suicide Prevention Lifeline. "With Help Comes Hope," http://www.suicidepreventionlifeline.org/ (cited February 22, 2012).

Ontl, Margaret. "Noted Young Adult Literature Author visits Hudson High School." *Hudson Star-Observer* (April 15, 2011), http://www.hudsonstarobserver.com/event/article/id/42623/ (cited February 22, 2012).

The Public Library of Cincinnati and Hamilton County. "Teenspace. Books and Reading," http://teenspace.cincinnatilibrary.org/books/ (cited February 22, 2012).

St. Cyr, Donna. "Connecting Kids with Authors." *School Library Monthly* 28, no. 6 (2012): 37–38.

U.S. Government. IRS. "Exemption Requirements IRS 501 (c)(3) Organizations," http://www.irs.gov/charities/charitable/article/0,,id=96099,00.html (cited February 22, 2012).

YALSA. "YALSA's Teens' Top Ten," http://www.ala.org/ala/mgrps/divs/yalsa/teenreading/teenstopten/teenstopten.cfm (cited February 22, 2012).

7

◇ ◇ ◇

POETRY SLAMS

Children LOVE poetry. They love the singsong rhythm of the poems we share with them before they can read. They love the poetry inherent in the songs that we teach them—remember singing *Twinkle, Twinkle Little Star, The Itsy Bitsy Spider,* or *I'm a Little Teapot?* Children learn these lyrics by rote by listening to their parents or librarians; they delight in repeating them over and over. But something happens as they progress through the grades.

Too often teen students have learned to **loathe** poetry! Instead of laughing at the silly poetry of Shel Silverstein, James Thurber, or Ogden Nash, these teens have graduated to classical poetry, often in Olde English or other seemingly archaic languages, which must be dissected and analyzed to death with little time to actually enjoy the rhythm or lyricism of the poems themselves. Why not wait to analyze poetry until students have read and enjoyed it first? Many librarians seek to make poetry an enjoyable experience again, by creating programs centered around verse, by running poetry workshops, and by creating their own poetry programs. In this chapter you'll find a number of approaches to using poetry as a program for teens. If you are interested in trying slam poetry, please note that it need not be limited to high school age students. Some very successful programs have been done with middle school students. The resource guide at the end of the chapter lists a number of resources that can help you to start a program of your own; in the meantime, let's consider some programs others have created.

COLLABORATION OPPORTUNITY MISSED

After reading about poetry slams in library literature, Rocky River High School Assistant Librarian Karen Naftzger thought of creating a poetry slam in the library. Since April had been deemed National Poetry Month, it seemed like the perfect excuse to gather students in the library to celebrate both poetry and National Library Week. Neither Karen nor Cherie thought to reach out to the public library for resources, advice, or assistance. What a shame! How much richer the experience would have been had they invited the local teen librarian to join them! They could have planned together and coordinated poetry events at both libraries. Poetry could have been displayed in both libraries. We lost the chance to have the teen librarian visit the school library to participate in poetry writing workshops. Finally, we could have expanded the audience for our poets by holding poetry slams at both sites—at the schools during the day and at the public library in the evening.

If you find yourself in a position of planning a poetry event for Poetry Month, call your partner library and see if the teen librarian is interested in helping you to promote and stage the event. Chances are the public library is also celebrating Poetry Month with displays about poets and poetry. If you are in a middle school, consider the fact that the children's librarian also deals with your preteen and young teen patrons. Reference librarians probably know many of your students from assisting them with their research and leisure reading needs, so they may be willing partners as well. If the public library has a TAB, these members can be great resources for brainstorming the format and selecting any prizes that you wish to offer.

COLLABORATION

Don't be afraid to invite a third party to join your program, they can add a unique perspective to your workshop and may offer you an alternate locale for your workshop. An art supply or craft store may be happy to provide discounted prices on fancy papers for teens' final copies of their poems. Local music stores may recommend a music teacher or musician who can provide tips on turning poems into song lyrics.

TEEN ADVISORY SERVICE PROJECT

Working together doesn't mean that you have to limit your audience to teens. Combine your TABs and suggest an afterschool activity that they can present with a twist on storytimes. Call them Rhyme Times and let your TAB members share their favorite childhood poems with younger patrons. Include some poems that can get children up and moving. Shel Silverstein's (2004, 45, 76–77) "Oh I'm Being Eaten by a Boa Constrictor" and "The Unicorn" are good choices. If you don't have a TAB at either library then have the school librarian survey the school's service clubs, for example, Key Club, National Honor Society, or Service Learning classes that enjoy this type of project.

Notes from the Field

Try Poetry!

In 2011, Loudoun County Public Library in Leesburg, Virginia, won the John Cotton Dana Public Relations award from the American Library Association (ALA) for its wonderful work with its Try Poetry project. Librarians created miniworkshops, invited poets, established a Poet-in-Residence position for the year, and planned poetry programs and contests. They created a separate Try Poetry web page, and schools filmed interviews with poets and added them to the local cable channel. They marketed the Try Poetry logo on magnets, flyers, shirts, and in the email signatures of all staff (Holtslander 2011, 7). Everyone was involved—poetry was read at the After Hours Teen Center, younger students worked with a poet to create a book of poems, and poetry was performed in many different settings by poets who spanned the generations. If you were to replicate this program be sure to invite school librarians to take part to help you with the workload. They can help with the planning, secure student volunteers, and provide for print and video production, usually, through students in broadcasting or drama classes.

SONG LYRICS

How else can you entice teenagers and preteens to enjoy poetry again? The Loudoun libraries found a way to immerse the entire community in their yearlong celebration of poetry. Others have done so by approaching poetry in the form of song lyrics, allowing students to write their own verses. Cable programs have tapped into a world where students see the rhythm of poetry in song lyrics. While these shows allow celebrities to express themselves in language that we would not find school or public library appropriate, they have found an audience with many teens, particularly in urban settings.

If you consider the fact that poetry abounds in every culture, is it much of a stretch to believe that there are many teen cultures that could contribute to the world of poetry? (Holtslander 2011, 7). Just as the teens of the 1950s listened to Beat poets, and hip-hop has appealed to more recent generations, the poetry found in today's song lyrics both reflects, and is defined by, the world around today's youth (Aptowicz 2008, 8). Students reluctant to try writing poetry might just attend a program that helps them to write songs. In many communities, teens spend hours practicing with their own garage bands. While they may be practicing with a computer software program as much as they practice in a basement or garage—they strive to share their thoughts, their angst, and even their joys with the outside world through their music.

Consider planning a joint song writing program; hold it at whichever library has a suitable software program for songwriting. If your school has keyboarding software from a music theory or music technology class plan to use their space and instruments; plan a performance night, either in the teen room or at a local coffeehouse.

One of the goals of creating a poetry project is to entice the often-unseen teen to take part. Numerous writers have found that poetry slams and other venues that allow students to share their voice have brought in students who are rarely seen together (Heeger 2006, 27). The self-described Goth might write poetry that differs from that of the preppy teen or the athlete, then again, they just might find a kinship that is hidden behind the clothing styles which they allow to define them.

POETRY CONTESTS

Depending on the grade level of your teens, you can try different types of contests and displays. At your library meetings discuss how and when you'll promote poetry. Middle school and teen librarians can create bulletin board displays that feature pictures of poets and ask teens to match pictures with the names of famous poets. In schools this type of display is sure to be popular with English Language Arts teachers. The same can be done with the first lines of poems. If both libraries have a TAB then teens could help to select lines, poets, and poems that are significant to teens. Students will be especially happy to take part if the contest involves a reward. Such a program can be done any time throughout the year as a simple way to celebrate poetry (Honnold 2003, 96–97). Poems can replace the pictures of poets in a contest, but don't be afraid to be silly.

In Our Experience

One year for Read Across America, the celebration of Dr. Seuss' birthday in March, staff in Cherie's high school dressed as Thing One, Thing Two, and the Cat in the Hat from the book *The Cat in the Hat*. Yes, Cherie did this in the high school during our afternoon "Read-in" whereby everyone in the library read. Teachers brought their classes to the library for a heavenly class period of silent reading. Later that week, Cherie ran a contest asking students to match a list of teachers with their favorite Dr. Seuss book; the staff were amazed not only at the positive response we received, but by the number of students who came in to talk about their favorite Seuss titles and to recite their favorite lines from the book. At this time we were without a teen librarian at the public library. Were we to do such a project again we would check with reference librarians instead to gather support from the public library.

LOCAL POETS

Before contracting with a commercial venture that provides poetry programming, be sure to check with your partner librarian, and with local writers' groups and universities. There are most likely poets living in your area, willing to present their work for a nominal fee, if not for free. This is another instance where the collaboration of school and public librarians can benefit from the combined network of both professionals and their colleagues; it creates a much wider net of options. Reference librarians often maintain lists of local writers and poets; writer's groups maintain lists of their members. Both librarians can post queries to their respective state associations' electronic lists requesting the names of poets who have presented successful programs. School and public librarians who meet on a regular basis (usually monthly or quarterly), use this time to share knowledge, discuss resources, and create programs that benefit all patrons. Workshops can then be planned for both libraries. Discussions with English teachers in the schools and children's and teen librarians in the public libraries will lead to an abundance of ideas for creative programming. Hold meetings, or communicate electronically, to decide the type of workshop sessions to hold. Would one library like a poetry workshop for its teens while the other wants a poetry reading to emphasize the enjoyment of poetry?

POETRY WORKSHOPS

Decades ago, Cleveland Heights-University Heights public and school librarians forged a special partnership allowing them to share their collections with each other. Through the years, the libraries partnered on many endeavors; but the 12-year-old Fall Poetry workshop and November Poetry Slam are two of their most popular and enduring success stories. Both teachers and librarians serve on the decision-making board while the district provides space for activities (Levin 2012).

Tutor Amy Rosenbluth has been working with slam poetry for three decades, nurturing student poets with writing and performance workshops. Workshops are held after school, with half of them held at the public library and the other half at the school with the poetry club. Students are bused from their respective afterschool programs to the workshop for a small fee.

Kathy Lawrence (2012), of Cleveland Heights-University Heights Schools, states that "We tap into each other's expertise regularly." She tells us that workshops have grown and that there are now "tons of kids and tons of volunteers" to help out each year. The school district supports the idea and provides space; Rosenbluth is now paid to present the workshops. She recruits students for Slam U competitions (held each March), and has had one student perform in national competition. Recently, Rosenbluth converted an unused school into a writing space called Lake Erie Ink, where she holds writing workshops and summer playwriting camps (Chilcote 2011).

READINGS VERSUS SLAMS

Two types of poetry performance programs can be held; one is a non-competitive set, where no scoring or winners are declared; the other is a competition with scores, judges, time limits, winners, and prizes. Make your decision as to the type of poetry program you will sponsor depending on your type of libraries, your setting, and the needs of your teens. Either of these programs can be held during the day at a school assembly or during school vacations at the public library. An evening poetry event is a better choice if you wish to invite parents and community members; it can be held at either library. The idea behind both types of events is to make poetry fun, cool, and relevant to the teens. Provide the venue, and make reading poetry optional to allow teens to have a voice, create, and express their feelings; allow them to choose, if they wish, not to share themselves with others (Aptowicz 2008, 345). For either activity, you need to find a venue. If neither library has an auditorium, set up a stage area with a microphone for the readers, a judges area (needed for the slam), and an area for coffee, snacks, or beverages (Alessio 2011, 75).

Poetry readings are generally noncompetitive programs. These are often called open mike readings, as poets are not judged (Aptowicz 2008, 34). Participants may either read their own work, or a favorite poem. Audience members are instructed to be respectful, and polite applause is expected. No prizes are given, no winners are declared, it is simply an enjoyment of the special literary genre of spoken poetry. Readings are an appropriate format for either library and both preteen and teen audiences; they are easily cross-promoted to patrons of either library.

Depending on the age group of the participants, props or costumes can be used so that the reading becomes a form of performance art. The school's drama department may be able to help with costuming. You can also host your own series of poetry readings in your library based on a theme for the month, a holiday, or anything else that works with your current programs or displays. If you have a TAB (see Chapter 10), give them the chance to discuss the type of program to be held and themes that would appeal to teens.

Notes from the Field

If you create a poetry slam, you need to decide whether to preview the poetry submitted by students. This will affect the spontaneity of the poems offered, and you will lose the ability to have teens create poetry on the spot; but you also gain more control over the event. A concern for us, in a conservative high school and community, was to be sure that our entries were school appropriate. We anticipated some negative feedback from students for this but did not receive any. If you decide to preview poetry, invite some of your local librarians to be on your preview committee.

True **poetry slams,** on the other hand, follow a strict set of rules that have evolved since 1980 when the slam began in New York City. Competitions soon followed in other cities, and the first national poetry slam took place in 1990 in San Francisco (Glazner 2000, 11). It is a highly competitive event, often well attended, with a master of ceremony called the slam master, who selects five judges and a timekeeper from the audience; the master of ceremony sets the tone for the slam and reads from a prepared script (Somers-Willett 2009, 149). Judges receive their printed instructions and are then required to score each competitor as if it were an event at the Olympics. Flashcards with numbers 1–10 (10 is the highest score) and a second set containing decimal numbers are often used for the scoring. The lowest and highest scores are eliminated so that the maximum possible score is 30. Often a "sacrificial poet" starts the proceedings; he or she is not part of the competition, but gives the judges a chance to practice their new task (Aptowicz 2008, 34).

Slams may consist of multiple rounds with readers with the highest scores moving on in the competition. All poems read must be the original work of the person doing the reading; no costumes, music, or props are allowed. (The exception to the rule of original poetry is made only if the event is promoted as a "dead poets' slam," that is, a reading of classical works by long-dead poets.) If readers advance to a second or third round, additional original poems must be performed, as no poem can be repeated (Somers-Willett 2009, 142). This rule holds true for groups as well as individual slammers. Readings are limited to three minutes, ten seconds, or less; longer readings have penalty points deducted from their scores (Jones 2009, 132). Besides the more formal rules governing poetry slams, the difference is in the attitude of the audience. Audiences attending slams are encouraged; and generally, they are happy to react—the idea being that poetry is fun and interactive. Cheering and applauding are encouraged; and in some events, booing is also considered appropriate behavior (Glazner 2000, 18). To create a nonthreatening slam, librarians may wish to modify the rules about appropriate behavior to include only positive comments.

If you feel inspired to try a poetry slam, consider watching the award-winning documentary film *Louder Than a Bomb* (http://www.loud erthanabombfilm.com). This film follows teams of young people truly sharing themselves and striving to achieve something amazing with the words they speak. After gaining the permission of parents, librarians wishing to conduct a spirited poetry slam are encouraged to share the story presented by this movie with as many potential participants as possible.

FEE-BASED PROGRAM ALTERNATIVES

Commercial companies provide poetry program opportunities whenever budgets or grants allow. Many offer interactive programs to schools, and will provide workshops for teachers as well for an additional fee. Poetry workshops can be created not just for artistic appreciation, but also to meet state standards as they pertain to communication skills. In

Arkansas, workshops emphasizing writing, speaking, and listening skills are used to meet standards known as the Arkansas Frameworks (Scott 2010, 89). Clayton Scott (2010, 90), a professional performer who provides these fee-based programs each year, thinks that teaching students to love poetry often leads to a better appreciation of reading and writing. In his four-day residencies he reinforces the lessons of English teachers by teaching concepts such as similes, metaphors, and alliteration. Students create their own poems and participate in a modified slam poetry event at the end of the week (ibid.).

Poetry Alive! is a 28-year-old company that runs Summer Residency Camps as well as single day assemblies. One great feature of their website is the online syllabus listing poems appropriate for each grade level grouping. Scrolling to the end of the syllabus leads to poems for grades K–1–2, 3–5, 6–8, and 9–12. If you are able to work in a computer lab setting, all students can read the same poem simultaneously, or it can be projected on a screen or whiteboard from a computer/projector workstation (http://poetryalive.com/services/shows/current_shows.html).

MARKETING

One of the most effective means of promoting your poetry activities to teens is through word-of-mouth marketing. Be sure to involve your TABs in the process, so that they are excited about the program and share the information with their friends both in school and the community. Remember to place bookmarks and flyers throughout the teen room; point them out to your regulars—the readers, the gamers, the students who come in every day after school to hang out for a few hours (Alessio 2011, 76).

Another marketing approach that has proven successful is promoting programs via "rave" cards. "Rave" cards are simply postcards carrying all the information that you would include on a flyer (Jones 2009, 13). These cards succeed because they can easily be passed around to friends. Prominently feature your events on the websites of both the school and the public libraries. Adding poetry websites or examples of different forms of poetry to the websites each month gives your teens a reason to keep returning to your website (Holtslander 2011, 7).

Another chance to cross-promote your program comes in the form of real-life demonstrations. The poems teens are working on in school can be tested out on peers in the teen area of the public library, which may spark the curiosity of teens who are not already involved. Of course, organized poetry readings or poetry slams can be offered as a school assembly for classmates, but consider also providing a larger community stage in the public library. As you plan your event, be sure that there is an element of fun in the workshops or performances. Allow your teens the freedom to express their feelings, emotions, and passion in a creative way. Let them help you to decide which format works best—simple writing, performance poetry, or songwriting; then let allow them to take center stage.

REFERENCES

Alessio, Amy J., and Kimberly A. Patton. *A Year of Programs for Teens 2*. Chicago, IL: ALA, 2011, 75–76.

Aptowicz, Cristin O'Keefe. *Words in Your Face: A Guided Tour Through Twenty Years of the New York City Poetry Slam*. New York: Soft Skull, 2008.

Chilcote, Lee. "Lake Erie Ink Inks Deal for Coventry School." *Freshwater*. September 1, 2011, http://www.freshwatercleveland.com/devnews/lakeerie ink090111.aspx (cited March 15, 2012).

Cuffe-Perez, Mary. "Story Quilt." *American Libraries* 39, no. 3: (2008): 50–52.

Glazner, Gary Mex, ed. *Poetry Slam: The Competitive Art of Performance Poetry*. San Francisco, CA: Manic D. Press, 2000, 11–21.

Heeger, Paula Brehm. "A Tie for Third Place." *School Library Journal* 52, no. 7 (2006): 27.

Holtslander, Linda. "Loudoun County Public Library: Try Poetry 2010." *Virginia Libraries* 57, no. 2 (2011): 5–12.

Honnold, RoseMary. *101+ Teen Programs That Work*. New York: Neal-Schuman Publishers, 2003.

Jones, Ella W. *Start to Finish: YA Programs Hip-Hop Symposiums, Summer Reading Programs, Virtual Tours, Poetry Slams, Teen Advisory Boards, Term Paper Clinics, and More!* New York: Neal Schuman Publishers Inc., 2009.

Lake Erie Link. "A Writing Space for Youth," http://lakeerieink.org/ (cited March 15, 2012).

Lawrence, Kathy. Phone interview by Cherie Pandora, March 12, 2012. Cleveland Heights, OH.

Levin, Nancy. Phone interview by Cherie Pandora, January 13, 2012. Cleveland, OH.

"Louder Than a Bomb," http://www.louderthanabombfilm.com (cited March 15, 2012).

Poetry Alive. "PoetryAlive! Assembly Show Syllabus," http://poetryalive.com/ services/shows/current_shows.html (cited March 15, 2012).

Project for Public Spaces. "Ray Oldenburg," http://www.pps.org/articles/rolden burg/ (cited March 15, 2012).

"Read Across America: An NEA Project," http://www.readacrossamerica.org/ (cited March 15, 2012).

Scott, W. Clayton. "Slamming Arkansas Schools!" *Teaching Artist Journal* 8, no. 2 (2010): 88–95.

Silverstein, Shel. *Where the Sidewalk Ends: the Poems and Drawings of Shel Silverstein, 30th Anniversary Edition*. New York: Harper Collins, 2004.

Somers-Willett, Susan B. A. *The Cultural Politics of Slam Poetry: Race, Identity, and the Performance of Popular Verse in America.* Ann Arbor: University of Michigan Press, 2009, 141–51.

FURTHER READING

Heeger, Paula Brehm. "A Tie for Third Place." *School Library Journal* 52, no. 7 (2006): 27.

Zalusky, Steve. "Winners of the 2011 John Cotton Dana Library Public Relations Awards," http://americanlibrariesmagazine.org/news/ala/winners-2011-john-cotton-dana-library-public-relations-awards (cited March 15, 2012).

8

◇ ◇ ◇

TECHNOLOGY AND SOCIAL NETWORKING

Not all teens depend on technology to get "connected," but the vast majority have an interest and knowledge of electronic gadgets, and participate in a variety of social networking sites on the Internet. Luckily, many libraries and librarians are ready, willing, and able to help teens find fun and safe ways to engage in these resources. Librarians have attempted to make the virtual component of the library just as important as the physical library (Valenza 2006, 54). There are, of course, also libraries that can only afford the bare minimum of options as well as librarians who are ambivalent, or even reluctant, to get involved after they consider the pros and cons of offering these options to their particular communities. But there are more than a few ideas in this chapter to help you think about new ways to approach any or all of these issues with your counterpart firmly by your side. Working with a partner can turn challenges that seemed insurmountable into smaller, manageable jobs that can be divided, shared, alternated, and accomplished.

SOCIAL MEDIA

Many librarians, teen librarians in particular, see social media as one more tool to reach their patrons, even when the teens can't be in the library itself (Farkas 2007, 242–243). Millennials, born between 1981 and 2000, have grown up with computers in diverse sizes and can't remember what the world was like before computers were readily available in public and school libraries, or homes (Flowers 2011, 20; Nowak 2011, 6). Even if there is no computer in their home, they know someone with a computer and expect reference tools to be available to them 24 hours a day, 7 days per week (ibid., 8). The 2009 PEW Research Center study "Trend Data for Teens: Teen Gadget Ownership" found that 69% of teens owned a computer while 75% owned a cell phone (see Figure 8.1). For these patrons, computers, the Internet, and social media aren't just tools—they are *the* way to have conversations with their peers.

As reported by *USA Today*, the American Academy of Pediatrics (AAP) sees social media as having both positive and negative aspects (Hellmich 2012). On the upside, the AAP has stated that these are wonderful tools, when used to build a personal network or to complete assignments. They caution that an overuse of the online network can lead to feelings of isolation and a greater risk of finding and using dangerous sites. Public libraries have tried to counter this sense of isolation by

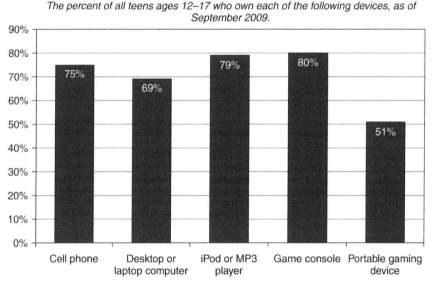

Figure 8.1: Teen Gadget Ownership

Source: PEW Research Center. "Trend Data for Teens: Teen Gadget Ownership," http:// www .pewinternet.org/Static-Pages/Trend-Data-for-Teens/Teen-Gadget-Ownership.aspx (cited April 15, 2012).

providing programs for patrons on Internet safety and by modeling appropriate use on their websites (Agosto and Abbas 2009, 33).

What will your library look like once you've achieved the level of electronic commitment your library can afford? This decision requires that you consider your facilities, your resources, your time, energy, and interest. Most of all, you must also consider the interests and needs of your teen patrons before making any decision. How much assistance can you provide at your library and still offer help to your counterpart? Should you both focus on providing primary access at one facility and direct interest toward those services, or should you try to share the burden equally so that teens are prepared to use either location as needed? Should you try to divide and conquer the endless amounts of technology with each library taking primary responsibility for services most natural for your organization to provide? Your final decision should be something unique to your community after all these variables have been taken into account. Be sure to consider the hours and access, as well as filtering issues, at both facilities.

Public and school librarians should have an open discussion about the extent, or reluctance, to filter the Internet at their library. What is the current attitude or approach your library director or school board are sharing with their staff and the public? The Children's Internet Protection Act (CIPA) law, passed in 2001, places restrictions on schools and public libraries receiving federal discounts on funding for Internet access (http://www.fcc.gov/guides/childrens-internet-protection-act). Many schools reacted by prohibiting the use of **all** interactive online tools. Schools are now starting to realize the potential of social media sites, and allow limited access by students and teachers. With such restrictions on access at school, students often flock to the public library after school to check their email, update their Facebook page, and check in with their peers.

Give serious consideration to creating policies and procedures concerning your teen, and preteen, population's use of social media at your facility. Share your library's forms with your counterpart as there may be some wording that you can use to improve your own Acceptable Use Policy (AUP) forms. Address issues of online privacy, Internet safety, appropriate use of library property, and what degree of responsibility your organization is willing to accept concerning the teens' online conduct. Will parents be involved in the policies conversation? Will they be asked to accept or decline their child's access to the Internet? Consider offering a program for parents of middle to high school students, informing them of the advantages and struggles of using these resources. This can be a great option for all concerned. (See Chapter 3 for details on Internet safety programs.)

Students view their phones first as sophisticated tools for entertainment and socializing. They love to add "apps" to equip these pocket-sized devices for sharing their favorite sites, downloading songs, posting pictures, and playing games with friends (Rosen 2010, 52–54). Teens don't always understand how these same tools can be used to make them more productive learners. Keeping that in mind, consider some of the social media opportunities available for your library staff and teens. Please remember that these technologies and the rules for participation are ever-changing. Also in constant flux are how these tools are used, by whom, and for what purpose. Both school and public libraries can use the following tools.

FACEBOOK

Facebook (https://www.facebook.com/), the successor to MySpace, the original online social community (http://www.myspace.com/), quickly became one of the most popular tools among teens. (MySpace is of significantly less interest to teens now.) For both professional and teen use, this might be the best spot to find, share, and discuss new music. To sign up, users must agree to a list of terms set forth by Facebook, and must identify themselves as users who are at least 13 years of age. Hopefully your YA patrons are working with their parents or guardians when they create their Facebook profile, and are persuaded to keep their profiles private. You or your counterpart may want to offer a workshop for young teens and their parents on the safe use of Facebook, but allow the final decision to be a family matter. Free online games and connecting with friends through status updates and online chatting are the most common reasons that teens want to join this community. There is a sense of belonging in the online world that can be had with a certain amount of anonymity. Teens are free to post their profiles and pictures without being shackled by rubrics imposed by teachers. Therein lies the danger! Teens often "over share" information, without realizing how vulnerable they are making themselves; this is yet another reason that you need to reach out to them. Consider offering searching and privacy tips; new book, movie, or music alerts; AND giveaways for teens who either join your group or "Like" your page. If your counterpart also has a Facebook page for her library, make sure you "Like" or "Follow" her page so teens have the chance to discover both profiles. Suggest that your teens also "Like" or "Follow" both libraries. Your public library can offer Facebook classes, including personal safety tips, and advanced search techniques. Have the school library cosponsor and promote your program; include sessions on the latest pictorial messages that can be captured and shared via Pinterest and Instagram.

Librarians should use Facebook as a free and easy way to see what your fellow librarians are promoting. Numerous groups and pages are dedicated to sharing ideas, tips, and tricks that others have tried successfully with their teens. Now that you're starting to have an abundance of enthusiasm and ideas of your own, consider creating some original pages or groups. This is a great way to brainstorm with colleagues everywhere and can provide that extra encouragement teen librarians sometimes truly need. Making a Facebook page to advertise teen events at your own library, at your counterpart's library, or for your collaborative efforts is a smart use of this communication tool. Facebook can also be used for book clubs and TABs in both public and school libraries.

Notes from the Field

In a telephone conversation with the author on July 27, 2011, Milena Streen, vice-president and chief information officer and librarian at Saint Ignatius High School, Cleveland, Ohio, explained that she uses social media to link students to new books, new applications, images, blogs, YouTube, and technology. "Students follow and interact with me more via Facebook by posting comments, clicking the 'Like' button, or telling me that they liked my comments," she says. Her advice to students is to "Look outside our walls, there's so much more out there."

So how can we use Milena's suggestion to foster collaboration? Our advice to every librarian is to post and share information, not just from your own library but from other libraries your teens use as well. In most communities teen librarians work with multiple public, private, and parochial schools. Why wouldn't the teen librarian place links to each school on the teen page? Wouldn't this make it easier for your patrons to shop your databases as well as those provided in the school? School librarians often borrow books from three or four neighboring library systems. It helps all students for links to each of these neighboring libraries to be posted on the school's web page. Encouraging our teens to use all their resources both within and outside of our own library walls is one of the goals we have in common. By cross-posting you make your web pages at both institutions far more valuable tools for your teens.

Why not try this approach with your partner librarian? Call and find out if your public library has a distinct Facebook page just for teens. If not, then design one together. The teen librarian can post items of interest from her department; the school librarian can email items for inclusion from her library's events calendar. We know that Twitter and Facebook are often blocked at schools so students simply view them at home or at public libraries. Schools that have wireless networks have brought huge changes in the ways that students accomplish research; students can now go online with their phones. Student smartphones have been a "seismic shift" that Milena compares to the progression "from slide rules to calculators." Streen (2012) feels that smartphones provide true one-to-one computing.

TWITTER

Twitter (http://twitter.com/) provides librarians with the chance to relay short (no more than 140 characters) and timely messages. While similar to texting, the goal is to create concise quick "tweets" that all your followers can read simultaneously. Small group conversations can quickly grow in numbers, becoming more of a town hall gathering. Professionals can locate and follow a variety of authors, organizations, publishers, fellow librarians, and other experts from a variety of fields. Both school and public librarians should consider using this as timely method of broadcasting any changes or reminders of upcoming events or teen meetings.

Trendy topics are often discussed via tweets. Twitter **topics** will start with a "#" called a hashtag as in #YALit for lovers of YA Literature or # hungergames for discussions of a favorite book. **People** create usernames beginning with the "@" symbol so you can search for your favorite author, professional organization (@aasl for the American Association of School Librarians) or librarian (@joycevalenza). Twitter provides a fast-paced flow of information that lends itself to brainstorming with an ever-changing group of people. It can quickly become a favorite source of inspiration and problem solving. Try sending tweets out to your teens to get fast feedback to an idea you find interesting, but do take into account that not all your teens can be or will be on Twitter. Consider placing your energy into quick tweets rather than formatting a library newsletter. #YAsaves became a hot topic on Twitter when someone posted the question, "Is YA Literature too dark?"

Notes from the Field

How do we go about using these tools with our teens? In a telephone conversation on July 29, 2011, Mariemont High School Librarian Emily Zauss Colpi (2012) explained that she is using Twitter heavily this year, since she found that "(S)tudents connect with other Twitter users and it presents another way for me to reach my students." She uses either a phone or tablet for efficiency and sends the Twitter feed directly to the library web page sharing both what she is reading and author information.

Colpi tried email to connect with her book club members but found that her students often didn't check their email while they do check their Twitter accounts. She sends reminders of meetings to Facebook via Twitter, which saves time, and posts her book review blog on Facebook as well. Twitter then becomes a conversational tool with both librarians posting quick messages about their own libraries. Short book reviews, especially those generated by your teens, will gain interest as will information on popular topics such as background on the latest, greatest teen read. The procedure is quick and easy and tweets are posted immediately; there are no newsletters to design, no graphics to resize. You will probably find that you will add new hashtags as teen interest grows. Check with your regular readers and your TAB to see what they are following and what they would like to see on your Twitter feed. You may, in fact, find that this is one of the quickest and easiest ways to communicate with your library partner; just create a new hashtag and reserve it for conversations between the two of you.

MOODLE

Moodle (http://moodle.com/) is a free classroom management tool that has grown in use in schools as an instructional tool. When used by librarians, it serves as a central hub to post lessons, quizzes, activities, websites, and links to citation guides. If the school librarian is using Moodle for Research instruction then the wise thing to do is to share the username and password with the teen librarian. While school policies may prohibit granting administrative privileges to the public librarian it makes sense to review the Moodle guide in one of your meetings; the teen librarian is sure to have suggestions that can be incorporated into your lessons. Colpi has done a great deal of professional development with teachers on the use of Twitter and Moodle and coteaches a college level class for teachers on 21st Century online skills. Luckily, she works in a school with "administrative support for innovative leadership with a focus on excellence in teaching" (Colpi 2012). Teachers tell her what they want to do and ask her advice. She experiments with different techniques and finds a way to accomplish the teacher's goal while saving the teacher's time. While this might not be a technology the public librarian can participate in directly, learning more about this tool now could bring great collaboration later. If the school librarian can provide access to a central hub for the teen librarian, the public library could have a better grasp of homework assignments as the teachers intended them to be accomplished.

BLOGS

Blogging is an activity often enjoyed by teens, as well as by authors and librarians. It is a popular way of publishing your thoughts, ideas, and information through a variety of free software platforms. Blogs can be simple or complex, but to be successful, they should have focus and frequent posting to attract, and keep, your audience interested enough to return to your blog.

If using blogs in a school setting, be sure to give your counterpart access to your blog. The school librarian can blog about the lesson just taught and the resources used. The teen librarian can add comments about appropriate resources at the public library; a real time saver for the student who needs to continue research at the public library after school hours.

The three most popular platforms for free blogs are: Blogger (http://www.blogger.com/), LiveJournal (http://www.livejournal.com/), and WordPress (http://wordpress.com/). If you decide to create a blog to share with the teens you serve or cocreate a blog with your counterpart, what should you include? Most platforms allow for a variety of access levels so you will be able to assign different roles to the different participants, keeping administrative control for the adults as well as the ability to approve postings before they become public. First you'll want to decide on a platform. Do you want to be chatty and informal in a blog, with links to additional blogs; or do you want to make concise educational and entertaining lists for your teens? What other sites might appeal to your teens? Hopefully your library will be able to provide access to a few paid databases, but will you supplement that list with free sites? What are some safe and free quality sites for entertainment? (See References at the end of the chapter for a listing of appropriate sites.)

Many teens have blogs of their own and enjoy the challenge of finding interesting ways to attract readers. Offering your library's TAB the opportunity to write a blog for the teen page might be just one more way to engage teens, both those in your volunteer group and those in the general population. Sometimes teens that are uninterested in writing on paper see blogs as a means of connecting with peers and enjoy writing for a blog (Godwin 2008, 169).

Librarians can create a blog of their own. Just don't forget to focus on the message you're trying to convey; and be sure to add new material via frequent updates. If you choose to create a blog with your counterpart it could ease the burden of time and effort as well as provide an interesting mix of topics for teens to enjoy. YAs tire of static content, and will move on to sites that stay current. Use your blog to connect with authors, publishers, and other librarians by reposting items of interest or using the blog roll to create a listing of recommended blogs. Or maybe only one of you has any interest or inclination to try blogging. Public libraries can share their upcoming programs, post program ideas for review, and add original book reviews by teens or librarians. School librarians can do the same and can pose and answer reference questions tied to homework assignments and research projects. And of course you'll want to make sure you post information relating to what's happening in your counterpart's library for interested teens.

PINTEREST

Pinterest (http://pinterest.com/) is a relatively new tool on the social media scene. Pinterest allows users to show and share original photographs and to indicate appreciation for other's photos as well. Users create their own themed boards, filled with pictures from all conceivable sources. They can follow other Pinterest users to access the boards they've created; access is available through Pinterest as well as through Facebook and Twitter feeds. An interesting, visual way to connect with fellow librarians and their teen patrons, this growing community is full of untapped potential. You and your counterpart might want to try building a few boards together with simple themes like read-a-likes for popular books or free images from a particular historical event. Use these boards to promote special monthly displays and activities occurring at both libraries.

TEXTING

Teens love to send and receive texts about everything and anything— at least the teens that are lucky enough to have parents willing to provide smartphones that years ago would have been considered a luxury. The PEW study on "Teens, Smartphones and Texting" revealed that three quarters of teens now text; the number of texts sent daily now averages 60 texts per day (Lenhart 2012, 2). As a librarian, you will find texting, like tweeting, a smart way to alert teens to last minute programming changes, or to announce breaking news about the latest hot title at the library. Many public libraries provide quick answers to reference questions via texting since teens prefer it to email and chat. Check in advance with your director or school principal concerning any limitations or exclusions your organization might have, since texting charges can add up for both the sender and the receiver. Have an honest discussion with your TAB before deciding to use it as a primary means of communicating. Texting is also an easy way to keep in touch with your counterpart, especially as neither of you will always be easy to locate within your own building or if you travel to multiple buildings.

YOUTUBE

YouTube (http://www.youtube.com/) features user-created videos with all manner of unrated content, from book trailers to online game solutions to postings by individuals. While teens often think of YouTube as just a fun place to kill time looking at random video clips, you can channel their creative energy into a worthwhile purpose. Consider helping teens to make videos to promote the teen area of the library. All you need is to provide teens with access to a digital camera; and they can easily make, and post, a video online. If your school is one of the many that produces daily video announcements, they may have sophisticated cameras, editing equipment, and even students enrolled in a production class, who can serve as your videographers. Public libraries may also have video equipment that can be borrowed for a teen program.

Having teens create original book trailers is an excellent way to promote books the kids have loved. Also, ask your teens to produce training videos (in their own words), demonstrating the use of various technology devices. Do you have an avid group of crafters? Have your teens create the video of a craft program as a marketing tool for the website. You could even have them tape some promotions for the adult programs hosted by your public library. If you have an immigrant population, can your teens help to create online tours of your library in other languages? If you find this medium works for you and your teens, consider setting up your own YouTube channel.

SKYPE

Skype (http://www.skype.com/intl/en-us/home) conversations, in voice and video, are free, no matter how distant the two users are from each other. This service lends itself to visual demonstrations and real-time conversations with others living far away or even your counterpart who isn't so far away. Why not try a team-teaching lesson using libraries, librarians, and materials from both locations to introduce new ideas to teens in a classroom? Or join a professional learning group without having to travel? Also be aware that many authors are willing to attend book groups for free through Skype (see also Chapters 3 and 4).

ONLINE BULLYING

We cannot leave the subject of social media without discussing recent occurrences of online bullying also known as cyberbullying. According to the 2010 U.S. Census Bureau report (searchable online at http://factfinder2 .census.gov/faces/nav/jsf/pages/index.xhtml) the community that Cherie and Stacey have been serving is 12.3% teens (ages 10–19), 10.5% of whom live with a single parent. It is important to share these statistics to make it clear that every community, with a similar or completely different set of demographics, should pay attention to the safety of their children and be aware of how teens will use or abuse their Internet privileges.

Notes from the Field

In an email message to the author on March 17, 2012, Police Sergeant George Lichman stated that the police work closely with schools in response to fairly regular complaints about teen online behavior. Sgt. Lichman (2012) offers Internet Safety Presentations free to local nonprofit organizations, alerting teens and adults about "multiple online threats, including predators, posting pictures, sharing information, passwords, cyberbullying, and SEXting." Check with your own police department to see if your police department has its own Internet Crimes Against Children (ICAC) liaison on staff who would be willing to speak to your teens. Feel free to check the following website for further information: http://www.ojp.usdoj.gov/ovc/publi cations/bulletins/internet_2_2001/welcome.html

It is also a challenge for public librarians, especially those in average to large size communities, to learn as much about the teens as the school librarians, who see these teens every day in a controlled environment. Generally speaking, teens you address by name have garnered your attention by being either outstanding patrons, or those who need reminders to correct their behavior. How can you tell if the teens you don't know by name are quietly doing their homework online, or if they're making mischief, intentionally or not, for another teen?

The nonprofit, nonpartisan organization PEW Research Center has studied the topic of teen behavior in the context of social networking and published their findings in a report, "Teens, Kindness and Cruelty on Social Network Sites" (Lenhart et al. 2011). It is an interesting study not just for the quantifiable facts and figures, but also for the insight into how influential parental involvement is for the online teenager. Librarians in both organizations can educate teens about responsible use and proper etiquette online through programs that educate and inform without being preachy. Talk with your counterpart about alternating your efforts to provide thoughtful guidelines and guidance so the frequency and presentation of your message is varied enough it has the best chance of being heard. Adult support fosters teen awareness of the consequences of their actions and can provide a sanctuary for teens who need to see a friendly face.

Knowing about negative aspects of social media doesn't mean that teens should be kept away from these resources. If used properly, with the best tools and knowledge the adults around these teens can provide, the online world can be used for a positive change. Learn as much as you can about the different applications available online, choose those you believe best suit your community, then teach the parents, guardians, instructors, and teens what you know; just be prepared to continue this cycle as new tools and websites become popular.

REFERENCES

Agosto, Denise E., and June Abbas. "Teens and Social networking: How Public Libraries are Responding to the Latest Online Trend." *Public Libraries* 48, no. 3 (2009): 32–37.

Colpi, Emily. Phone interview by Cherie Pandora. July 29, 2012. Mariemont, OH.

Farkas, Meredith. *Social Software in Libraries: Building Collaboration, Communication, and Community Online.* Medford, NJ: Information Today, 2007.

Flowers, Sarah. *Young Adults Deserve the Best: YALSA's Competencies in Action.* Chicago, IL: ALA, 2011.

Godwin, Peter, and Jo Parker, ed. *Information Literacy Meets Library 2.0.* London: Facet Publishing, 2008.

Hellmich, Nanci. "Social Media Websites Can Help and Harm Kids." *USA Today* (March 28, 2011). http://www.usatoday.com/yourlife/parenting-family/2011-03-28-pediatrics28_ST_N.htm?csp=34 (cited April 15, 2012).

Lenhart, Amanda. "PEW Internet and American Life Project: Teens, Smartphones and Texting," http://pewinternet.org/topics/Teens.aspx (cited April 15, 2012).

Lichman, George. Email interview with Stacey Hayman. March 17, 2012. Rocky River, OH.

Nowak, Kristine. "Serving Teens in the Public Library." *Kentucky Libraries* 75, no. 3 (2011): 611.

PEW Research Center. "Trend Data for Teens: Teen Gadget Ownership," http://www.pewinternet.org/Static-Pages/Trend-Data-for-Teens/Teen-Gadget-Ownership.aspx (cited April 15, 2012).

Rosen, Larry D. with Mark Carrier and Nancy Cheever. *Rewired: Understanding the iGeneration and the Way They Learn.* New York: Palgrave Macmillan, 2010.

Streen, Milena. Phone interview by Cherie Pandora. July 27, 2011. Cleveland, OH.

U.S. Census Bureau. "American Factfinder," http://factfinder2.census.gov/faces/nav/jsf/pages/index.xhtml (cited April 15, 2012).

Valenza, Joyce Kasman. "The Virtual Library." *Educational Leadership* 63, no. 3 (2005): 54–59.

FURTHER READING

Lenhart, Amanda, M. Madden, A. Smith, K. Purcell, K. Zickuhr, and L. Rainie. "PEW Internet and American Life Project: Teens, Kindness and Cruelty on Social Network Sites," http://www.pewinternet.org/Reports/2011/Teens-and-social-media.aspx (cited April 15, 2012).

Parkes, Dave, and Geoff Walton, ed. *Web 2.0 and Libraries: Impacts, Technologies and Trends.* Oxford: Chandos Publishing, 2010.

Here are just a few suggestions to consider for blogs and teen pages (all cited April 15, 2012).

Educational

NASA (for grades 5–8)
http://www.nasa.gov/audience/forstudents/5-8/features/homework-topics-index.html

NASA (for grades 9–12)
http://www.nasa.gov/audience/forstudents/9-12/A-Z/index.html

Library of Congress (for all ages)
http://www.loc.gov/families/

OneLook Dictionary
http://onelook.com

ipl2: information you can trust
http://www.ipl.org/

Best of History Web Sites by EdTech Teacher Inc.
http://www.besthistorysites.net/

The Math Forum
http://mathforum.org/dr.math/

College Board Resume Writing
http://www.collegeboard.com/student/plan/high-school/36957
   .html

Pure Entertainment (Some Suitable for Your Preteens)

Disney
http://www.disney.go.com/games/

Club Penguin
http://www.clubpenguin.com/

NASA (for grades 5–8)
http://www.nasa.gov/audience/forstudents/5-8/multimedia/funa
   ndgames_archive_1.html

Pogo.com (You are not required to register, but must be 18 if you want
   to create an account)
http://www.pogo.com/

Scholastic: The Stacks
http://www.scholastic.com/kids/stacks/games/

Free Yahoo Games
http://games.yahoo.com/free-games

9
◇ ◇ ◇

HOMEWORK HELP

Homework, the bane of every teen's existence, is one of your best opportunities to connect with the most diverse population of teens you can imagine. The school librarian has a better chance at catching teen walkthrough traffic, but the public librarian will be able to provide access to more materials for a longer period of time, due to the hours the public library is open. In any given community, there are many homes that do not have home computers; other homes have computers but do not have Internet access; most home libraries can't hope to compete with the library's reference books, which often contain the best information for students. Teens with computers and connectivity at home might not have a working printer, have a system-crashing computer virus, or lack computer paper needed to finish their latest report, and no money to fix the problem. Due to the limitations on hours and resources, the school library cannot always meet the demands of students. Often due to necessity, the public library becomes the place of choice for homework and research during evening and weekend hours. How can we collaborate to make the most out of both situations? We'll cover that in this chapter.

If you work in an area with high levels of poverty (e.g., where a large percentage of students receive free and reduced school lunches), your patrons are even more in need of your services and assistance as they are less likely to have home access to computers, the Internet, or perhaps even the advanced skills needed to most effectively use these tools to their advantage. In addition, teachers and librarians agree that the Internet cannot replace the wealth of resources found in print or in the "gated web" (those password-protected resources such as online databases that are purchased by libraries or consortiums for the sole use of their patrons; Siu-Runyan 2011, 29).

In Our Experience

Cherie's high school library contained walls of literature reference books, many donated by the public library, which we used extensively during the intense spring research paper season. Eighteen classes of English students used them to craft literature critiques on the novels they'd read. When the publisher began to digitize these works, they admitted that their database carried just a selection of the hundreds of books we had on our shelves. To students, the thick, weighty books looked boring with their worn brown covers. Students were attracted instead by what seemed like a decent, and easier, way to find their information—by searching databases, unaware that they were missing quality analysis in print resources. Given some guidance from librarians in both libraries, these "boring" books became the tools that helped them to be successful in analyzing their topics.

What is a student to do after the school library is closed for the day? Where will he or she go for guidance in completing assignments, reports, and projects? The answer lies in their access to the resources and the staff of the public library—the reference staff, and, if there is one, the teen librarian.

How can school librarians help their partners in public libraries deal with the avalanche of adolescents who rush to them after the final bell? The key, as always, is communication. Communication between school and public librarians benefits all of our teen, and preteen, patrons. Good communication can help students and librarians maneuver through some exciting, as well as some ghastly, assignments.

ASSIGNMENT ALERTS

Whenever possible, school librarians should alert the public library to classroom research assignments via assignment alert forms (Figure 1.1). School librarians are also encouraged to forewarn the reference and teen librarians of any "poorly designed" projects, and how the problem of finding information to help students can be solved. All librarians have dealt with assignments that are almost unsearchable, for example, finding primary sources for an obscure historical event or a topic that might require expert knowledge to begin the hunt. Some teachers are apparently clueless about how to use a library; and their assignments reflect their inability to create topics that allow students to easily determine the best search terms to use (Vaillancourt 2000, 57). Wouldn't it be wonderful if *all* teachers shared their syllabi, their reading lists, and copies of their assignments with both the school librarian and the teen or reference librarians? (Vaillancourt 2000, 58). While many teachers are forgetful or simply won't take the time to share their work, school librarians must make every effort to retrieve this information and pass it on to their counterpart at the public library.

ENHANCING COMMUNICATION

As discussed in Chapter 2, one of the best ways to keep on top of these projects is to hold regular meetings attended by the library staffs of both the middle school and the high school, with the teen librarian from the public library. These monthly, or quarterly, meetings allow librarians to share more information than can be shared via email, fax, or phone. Teen librarians can provide information about their resources, and air their frustrations with research and homework assignments. (This is also a good time to discuss background on teens who might be interested in volunteering, or to inquire about these teens that are less than well behaved.) Unfortunately, school librarians may not be cognizant of every homework assignment that is assigned. Ideally, the school librarian would be informed about assignments that are difficult or poorly worded before they have been given to students, so they can approach the teacher and suggest modifications to the project.

If meeting locations rotate between public and school libraries, teen librarians can easily share their newest acquisitions by passing around print materials and demonstrating new databases. Public librarians may be able to suggest materials that would benefit the school, and school librarians can do likewise for public librarians.

In Our Experience

Cherie remembers a meeting where the teen librarian shared some wonderful business and literature databases that they were planning to purchase in order to support our teens. While the business materials also helped the adults of our community, the literature materials were meant almost solely for the use of high school students from all of the local parochial, public, and private schools.

HOMEWORK HELP CENTERS

Some public libraries have established homework help centers for students. These range from a simple collection of general resources—a dictionary, an encyclopedia set, database access—to complex centers with banks of computers, extensive collections, and staff or volunteers who offer tutoring and coaching during afterschool and evening hours.

Why would you want to add a homework center to your teen space? The answer is simply to improve customer service, and to provide access to materials and equipment teens might not have at home. One of the best ways to support all the teens in your community is to offer to help with one of the most prevalent, parts of their life—homework. Teens that would never show up for a recreational program are more likely to use your resources to complete assignments and research projects (Vaillancourt 2000, 52). While no one expects that the public library should supplant the school library in purchasing curriculum-related materials, the truth is that students rely on public libraries for their day-to-day needs, just as adults rely on the public library for the latest business resources (Vaillancourt 2000, 53).

Some public libraries don't have formal homework help centers, but do have computers available exclusively for teens after school. Having a complete and current reference collection of middle school and high school textbooks, furnished by the school system, for use within the library helps students catch up on classroom reading, finish homework, and review material before exams.

SETTING UP A HOMEWORK HELP CENTER

It's never too early to start collaborating on supporting students. When considering adding a homework help center to your library, find out first whether you are duplicating the efforts of the school. Contact the school librarian and find out—does your local school provide after school tutoring programs, homework sessions, or help preparing for state standardized tests? If not, there is an opportunity for you to work together with the school library and make this a worthwhile collaborative effort. School programs are often heavily structured, requiring mandatory attendance, formal goals that must be met by the tutor and the student. Students often prefer a less-regulated place to start homework; a place where assistance is available, but no one hovers over them and their work.

Decisions

Planning your homework center requires many decisions and using your counterpart to bounce around possible choices could help you think through potentially problematic ideas. Do you want to provide a space for teens to do homework, or reserve a group of computers for them? Will the center be available every weekday or on limited days? Will there be specific hours for the homework center? Will the small number of computers necessitate a time limit (perhaps a half hour) of computer time per student when others are waiting? If you want to provide more than your existing teen space, how will you staff the center? Will it be staffed by adults or peers? Will the adults be volunteers or paid staff? Will students need to preregister for the sessions or will it be a drop-in center?

Space

Do you have an area in your library that you can dedicate to a homework help center? Can you find space in a nook, a corner, a multipurpose room, or are you lucky enough to have a larger area you can remodel with this idea in mind? What supplies will you need? How many people would occupy the space at any given time? Consider how well you will be able to control the noise level of both the help center and the surrounding area. Discuss your ideas with your counterpart at the school library, asking for suggestions about supplies and furnishings that would work. If you are able to dedicate a specific area to this endeavor, what other uses can you wring out of this space to get the maximum "bang for your buck?" Often, libraries designate small conference rooms as tutoring rooms for adults. Parents can make arrangements with tutors and the space is available without cost as a benefit for community members.

Hours

One of the first decisions that you need to make is to decide on the months, days, and hours that you wish to operate your homework center. Will you have afterschool hours or evening hours? Ask your counterpart at the school library what time school lets out, and which holidays are observed. Hours may be immediately after school from 3:30 to 4:45 P.M., from 4:45 to 6 P.M. in the evening, or some other combination that works for your library. Some centers operate Monday through Thursday and only from October through May of each school year. The **drop-in**

center option: St. Paul Public Library, Minnesota, uses a different approach; they have a drop-in philosophy for their centers. The centers have determined their own brands with teen-friendly names like The Zone and Hot Spot; others like Community Learning Center make it easy for parents to understand the purpose. A Sunday afternoon homework group is known as STARS—Students Together Afterschool @ Rice Street branch (Saint Paul Public Library 2012). The library website also provides what they call Homework Rescue with online tutoring available 24/7 in both English and Spanish, available via both chat or email. Resources online include flash video tutorials, while specialized databases for the state of Minnesota are available for students doing research for History Day competitions (St. Paul Public Library 2012).

Materials and Equipment

If you're providing computers, will they have Internet access, or only basic software programs and access to online databases? Reference books, basic school supplies, and printers also should be allocated to this dedicated area. Access to computers is essential for any library providing homework support to teens and preteens. Many children do not have computer access anywhere other than their school or their public library. If this is their situation, it means that your library may be the ONLY place that these students can research, organize, and word process their papers. Having a computer area designated just for teens is ideal, but that's not always possible, given the limitations of space and budget. If this is the case for you, consider allotting specific hours on specific days as teen homework time.

Supervision

Before considering potential homework center supervisors, establish guidelines for selecting and using anyone working with children under 18. Each state has its own set of laws that have come out of the National Child Protective Act of 1993, and public institutions are held to those standards (http://www.ojjdp.gov/pubs/guidelines/appen-a.html). It is no small task for either the individual or the institution to screen adult volunteer candidates, so be sure to recognize this fact when staffing choices are debated. After your procedural policies are put into place, different groups can be analyzed for their strengths and weaknesses within your vision of a homework center. Regardless of how you decide to staff such a center, be sure to assign a library employee to coordinate the efforts of those you choose to staff the center.

HOMEWORK CLUBS

Essentially, a homework club is a group of teens that meet on a regular basis. Homework clubs can be created to meet most needs expressed by your teens. With preteens you may want to allow them to select a name that sounds like a fun organization, one that eliminates the word homework. Unlike drop-in centers, where teens come whenever they need help, in a homework club, teens plan to visit your center at a regular time, often for a specific period of time, so you know the numbers that will attend and can plan accordingly as to your staff needs.

Do your teens need help with science fair preparation? Perhaps you should consider a science club that meets every Wednesday afternoon after school for the months that lead up to the science fair symposium. Have teachers asked for writing centers? Would your teens appreciate a special writing center that meets only for the two weeks prior to midterms and finals? Do your patrons reflect a number of immigrant groups new to your area? All of these situations will benefit from a homework club.

English as a Second Language

In Pittsburgh, Pennsylvania, Whitehall Public Library's Teen Services Librarian Licia Slimon created a tutoring area for students who struggle with English as a second language. English Language Learners (ELL) club students represented numerous countries, but shared similar experiences. All were reading far below grade level, many were afraid to read in class, and some had little formal schooling due to the political climates or danger of attending school in their homeland (Slimon 2010, 134–135). Since money was not available to hire additional staff, Slimon became their first tutor, meeting with them every Wednesday after school. Partnering went beyond talking to teachers and school librarians; it included contacting religious groups and literacy programs aimed at the parents of these teens. Other libraries provide tutoring and a writing center throughout the year to assist students with homework, research, and essay assignments. The Williamsburgh branch of the Brooklyn Public Library in New York City is one library that has done just that (Shaffer 2006, 38).

Library Staff

Since they are already employed, you can presume that staff has already passed the required screening. This would seem to be the easiest route *if* staffing levels within the library are solid, with the obvious first choice on staff being the teen librarian. If staffing is tight and the teen librarian is required to wear many other hats, such as working as a reference librarian or supervising the children's room, then who can be the adult presence in a homework center?

Library Volunteers

Many public libraries without strong funding rely on volunteers to act as unpaid staff in a variety of ways, from sorting donated books to shelving returned items, from presenting storytimes to hosting adult programs. Library volunteers come in all ages and have wonderful talents to share with their fellow patrons, but they are volunteers and cannot always be asked to make the same commitments as a paid staff member. There are certain groups of individuals who are especially appealing as volunteers at the homework center.

Current Teachers

Teachers willing to donate their time and expertise should be at the top of every hopeful list. Current teachers or even college faculty come with insider knowledge of the curriculum, the best understanding of the students needing assistance, and unparalleled access to their fellow teachers for questions that come up in the assignments. Currently employed teachers, however, need to complete their own work, tutor their own students, and live lives of their own as well so they may not be as likely to devote additional volunteer hours to your project. On the other hand, some teachers are not employed full-time, and this may be an opportunity for them to add to their experience.

Retired Teachers

Retired teachers come with most of the same basic pros and cons as current teachers. Small differences do appear, the most obvious being that retired teachers have the potential for greater availability, but may not have the same timely knowledge as their currently employed counterparts.

Peer Tutoring

There have been discussions of Key Club or National Honor Society members from the high school working as tutors, but this works best if the students needing help are upper elementary or middle school age to ensure the tutor's mastery of the skill being taught, and to prevent any chance of an older teen feeling uncomfortable seeking the guidance of a direct peer. Also, be sure to discuss how much adult supervision is needed for teen tutoring, and who might best shoulder that responsibility.

College Students

College students seeking a degree in education could be the most natural fit for your homework center, but consider students with expertise in specific subjects as well. Is it possible to partner with a local university? Would the university allow students to receive college credit or service credits for their assistance? If college students are to receive college credit, how will their assistance be reported? How will missing a scheduled time be handled? If there is no college credit offered, what motivation can you provide besides a recommendation letter for future employers?

Concerned Parents

Parents are perhaps the most vocal advocates, but based on our experience, they are often the least dependable group of volunteers. Both working and stay-at-home parents have plenty of personal investment in making a homework center successful; but by the very nature of being parents, they will also have school and child commitments of their own to keep. If their child falls ill, has a sports practice, or scout meeting, their personal life will, and should, take precedence over their volunteer commitment. It is also worth considering whether their own teen is being tutored. Will it make that student feel awkward to have their parent present?

In Our Experience

Providing a space, a welcoming atmosphere, great print resources, and computer access are things that make teens WANT to return to your library. Some teens feel claustrophobic after six hours of sitting in classes. No matter how interactive the work in classes may be, preteens and teens need a little time to relax. This means that your afterschool crowd may not be as quiet as the groups that come in after the dinner hour. They mean no disrespect for the rules or for the staff. They simply have felt a bit "caged" in class, and need a bit of time to change modes. In an effort to keep a balance between out-of-control behavior and overly controlling staff, post simple guidelines and hold teens accountable from the first day of school. Once teens understand what you find acceptable, they will behave appropriately and stay as long as they like. If they are not interested in making the space inviting for everyone, they might be better served by leaving the library for a brief time to work off some of their energy, and return when calmer.

ORGANIZATIONAL STRUCTURE

You've found the proper space and you've selected your supervisory staff; now you need to set the parameters for your center. You need to set hours and days of the week that it will be available and create guidelines as to how students will be granted, or denied, access to these special resources. Again, collaborating with a school librarian can help you improve the quality of your homework center, and ensure its success.

The sections below will guide you through the process of setting up such a center for your library. If teens are tutoring, how will their time be structured and recorded? Can students come and go at will, or will they be required to schedule appointments? Consider how you will handle students who request help with one-time projects versus those needing long-term assistance with recurring homework issues.

INITIAL VERSUS ONGOING COSTS

Costs for space, staffing, and supplies do add up, and are often the deciding factor in what, if any, style of homework help center your library chooses to create. Will your library consider set-up to be a one-time expense, or will the cost be determined by the continued consumption of resources? Are there support groups or grants that can be applied to the cost of this project? Will the Friends of the Library or the school's PTA or Educational Foundation assist you with funding? (See also Chapter 12.)

JUDGING THE END RESULT

How will you know if your efforts have been worthwhile? Are you looking to see a change in grades or in attitude? Maybe you're simply collecting statistics on the number of hours and participants present in the homework center. What kind of response do you need to see, or report, to determine if your homework help center is needed and a success, or if your time and money would be better spent on other projects? Can the school librarian help by providing anecdotal evidence from their own experience or from interviewing teachers? Use these questions above to guide you as you evaluate the effectiveness of your homework help center. It is best to gather both statistical information and anecdotal evidence from your patrons. Simple numbers alone are not enough, particularly, if you need to report back to the source that helped fund your center. You need to also use surveys, Likert scales of effectiveness, success stories, criticisms, and positive comments to discover whether you are meeting the needs of your patrons, both teens and their parents. For more information on evaluation, see Chapter 15.

Notes from the Field

Cuyahoga County Public Library in Greater Cleveland (Ohio) maintains three homework centers for grades 7–10 (and seven centers for grades K–6) throughout the system. Registration is required to make sure that the centers are adequately staffed for the number of students who need help; grants from the Cleveland Foundation help with the costs. Websites list the homework centers that exist, their hours, and the grades that are served in each time period. Tutors are often college students from nearby Baldwin Wallace, John Carroll, and Cleveland State Universities.

Special events are held monthly at different branches. Family Literacy "Nites" provide help with online and science fair projects. The Maple Heights branch presented Tech Thursday evening programs each week from January through May for secondary students. Topics that appealed to teens include creating your own website, creating digital animation, creating video games, and developing 3D models. What technical skills would your teens be interested in learning? Who on your staff, or on the staff of the local school, would be a great resource person for such a specialized topic? Teens were also offered programs on college planning with workshops later in the year to help sophomores and juniors to prepare for ACT and SAT college entrance exams.

Notes from the Field

Recognizing that many local schools no longer have school librarians and that the needs of students to learn how to research are not being met, many public libraries are paying more attention to information literacy skills from a teaching standpoint. The Public Library of Charlotte and Mecklenberg County (PLCMC) created a computer room called Tech Central to serve the needs of 'tweens as part of their ImaginOn building. While some computers are available for fun, browsing, and games; 15 are reserved in a lab for instruction in productivity tools or research with instruction provided by full-time staff members (Kenney 2005, 54).

MARKETING THE CENTER TO PARENTS

Your homework help center can't be successful unless your teens know of its existence. In addition to letting your school library counterpart know about this service, it would also be helpful to reach out to parents as they will often be your biggest supporters and advocates. Consider this success story of two librarians who reached out to parents as a means of reaching students. Through a special partnership with Bay Public Library (Bay Village, OH, part of Cuyahoga County Public Library system) YA Librarian Cathy Schultis and Bay High School Librarian Sheila Benedum made presentations to parents, PTA groups, and other community sources showcasing the resources of each library and explaining how they work together to help students of all ages with homework and research projects. They called their collaboration *Parents as Partners: Homework Help @ Home.* Their mutual goal was to help parents to steer their children away from simple Internet searches by using high-quality resources found in databases at their local libraries. They informed parents about databases purchased by state agencies INFO-hio (for K–12 schools) and OPLIN (for public libraries) (Benedum 2001). They provided a handout for parents listing websites for both libraries and detailed instructions on the use of the online public access catalogs and periodical databases. They also provided a short demonstration of Internet Public Library and its various pages of reference materials for teens and children (Benedum 2001).

How do you reach families that don't often enter your library? The school librarian can personally alert teachers to what's happening at the public library, or perhaps announce the information in a school newsletter parents receive. Once teachers have been told, they can share the information with teens they think might benefit. A simple brochure can be made available for teachers, teens, or parents to pick up in the school office, as well as in the public library for interested parents or teens.

You can also rely on your web tools—email blasts, your own web pages, and the web pages of the local schools. Add the homework center to the list of services that are talked about in your social networking tools (Adams 2010, 11). Make sure that you don't overpower web pages with too many visuals or "flash" technology as this will limit the homes that can easily access your pages. If your web page takes too long to load or the patron's computer is older and doesn't support your newest add-in, you may lose a potential patron. If you have an already-established blog that patrons use to communicate with you, then by all means, use this as well.

TERM PAPER AND WRITING CLINICS

How else can we jointly help students to succeed? Who else but librarians would see the need and work together to create after hours Term Paper Clinics? This type of homework program has a very narrow focus—to assist students in completing one single, specific classroom assignment—their research paper. The beauty of the project is the fact that it can be replicated in either school or public library, and it can even be taken outside the library to another location, such as club or scout meetings, as well as to the homes of homeschooled teens. It can be done as a short one-hour program or done as a series of meetings (Jones 2009, 56).

Staff your clinic with librarians from both buildings along with any willing teachers you can entice to join you. Your clinic will work best if teachers provide assignments and due dates in advance, so that you have time to prepare for your workshop. One way to conduct such a workshop is to provide easy-to-follow directions for prewriting, writing, and proofreading your paper. Select your favorite presentation format, that is, PowerPoint to Smartboard or Prezi, for the workshop but test it to be sure that your website is compatible and will allow its posting to the teen web page (ibid., 56–57).

Creative writing labs can be loads of fun for YAs, but that doesn't mean they aren't improving their literacy skills through writing at the same time. Story writing workshops have proven successful in helping inner-city middle school students in Brooklyn, New York. Their center helps pre-teens freely express their thoughts and emotions without the constraint of rubrics or grades. The area where they hold their workshops is called the Superman Annex. Sounds like a place you want to go to, doesn't it? (Shaffer 2006, 38). The partners here are the public library and an educational group called 826 Valencia. 826 Valencia is a nonprofit group that strives to help children from ages 6 to 18 to improve their writing. While it did not start in a library, but with collaboration between author Dave Eggers and a teacher named Nínive Calegari, the connection to schools, the commitment to students, and the commitment of volunteers are remarkable. If you wish to start a writing program, begin by investigating their publishing website http://826valencia.org/; it lists writing prompts they've used over the years that have been successful with students (826 Valencia).

Somewhere in all of these ideas and suggestions, there should be more than a few to get you and your fellow librarians thinking. We all know the teens will be assigned a paper, or need access to online materials, or even just a quiet place to work. We know we can provide all of these needs to varying degrees. It is now up to us to seize every chance we are being provided to make those connections that create lifelong learners and library users. Homework help centers are one means of fulfilling a need and serving both parents and teens.

REFERENCES

"826 Valencia Annual Report, 2010–2011," http://826valencia.org/our-programs/publishing/#tabs-173-0-0 (cited March 27, 2012).

Adams, Suellen S. "Marketing the Homework Center Digitally." *Young Adult Library Services* 8, no. 2 (2010): 11–12.

Benedum, Sheila, and Cathy Schultis. "Building Strong Partnership between School & Public Libraries." PowerPoint presentation, 2001. Modified December 5, 2005.

Benedum, Sheila, and Cathy Schultis. "Parents as Partners: Homework Help @ Home." PowerPoint presentation to the West Shore Librarian's group, 2001. Modified August 17, 2009.

Cuyahoga County Public Library. "Free Homework Centers," http://www.cuyahogalibrary.org/HomeworkCenters.aspx (cited March 27, 2012).

Jones, Ella W. *Start to Finish Young Adult Programs: Hip-Hop Symposiums, Summer Reading Programs Virtual Tours, Poetry Slams, Teen Advisory Boards, Term Paper Clinics and More.* New York: Neal-Schuman Publishers, 2009.

Kenney, Brian. "Imagine This." *School Library Journal* 51, no. 12 (2005): 53–55.

Office of Juvenile Justice and Delinquency Prevention. "Appendix A: National Child Protection Act of 1993," http://www.ojjdp.gov/pubs/guidelines/appen-a.html (cited March 27, 2012).

Saint Paul Public Library. "Homework Centers," http://www.sppl.org/services/homework-help/homework-centers (cited March 27, 2012).

Shaffer, Gary. "Stop the Presses!" *School Library Journal* 52, no. 7 (2006): 38–39.

Siu-Runyan, Yvonne. "Public and School Libraries in Decline: When We Need Them." *The Council Chronicle, The National Council of Teachers of English* 21 no. 1 (2011): 28–29.

Slimon, Licia. "Homework Club for English Language Learners." In Smallwood, Carol, ed. *Librarians as Community Partners: An Outreach Handbook.* Chicago, IL: ALA, 2010, 134–36. http://www.flickr.com/photos/whitehallpub/sets/72157619649699120/show

StartSpot Mediaworks. "Homework Spot," http://homeworkspot.com/ (cited March 27, 2012).

Vaillancourt, Renée J. *Bare Bones Young Adult Services: Tips for Public Library Generalists.* Chicago, IL: Young Adult Library Services Association, 2000, 52–67.

FURTHER READING

IXL. "Sixth Grade Math Practice," http://www.ixl.com/math/grade-6 (cited March 27, 2012).

10

◇ ◇ ◇

TEEN ADVISORY BOARDS

How do you determine exactly what programs, ideas, books, and other resources will appeal to your teen patrons? The answer may be simply to ask them! You can create an online survey tied to their portion of the library web page, although you might prefer to talk with them face-to-face. After all, you have a passion for the wants and needs of teen and preteen patrons, so you shouldn't be afraid to start an ongoing dialogue with them. Once you've identified teens who have shown an interest in providing feedback, **don't let them go!** These are the patrons you want to form into your own, ongoing teen advisory group. It doesn't matter whether you work in a public library or a school library, such groups work well in either setting. Whether you call your group a teen advisory board (TAB), a teen advisory group (TAG), a library advisory board (LAB), or some other acronym, the purpose is the same—to give your teen patrons a voice in what happens in their own portion of the library. (For simplicity's sake the acronym TAB is used throughout this chapter to refer to any kind of advisory board). This group can act as a sounding board for your ideas, and can also present ideas of their own. TAB members could also be your greatest supporters providing "word-of-mouth" publicity for your programs when they are given the opportunity to brainstorm ideas and carry out the programs they've designed. And yes, TABs provide even more opportunities for collaboration. A single group can serve both public and school libraries; or two separate groups can be formed that sometimes collaborate on specific projects.

Before approaching your teens about joining a TAB, brainstorm ideas with fellow librarians or teachers and ask yourself WHY you want to form such a group. Which ages make the most sense to grow a core volunteer group for your library? Do you want to work with middle school students, high school students, or a mix of the two groups? What do you see as the purpose of the group? Will they help with collection development and resource selection? Will they work as library volunteers, shelving books, or creating promotional displays? Will they be book reviewers who place their commentary on the teen web pages? Will they find sites for the web page that have strong appeal to teens or preteens? Will they conduct programs for teens during the year? Will they primarily meet to read and discuss books? Should there be two separate TABs for school and public libraries, or could one group meet the needs of both? Meet with your counterpart librarian to discuss forming a TAB. Plan to use the questions above to start your discussion; record your answers on the planning tool found in Figure 10.1. Be sure that you do not overlook teens who are already playing a role in your library. Ensure that your library pages, your voracious readers, and your volunteers who work with summer reading programs for younger children are informed that you are starting such a group (Vaillancourt 2000, 18).

How much autonomy are you willing to give these teens in decision-making? Some adults, usually those who do not work with teens on a regular basis, are fearful of allowing teens to have a substantial voice in matters that affect their lives, even in planning for the teen room and the materials that are purchased for them. Teen librarians and school librarians usually have a different feel for their clientele, and are willing to trust within limits. They generally allow teens to offer suggestions and to try different avenues of achieving the central goal of improving their space. If your eventual goal is to have teens initiate, and be responsible for, programming, book selection, or additions to the website, refer your reluctant colleagues to the various degrees of participation found on Sociologist Roger Hart's (1992, 8) "Ladder of Youth Participation." This pamphlet showcases the benefits of giving children more voice. You can use his ladder, or the updated ladder and rubric, to decide how much autonomy you would like your teens to have in making decisions (Fletcher, 2011). Know that as your TAB grows over the years, the reluctance of staff members may diminish as they see the vast benefits in giving students a voice in planning for the teen area.

	Task	Assigned to:

1	Purpose of the Teen Advisory Board
	
	   a. Tasks
	
	   b. Fun!	

2	Formality
	
	   a. Type of applications
	
	   b. Teacher recommendations needed?
	
	   c. Parent signature required?	

3	Joint Ventures	

4	Meeting Schedules
	
	   a. Frequency
	
	   b. Location	

5	Recruiting teens and/or 'tweens
	
	   a. Age groups
	
	   b. Single group or many	

6	Other topics	

Figure 10.1: Planning Meeting of Librarians

From *Better Serving Teens through School Library–Public Library Collaborations* by Cherie P. Pandora and Stacey Hayman Santa Barbara, CA: Libraries Unlimited, Copyright © 2013.

Your brainstorming phase with colleagues should involve discussions with those colleagues who are already advocates for these patrons. Discuss your budget, or the lack thereof, with the proper manager, director, headmaster, or principal. Ask if there are any line items in your budget that can be used to purchase inexpensive refreshments for meetings. The snacks could be as simple and inexpensive as a drink mix and pretzels.

Does your director or principal have any discretionary funds that can be tapped for special projects? If not, are there any library booster groups that might support your project, for example, Friends of the Library in the public library or the PTA in the school library?

GETTING STARTED

Consider starting small and with a single purpose for your group. As interest grows, the size or scope of the group can be altered. You can even form a second more specialized group if the teens are clamoring for it! The tasks listed above may appeal to different segments of your teen population. Your artistic students may relish the chance to create displays, while some of your most avid readers may enjoy reviewing books or participating in book discussion groups. Your tech-savvy students may embrace the opportunity to use your computers to update teen websites for their peers.

Before proceeding further, determine the tasks that not only best serve your needs and the needs of your library but will also be well received by your YA patrons. It always helps to have one common goal to measure all activities against (Chapman 2003, 153). Is it your overriding goal to create a more vibrant space and a more welcoming atmosphere in the teen area? (Tuccillo 2010, 188). Do you wish to receive help in programming or book selection? Perhaps you want to make the teen websites more attractive and relevant. Pick one larger goal and then select specific tasks that will help your group to reach that goal.

SELECTION

Once you have determined your main purpose for the teens, determine the optimum group size you can accommodate. (No, you might not receive a large outpouring of requests to join at first, but you are still in the conceptual stage here.) Your next step is to refine your selection process and create your marketing campaign. Some of these procedures will be influenced by the purpose you have chosen. Do you want your new group to be chosen based on a formal application or recommendation? If so, be sure to discuss and define just who is qualified to offer a recommendation. Here is an opportunity for you to draw on your library counterpart, and ask for recommendations. Will you request recommendations from teachers, from coaches? Would you prefer that students refer themselves (self-refer) rather than be selected by a committee of librarians? How do you feel about peer nominations?

Whichever route you choose, it will require that you mount a marketing campaign to inform teens of your intent to form the group, to share the procedures for selecting members, and to provide applications and any recommendation forms. Create flyers that can be displayed online as well as at your own library, at school libraries, and at other teen hangouts, any place where teens congregate—coffeehouses, the mall, recreation centers and workout facilities, music stores, and fast food restaurants.

You also need to decide about the organizational structure and formality of the group. Do you want to have officers or a board of directors? (Vaillancourt 2000, 92–94). If so, will they be elected or appointed? Some groups manage just fine without student directors, while others prosper with a formal, organizational structure and a set of bylaws (Tuccillo 2005, 44–47). Consider the ages of your volunteers; younger students might need more structure than older students who should be better able to handle self-directed tasks.

INITIAL MEETING

For your first meeting, make sure that you've dangled the lure of refreshments. You need not supply a meal, but be sure that teens know that snacks will be available. Remember, your participants have been in class all day and will need some downtime and socializing before they get down to business. Decide if you want teens to preregister for your meeting. Discuss with your counterpart whether such preplanning will deter teens from attending. Consider having registration and reminder phone calls to help students feel more committed to attending.

At the first meeting, present teens with your ideas and ask them for feedback. (See Figure 10.2 for some ideas.) Be sure to allow plenty of time for teens to suggest totally new ideas and be flexible if their ideas don't easily mesh with your original plan. Compromises on some tasks and goals may help to create a more enthusiastic group of teens. Make sure that teens understand that they will have to make detailed plans to enact their ideas.

Discussion topics for the first meeting:

1. What will be our main tasks? Provide a list of suggestions to start the discussion.

2. What are the duties of each member? Should these duties be assigned to one person or should there be a rotating schedule?

3. How often should we meet? Will there be consequences if someone misses meetings? How many meetings can be missed before there are consequences? What are the consequences?

4. How will we communicate between meetings—email, text, website?

5. We need to create a name for ourselves. While we won't make that decision today, what names would you suggest? Offer some suggestions if students are having trouble. Waiting until the second, or a later meeting, gives them time to think about names or to dream up a clever acronym.

Figure 10.2: Sample Agenda for First TAB Meeting

From *Better Serving Teens through School Library–Public Library Collaborations* by Cherie P. Pandora and Stacey Hayman Santa Barbara, CA: Libraries Unlimited, Copyright © 2013.

It might be helpful to have another adult to serve as a recorder, so that all ideas are carefully noted. Consider tracking these suggestions on a computer that is projected on a whiteboard or flip chart to make it easy for everyone to see the list; it will also make it easier to place this list on the website when you are ready to publicly announce your plans. Have a plan for the second meeting and share this with students before your first meeting ends. This will help teens feel that they are accomplishing something and making progress. Start off your second meeting by soliciting suggestions for an official name for the group and whittling down to a manageable size the list of activities suggested by your teens. This helps your teen volunteers feel invested in the future success and staying power of the group.

Whether your TAB is selected by librarians or consists of teens who volunteered, you may want to postpone creating your website just yet. Allow the teens to settle in over a few meetings, and let everyone get to a level of comfort before becoming "official" and going public with website postings. If you wish, the name and activities can be formalized after the second meeting; just remember that this process may change annually, when the membership changes each year.

Be flexible! Be open to suggestions for your group's name and purpose. If you have an ongoing group, chances are teens new to the TAB have joined because they've heard about the interesting things this group has done in the past, and they'll want to keep those traditions alive. If your teens are impatient to start big with a web page promotion, remind everyone to allow some time to think over their options before placing anything in writing on the Internet. You can reevaluate any part of the process at three-month intervals and make changes as needed (Tuccillo 2005, 40). If technology gets the biggest push from the teens, check with your IT person, your director, or your principal to see if you can create a password-protected portion of the website for communications between members of the group.

MEETING REGULARLY

Once you have determined how often you will meet (perhaps monthly) be sure to book the space at your libraries. If you are creating a joint TAB, involving members recruited from both the public and the school library, you may want to alternate the meeting sites. If you know that you will need a room with a computer, be sure to book such a space for the next few months to ensure the equipment is available to you when you need it. Setting a regular time and place for your meetings allows students to plan the rest of their commitments appropriately.

Provide a list of three or four days and times for students to prioritize, hopefully the most popular day and time will work best for everyone. If there are many conflicts, consider varying the meeting days, for example, have one month's meeting on a Wednesday and the next month's meeting on a Thursday. If you run a TAB in a school setting, can you have meetings during the lunch period? Is that a convenient time for the teen librarian to come to your school? Such a meeting time during lunch, before, or after school in the school library solves the problem of transportation for many students and only the teen librarian will need to travel (Brown 2005, 139).

Be aware that your TAB meetings will likely run into the occasional conflict with special events, such as play practice, sports banquets, or special classes or programs at the public library that have been scheduled for the same date and time. In many cases these special event dates would not be known to your teens until a few weeks ahead of the date. This is one more reason to communicate with your counterpart. School librarians should have access to yearlong school calendars that include these events and dates, and can easily share this information with you. Public librarians should have room schedules that include special events and classes.

If schedule conflicts arise, ask your teens to think of possible solutions. Do you want to hold a meeting for the teens who are still available? Would you hold the meeting only if a quorum of students can attend? Do you want to allow teens a certain number of "excused absences" when this kind of double booking occurs?

In Our Experience

The timing of a TAB meeting will partially be determined by the ages of the teens in your group. While many middle school students might be able to meet right after school, your high school students are more likely to have prior commitments at that time for athletics, clubs, or extracurricular activities and would prefer to meet in the evening or even before school (Brown 2005, 139). In many public libraries, middle school students can already be found hanging out during nonschool hours. Parents discover that their children are eventually too old for afterschool programs and often expect their preteens to stay at the local library until they can pick them up after work.

GIVE THEM A REASON TO JOIN

Why might students want to join your new group? TAB groups hold appeal for teens. For some teens, the library, whether at school or the public library, is their favorite refuge away from home. Your library may be the place where they feel most comfortable and they would welcome any excuse to spend more time in the space where they feel most "at home." Then again, you may have intrigued them with the idea that they can have some say in shaping the teen areas, whether physically or virtually on the web. Some may be regular readers who are looking to share their experiences with other bibliophiles. Other teens may think your TAB is an easy way to earn hours for service learning commitments. They may just see it as a great way to socialize with other teens who enjoy the library.

Even with all these reasons for participating, you should expect that at some point some of your TAB members will drop out of the group. Do not take this personally! As preteens and teens explore different options in their lives they find activities that suit them and others that do not. Be sure that they are not made to feel guilty by you, or by those members who remain. Just as you want your new members to feel welcome, you want to avoid having your group become a clique more interested in excluding others than in welcoming them (Chapman 2003, 153).

DISPLAYS

Some teens may enjoy creating displays in the teen area, the children's room, or the lobby. Those who have a creative flair may want to be able to share it with as many people as possible. Any public space, a bulletin board, a top shelf, or display cases, all make the perfect backdrop for these artistic students. However, before enlisting the young artists, be sure to approve sample sketches or receive detailed explanations of what they'd like to create, both to keep supply costs down and to make sure they don't indulge in projects inappropriate to the library setting. When they are ready to mount the display, be sure you're available for advice, assistance, for ensuring that the right kind of supplies (e.g., tacks, staples) are used, and for ensuring their safety and the safety of other patrons.

A schedule may need to be devised for displays each month rotating assignments, so that each person who expresses interest gets the chance to serve as lead designer. The group will definitely want to come to a consensus on the length of time each display is to be showcased. If a display celebrates a time-specific event, for example, women's history month, it needs to be changed out in a timely fashion to make room for the next month's special display.

PROGRAMMING

Programming for, and by, your TAB members is another possibility for teen involvement. Programs designed by teens might be something you offer once a season; depending on the complexity of the programs and the commitment of the teens involved, it could happen more often. With this in mind, teens programming for teens should be pretty successful! However, be aware that this can result in more work than simply designing programs on your own. After all, these are teenagers: they dream big and don't always understand the time commitment, and cost involved in creating and leading a program. This activity will provide a wonderful learning experience for them!

Be prepared to be both encouraging, and the voice of reason at the same time. Determine exactly which parts teens will be responsible for accomplishing, and then be prepared to continually check to make sure they are getting their self-appointed tasks done in time. Find out if they want to be in charge of their own publicity. Do they need a certain amount of space, supplies, or equipment? What, if any, cost will there be for the library? As the date of the program approaches, you need to double-check their progress and be ready to suggest alternatives depending on how smoothly their program is, or is not, coming together.

After the program is over, solicit feedback from both the teens that put on the program and the teens who attended. What did everyone, including you, enjoy most and enjoy least about the experience? What should you continue to do? What would you do differently? Meet with your counterpart to review all the comments and note changes you'd like to make in the future.

Socializing is a necessary and attractive component of such clubs. Don't expect your teens will spend all their time working! They need some time to have fun being together and to get to know each other. They also need to have some time to get to better know you and any other staff members who will be working with them. Plan to infuse some fun and socializing time into each meeting. Add some "icebreakers" or fun activities at the beginning of randomly selected meetings. Surprise the teens with unexpected games—the teens will love this. Although they may initially try to hide their pleasure by rolling their eyes and groaning at you, do it anyway. They'll have a blast! (Chapman 2003, 152).

SERVICE HOURS

Teens can be sensitive, so when they request that you be in charge of recording and verifying their hours, it might be kindest to grin and bear it. Teens have incredibly busy schedules with classes, religious education, family commitments, athletics, clubs, and work. Throw in requirements

Name: _____   Date: _____

Please check any activities that you completed today.

	Activity	# of Hours/Minutes
_____	Teen Advisory Board meeting	_____
_____	Working with summer reading games	_____
_____	Creating displays	_____
_____	Reviewing materials—books, software, movies, games, music, websites, etc.	_____
_____	Participating in book discussions	_____
_____	Serving on strategic planning committee	_____
_____	Shelving books	_____
_____	Assisting senior citizens in computer lab	_____
	Total hours	_____

Name of Supervisor: _____   Job title: _____

Signature of Supervisor: _____   Date: _____

Figure 10.3: Service Hours Form

From *Better Serving Teens through School Library–Public Library Collaborations* by Cherie P. Pandora and Stacey Hayman Santa Barbara, CA: Libraries Unlimited, Copyright © 2013.

that they volunteer their services to a nonprofit for school clubs, as part of a religious program—confirmation or bat or bar mitzvahs—or even as a graduation requirement, and you have a student who sees a silver lining in the chance to complete their hours by volunteering at the library. Realize that tracking hours for your TAB members might take a little time on your part, but will result in great advantages for your teens. If you don't have a form or logbook you've previously used for other volunteer groups feel free to use, or modify, the form found in Figure 10.3. Most organizations need simply the name of the student, the hours worked with a simple description, a total of the volunteer hours worked over the course of the month or semester as well as your name, title, and date.

After you get to know your group a little better, students may offer to record their own hours. You can list a variety of tasks and have students check those that apply with space left for additional projects that were not included in the form. This verification sheet can be done on paper, or if your website will allow, online in a form that students complete after each meeting or activity. Be sure to verify each activity with your signature as soon as possible; it's very difficult to recreate this information after the fact! If you use an online form, ask your IT person to create the forms so that reports can be printed as spreadsheets for each individual teen and for the entire group. This will simplify recordkeeping, as well as provide data that can be presented to your manager. (See Chapter 15 for additional ideas.) Expect to be asked to prepare recommendations for your TAB teens when they apply for jobs, to colleges, or for scholarships just as you would for any other volunteer worker. Retain these files for a few years, just in case you need to refer to them for subsequent recommendations.

COLLECTION DEVELOPMENT

If you want your TAB to be involved in collection development, you need to determine the process for doing so. Will you share catalogs, online or paper, with your students? Do you have a nearby bookstore that would welcome a visit or field trip from a group of teens interested in selecting fiction for the collection? (Mitchell 2005, 133).

In Our Experience

Rocky River High School was lucky enough to be able to do this with a reading class; they became our Reading Advisory Club. Students loved the chance to select books for their classmates. After a short welcome from the bookstore's community representative, our students were taken on a tour that showed them the locations of each section of the store, fiction, nonfiction, poetry, biographies. Our rules were simple. We established a budget prior to the trip and made arrangements with the store to take a purchase order from our school. We reserved $200 from our budget for discretionary use by the librarian. The remainder of our budget was divided by the number of students on the field trip. Each student was encouraged to find appealing books within their budgetary limit. All books had to be approved by the librarian prior to purchase, so that they were deemed school appropriate and did not duplicate a choice made by another student. Books were reserved for the semester for the exclusive use of the students in the reading class. We stamped and processed these books that same day, enabling each person to read their book as soon as possible. After they read their own selections, these titles were made available to all the other students in the reading class. Allow teens to search the online catalog of the public library, either with a mobile app or once you return to school, to see if a particular title might already be available. Or if a title was determined not appropriate for the school setting, alert your counterpart of the interest and perhaps it can be purchased through the public library. Don't forget to offer the teen requesting the title the opportunity to be first on the waiting list at the public library.

To get the full value from the experience, ask students to evaluate their purchase after they finish the book they selected; then ask these students to evaluate some (or all) of the other titles their group purchased. How well do they think they did? What might they do differently next time? Was it harder or easier than they expected to find books with wide appeal?

BENEFITS

The benefits of TAB membership are many. Besides the privilege of being the first to review new books, select new materials, and hang out at the library, teens will have the chance to work on projects that interest them without worrying about rubrics, grades, or pressure. The sense of accomplishment can do a great deal for the self-esteem of your teens (Chapman 2003, 152). Students should be given special privileges when authors visit. They can serve as hosts who introduce the author, or be the first to ask him or her questions. If dinner is planned before, or after the talk, plan on having some, if not all, of your TAB members attend. Be sure that you recognize your TAB members whenever other library volunteers are recognized (Vaillancourt 2000, 20). A nice gesture is to provide each with a certificate at the end of each year. Students will want to include this service activity on their applications to honor societies, school offices, college, and scholarships; a certificate will help them to remember the years that they participated and will provide them with the name of a contact person in case that is also required.

Notes from the Field

Homeschooled Students!

For public libraries, TABs can become an opportunity to introduce and unite homeschooled students with public and private school teens. In Ohio, it is possible to search the state's Department of Education page to find homeschooling information. From there, librarians interested in reaching out to homeschooled teens can find a list of educational contacts for their geographic area. Look at your own state's Department of Education website, locate state or local contacts, and offer to support their curriculum with programs to further their educational aims. It's worth noting that the social aspect of your TAB might be difficult for teens who spend much of their time surrounded by family, but few of their peers. Be sensitive to the struggle some experience, but allow them this independence and both the homeschooled and traditionally schooled teens should emerge with greater understanding of each other. Gaining just one homeschooled student can open the door for a new group of teens who could benefit from your expertise and your services.

ADVOCATES FOR YOUR LIBRARY

Another benefit for your library is having impassioned library users who are willing to work toward making the library a better place. These teens who serve on your TAB might be a better voice to advocate for "their" space than the teen librarian! As your group progresses throughout the year, you will likely see leaders emerge; and hopefully everyone will have a turn, if they so choose, to be both leader and follower. These emerging leaders may be a great representative to the strategic planning process, whether at the public library or at the school. Schools often give high school students a voice in building leadership teams as they bring a totally different perspective to the table. Students also take back information to their peers as to why certain projects cannot occur as hoped. Remember, in just a few years these teen patrons, including your TAB members, will be among the voting public. If your library relies on ballot issues for its operating monies or construction budget your director or principal will be happy to have this new additional group of library-friendly voters on your side.

REFERENCES

Brown, Margaret. "Teen Advisory Board (TAB)." In Tuccillo, Diane P., ed. *Library Teen Advisory Groups.* Lanham, MD: VOYA Guides, Scarecrow Press, 2005, 139–40.

Chapman, Jan. "The Care and Feeding of a TAB." In Tuccillo, Diane P., ed. *Library Teen Advisory Groups.* Lanham, MD: VOYA Guides, Scarecrow Press, 2005, 152–53.

Hart, Roger A. *Children's Participation: From Tokenism to Citizenship.* Florence: UNICEF, 1992, 8.

Mitchell, Connie. "Schools Can Have Advisory Groups, Too! Writers and Readers Advisory Panel (WRAP)." In Tuccillo, Diane P., ed. *Library Teen Advisory Groups.* Lanham, MD: VOYA Guides, Scarecrow Press, 2005, 133.

Tuccillo, Diane P. *Library Teen Advisory Groups.* Lanham, MD: VOYA Guides, Scarecrow Press, 2005.

Tuccillo, Diane P. *Teen-Centered Library Service: Putting Youth Participation into Practice.* Santa Barbara, CA: Libraries Unlimited, 2010.

Vaillancourt, Renée J. *Bare Bones Young Adult Services: Tips for Public Library Generalists.* Chicago, IL: ALA, 2000.

FURTHER READING

Alessio, Amy J., and Kimberly A. Patton. *A Year of Programs for Teens2.* Chicago, IL: ALA, 2011.

Fletcher, Adam. "Ladder of Youth Voice," http://www.freechild.org/ladder.htm (cited March 21, 2012).

Kunzel, Bonnie, and Constance Hardesty. *The Teen-Centered Book Club: Readers into Leaders.* Westport, CT: Libraries Unlimited, 2006.

11

◆ ◆ ◆

BUDGET/FINANCE

FUNDING OVERVIEW

The mere word budget scares many people away, trying to figure out all those different accounts and categories is challenging. Equally difficult is finding the money to meet all the needs that patrons, librarians, teachers, or staff bring to the table. It probably seems that each year you are asked to do so much more with much less funding. How do you solve the headache of diminishing funds at a time of rising costs? In this chapter, you'll find some ideas gleaned from reading the literature and talking to colleagues who have found a way to do just that. Too few school and public librarians currently collaborate. When *SLJ* compiled its first survey of Public Library Spending it learned that 91% of public libraries do not yet work with school libraries when it comes to spending decisions (Miller and Girmscheid 2013, 27). The good news is that collaboration provides you and your counterpart with more options for financing your joint projects.

Notes from the Field

Bob Smith (2012), former director of Medina County District Libraries (Ohio) explained that your type of library determines who else you must report to outside of the library board. Depending on the type of library and the rules for any given state or province, the director may have to gain approval from assorted governmental agencies (e.g., county commissioners, city councils, mayors, trustees, or the school board) before taking it to the people on the ballot.

Each state and province has its own unique set of laws that define the creation of libraries and detail their financial structure and funding. Within legal boundaries, it is difficult to make generalizations about finances that apply to all libraries throughout North America. Instead, let's concentrate on an overview of library funding, both public and school, and explain how their budgets are organized.

Where does the operating money for public libraries originate? There is no national database, compendium, or website that explains this on a national or international level, so here is a simplified version of how public library budgets operate in general. Some public libraries are funded, at least in part, by state or provincial funds while others are financially tied to their cities or counties. Public libraries can be part of a large network that maintains multiple branches with centralized administration while still others operate independently funding only a single branch.

Again, there isn't one source for discovering how media centers, or libraries, receive money in public schools. In general, public school libraries gain some funding from their state or province with additional monies being voted on by the community. Private, and parochial, school libraries are financed in a variety of ways through tuition, endowments, fundraisers, alumni donations, and/or allotments coming from religious organizations.

Even if you aren't the person who controls the purse strings for teens in your library, it is important to be aware of how your own system works. Take the time to research how your own library is funded, and you'll find the return on your investment is great. The list of websites in Appendix B can help you to begin your research. Being aware of budgetary factors and concerns can help you when you need to request funding from your manager, director, or principal (Chudnov 2008, 27). If you have a great idea, don't be afraid to ask, even if the regular funding cycle has passed! "If approached by an employee with a project idea I will try to find the money to do so," says Bob Smith (2012).

Notes from the Field

Catherine Hakala-Ausperk (2011, 133–134), director of the Northeast Ohio Regional Library System (NEORLS), suggests a team approach to budgeting that starts with a needs assessment. She begins by meeting with her managers to discuss the library's mission and goals, set priorities, create a plan, and share fiscal knowledge to benefit all staff.

WORKING TOGETHER

The team approach is a great suggestion for teen and school librarians. Meet with your partner librarian to compare notes and to discuss the missions and goals of your respective libraries. Review priorities set by your management team, the trustees, or the board of education. Add your own priorities for teens to the list and search for those goals that are common to both agencies. Discuss your budget categories and look for ways in which you can help each other to save money while still serving the needs of your teens and preteens.

Brainstorm an action plan that will help you to meet your joint goals. Do you want to add an author visit to your teen program? Can you purchase and share audiobooks, graphic novels, or DVDs? Can you collaborate on collection development of your nonfiction collections now that Common Core Standards (for schools) emphasize the reading of informational texts? Review your electronic databases to determine if you are duplicating the resources provided by your partner. Perhaps you can subscribe to two different business databases rather than the same one. Revise your new wish list; place your ideas in priority order, and create a rationale for each item on your list.

When planning to invite an author or speaker reach out via email and invite partners from local schools and public libraries to collaborate. Having others willing to share in the costs of the speaker's fee and details such as food, transportation, and lodging make the venture more affordable (see Chapter 6 for more information on sharing costs).

FUNDING SOURCES

Your first step after deciding to collaborate is to determine the amount of money that you have at your disposal. Approach your director or principal to request your budget for the upcoming year. Armed with this information you can brainstorm to decide what you want to purchase that will benefit your common patrons. Perhaps you can join forces with other libraries to negotiate group discounted prices on subscriptions. Revise your new wish list; place your ideas in priority order and create a rationale for each item on your list.

Your wish list will most likely have a larger price tag than either budget can handle. Determine which items from the list can be paid for within the amounts and regulations that govern your budgets; for example, speaker's fees may legally be paid for by many public libraries but most school library budgets do not have a line item for these services. Be sure to keep a written record of your requests, both dollar amounts and descriptions of each item, what used to be called a "consideration file." Such a list is helpful when you desire to approach other sponsors or in case money suddenly becomes available (Cox 2008, 25).

DOCUMENT YOUR NEEDS

Even if you don't have direct input into the budgeting process, it is worthwhile to document your needs and wants (see Figure 11.1). Be sure that your budgetary requests provide rationale explaining the impact these purchases will have on your teens. For school budgets, it is most effective to place your rationale within the context of per pupil statistics (Young 2008, 26). Requesting $3,000 with a list of books and eBooks is a great beginning; adding the per pupil expenditure (for a school of 1,500 students) means that you are requesting only $2.00 per pupil. It has a greater impact on your administrators. Librarians must identify the impact the project will have on teens and which of the 40 Developmental Assets the project should address (http://www.search-institute.org/content/40-developmental-assets-adolescents-ages-12-18). Whenever possible use a spreadsheet program to create charts and graphs to accompany your rationale; your principal may be able to use them to gather monetary support from the superintendent, a booster group, or a PTO.

LOCAL SUPPORT GROUPS

Items such as speaker's fees, programming, supplies, food, and prizes often aren't written into existing budgets. When allocated budgets aren't quite enough, you need to change your focus from developing wish lists to brainstorming alternate sources of funding. Public libraries usually have a Friends of the Library group that provides volunteer and monetary support for special projects; schools usually have a PTA that does likewise.

You may not have a formal plan that allows you input into the budgeting process, but you should consider documenting current, and desired, expenditures to help you plan for the future.

Category	Items (prioritize within each category)	Cost	Rationale
Materials Books, eBooks, music, DVDs, games	1. 2. 3. 4. 5.		
Periodicals and databases	1. 2. 3. 4. 5.		
Speakers and authors	1. 2. 3. 4. 5.		
Programming supplies and prizes	1. 2. 3. 4. 5.		
Equipment—computers, gaming stations, furniture	1. 2. 3. 4. 5.		

Figure 11.1: Budget Planning Tool

Talk first with your manager or principal as most organizations do not want individuals to approach these groups without prior approval. Once granted approval, make an appointment with the Friends or PTA and do the interview as a team. Present your plan, budget, and rationale. Always put the emphasis on how your community's teens will benefit.

LOCAL FOUNDATIONS

Once you've explored the possibility of funding from budgets, group discounts, PTAs, and Friends of the Library groups determine if your local schools have their own educational foundation. As budgets have been reduced, many schools, and some public libraries, have created foundations gathering donations with the enticement that all donations are tax deductible. Again you'll need the approval of your managers before approaching the foundation. For some library foundations only a formal letter, drafted and signed by both of you explaining the project, providing a rationale, and a budget are required. On the other hand, educational foundations, those that support a particular school or district, often require a more formal application process. While the application is usually short, it will require additional information stating the state and national standards that will be met through the grant. Letters of support from the library director, superintendent, or headmaster are required. For additional information on cowriting grants please turn to Chapter 12.

SAVING MONEY THROUGH INTER-LIBRARY LOAN

In times of financial difficulties, it is more important than ever to partner with other libraries to save money and to collaborate on projects that better serve your patrons. Smith's (2012) hope when he was in Medina was that his public library multibranch system and the county school district could share materials through a delivery system between organizations to create a unique countywide Inter-Library Loan (ILL) delivery system. Teachers and teens would go online to order books for delivery to each school from the public library as well as from the other school libraries. At the time, the effort was stymied by reluctant school administrators and the technical difficulty of creating library cards that worked with multiple circulation systems. Some states have adopted such plans for their academic libraries, but often state funding for such a delivery system between public and school libraries does not occur due to costs and technical requirements. Since many states do not yet have an ILL system for school and public libraries, librarians have solved this problem by emailing request to each other and using their own vehicles to retrieve books from partner libraries. The State Library of Ohio created such an ILL system called MORE—Moving Ohio Resources Everywhere. Most of the partners are public libraries but some school libraries participate as well. In some areas of the state public libraries are serving as the conduit for school libraries to extend their collections through the use of MORE.

VOLUME DISCOUNTS

After learning the limits of your budgets each librarian should check with appropriate state and regional library groups to see if a buying consortium exits. If there is a consortium within one of the systems, either the school or public library, inquire if the guidelines allow the inclusion of your partner library. Considerable money can be saved when you purchase books, library supplies, equipment, and databases. If your region or state doesn't have such a consortium as yet, this is the time to start one!

JUST DO IT!

Whether you enjoy working with numbers or hate working on budgets, learning how to ask for and find money is a skill worth acquiring. Learning how budget decisions are made within your organization and within your own department is vitally important. Once you understand how money is allocated, you will be better prepared to provide your manager with rationale that clarifies your requests. Be sure to explain the impact that each budget item will have on your teens. Remember, information is powerful.

REFERENCES

Chudnov, Daniel. "Show Me the Budget." *Computers in Libraries* 31, no. 3 (September 2008): 28–29.

Cox, Marge. "10 Tips for Budgeting." *Library Media Connection* 26, no. 4 (January 2008): 24–25.

Hakala-Ausperk, Catherine. *Be a Great Boss: One Year to Success.* Chicago, IL: ALA, 2011.

Miller, Rebecca T. "We Need Tag-Team Leadership." *School Library Journal* 58, no. 5 (May 2012): 11 (editorial).

Miller, Rebecca T., and Girmscheid, Laura. "It Takes Two." *School Library Journal* 58, no. 5 (May 2012): 26–29.

Search Institute. "40 Developmental Assets for Adolescents," http://www.search-institute.org/content/40-developmental-assets-adolescents-ages-12-18 (cited February 22, 2013).

Smith, Bob. Interview with Cherie Pandora. Phone. March 26, 2012. Medina, OH.

FURTHER READING

Berry III, John N. "Transformed by Teamwork." *Library Journal* 137, no. 2 (2012): 20–23.

Payne, Mary Ann. *Grant Writing DeMystified: Hard Stuff Made Easy.* Dubuque, IA: McGraw-Hill, 2011.

Young, Robyn R. "Eight Easy Steps to Maintain and Increase the Library Media Center Budget." *Library Media Connection* 26, no. 4 (January 2008): 26–27.

12

◇ ◇ ◇

GRANTS

Quickly, list three things you would buy for your library **if money were no object**. No restrictions—your wish list of items could start at the expensive end with popular gaming systems, lendable preloaded eReaders, mobile devices, lounge chairs, and continue to less expensive posters, gift card prizes, or pizza parties, anything you can use to celebrate your YA patrons. Maybe you want a beloved author to speak with your teens. Your list can include something you covet which falls outside of regular budgetary lines. Write them down! We'll wait! . . . Congratulations! You have conquered the toughest step and are now on the way to securing your first, or your next, grant.

DONATIONS ARE AN EASY FORM OF GRANT

Sometimes the only way to get what you want, and to serve your teens, is to beg, borrow, or cajole donations from local businesses and restaurants. Start small by requesting donations from local businesses. Remember that donations don't always mean cash! Sometimes you can borrow items for short-term use and won't need to purchase items at all. Besides cash and food donations you can ask for donations that will help you with your programming activities. A craft store can donate supplies. A take-out restaurant that can't donate food may be able to donate plates, cups, and napkins.

In Our Experience

For our first poetry slam we secured free coffee and hot chocolate from a local coffee shop. For a senior project that involved painting library walls, we received discounted paint and supplies. These experiences highlight what's possible if you're willing to be shameless by asking help from anyone and everyone.

For cash donations we found that local businesses are very generous to hometown agencies. Make a list of the places where your teens congregate or work, the coffeehouses, the athletic clubs and recreation centers, the music stores. Grocery stores, pizza parlors, local restaurants are often willing to donate small amounts of food, or beverages to nonprofit organizations within the community. (Note that many fast food franchises must request approval from corporate headquarters so they will need a few months' notice to receive permission to donate food.) If corporate policies negate donating food, the restaurant may discount the cost of any purchases that you make.

Few libraries work with a budget large enough to support the teens we adore; we must rely on donations from local agencies to help us to fund our programs. Often community groups are happy to provide small amounts of seed money for your project. To identify those groups within your city who are most likely to provide such donations, we suggest that you check the following publications: community newsletters and newspapers; athletic programs for high school and community sports; programs for band, choir, and dance events; local church bulletins; and the high school newspaper; and yearbook's advertising pages. Depending on the scope of your project you might want to check with community agencies such as the PTO/PTA or local antidrug organizations that work with your schools and libraries. Be persistent in calling all possible businesses and organizations; you'll be surprised at how often your efforts will be rewarded.

The fact that there are two of you means you have double the number of connections to approach, and double the people power in getting the job done. When brainstorming what you need for your event or endeavor, be sure to list any and all contacts that both of you have who might be of assistance. Remember the "six degrees of separation" principle too. If you want someone to furnish pizza, chances are you or your counterpart knows someone who knows someone who owns a pizza shop.

In Our Experience

When Cherie advised the high school yearbook she was surprised to learn that some of the most generous businesses in town were insurance and printing companies, and funeral homes. Fraternal and professional organizations are powerful allies for your projects; they raise large amounts of money, which they donate to nonprofit organizations; others are willing to work as advisors for your projects. Be sure to check your Chamber of Commerce website for references to local chapters of the Rotary, Kiwanis, Eagles, Elks, American Legion, Veterans of Foreign Wars, Garden Clubs, Junior League, Women's Clubs, and similar organizations. Donations for public libraries can be anything from pizza supplied by a local business for a gaming program or a grant to supplement the summer reading program.

If these tactics don't work, sometimes you simply have to learn to write a grant. Grant writing to fund your collaborative project can be a natural fit for librarians. You have already completed the first two steps needed in writing a grant. You have identified both a collaborative partner in your sister library and have demonstrated a genuine passion for assisting teens, your target audience. Grant writing is often a new task for librarians since we don't usually have the luxury of a professional grant writer on staff at our libraries. Rest assured that not all grants are lengthy and complicated; some are remarkably **short and sweet.**

From Our Experience

The first grant application that Cherie wrote was written to the PTA at her high school. The application asked two questions, and answers were limited to 25 words each, which was a challenge for a wordy person like her. She requested $25 to purchase a globe for the library; at Open House that year a father had complained to the principal that the globe was outdated. He was correct about the globe—it did need to be replaced; however, since he didn't offer a donation she needed a creative funding solution.

THE PROCESS

Before you start the search for a funding source you need to identify exactly what you need. Since you did so when you read the first paragraph you next need to record your ideas; meet with your counterpart librarian to plan how your work together can benefit your teen patrons and both libraries. Identify the basic information you need for any grant application using the bulleted list below. Included in the list are sample categories you will find on many applications and a list of questions you can ask yourself as you work through the process. A sample form is available from the Foundation Center's Wisdom Exchange Project (http://www.yep.cohhio

.org/pdf/Grantsmanship061208/FCblue.pdf). Your approach should be to modify this form each time you use it to meet the needs of both libraries and to suit the requirements of each grant.

You should be able to answer the following questions:

1. **Description/ Purpose:** What do you want to do?
2. **Need:** Why is this needed?
3. **Collaboration:** Who will be your partner(s)?
4. **Impact:** How many teens will participate?
5. **Budget:** What is the approximate cost?
6. **Timeline:** What is the timetable for the project?
7. **Goals and Objectives:** What are your goals and objectives?
8. **Evaluation:** How will you measure success?
9. **Sustainability:** Can the project be sustained after grant funding ends?
10. **Model:** Is it replicable? Can others use your project as a model?

If you work in a school library then you also need to identify how your project ties into the curriculum; identify local, state, and national standards that will be met, and include these standards in your appendices. If you work in a public library you need instead to identify how your project ties into the goals and mission of your library. Some educational foundations require that you also identify problem-solving techniques and critical thinking components. If you are a public library, your scope will be broader but you might just edge out the competition if you can explain how your project will support curriculum standards as well.

Notes from the Field

Follow the format, SERIOUSLY! Failing to format properly can have dire results. In 2003, respected Case Western Reserve University (Cleveland, Ohio) lost a two-million dollar grant to study the West Nile Virus; they formatted the grant incorrectly by using the wrong font (Mezger 2003). Grant reviewers can't read grants that have ignored the format guidelines. They are disqualified and never reviewed. The format guidelines should serve as your rubric. Format guidelines make your job easier, they allow you to focus on content, and if you're wordy they force you to revise your document until it is concise and clear. (Note: The National Science Foundation allowed CWRU to resubmit the grant with the proper font and their grant was funded.)

In Our Experience—

How we started

Stacey and I started our partnership over a decade ago writing a grant requesting $26,000 to create research training labs in both libraries. We spent many hours brainstorming our needs, identifying databases, and comparing computer prices. We regularly met with our supervisors to ensure that we had their support. While our grant was unsuccessful it led to years of collaborative projects between our two agencies and was a great learning experience for both of us.

SHOW ME THE MONEY!

Whether you are writing your first grant or are an experienced grant writer, finding a grant to match your intended project is made easier by knowing where to search. Cynthia Anderson and Kathi Knop, in their article, "Go Where the Grants Are" suggest that you first check with your treasurer to see if your library has a corporate partner; they also provide an impressive list of grant sources (Anderson 2008, 12–13). It is important that both libraries do so as each might have different corporate partners who can be brought into the process. As a seasoned researcher you will automatically begin by locating books and articles on grant writing, all the while perusing their bibliographies for additional grant sources. Check for local community organizations and school educational foundations. Public libraries also have a Friends Group, and, often, a foundation of their own that donates cash or items to promote the library. To simplify your recordkeeping, create a reading log, or source journal or subscribe to RSS feeds. Look to your colleagues for advice, considering both what to do and what missteps to avoid. For the latter you will want to expand your search to include the archives for the international listserv known as LM_NET as well as the listservs for your state library organizations. Don't be afraid to post queries on social networking sites such as Facebook and Twitter.

You may also have the option to input search terms into your favorite periodical database to receive emailed "alerts" which send relevant articles directly to your email inbox. Confer with your counterpart and divide your databases into two groups with each of you receiving alerts from a different database. If your options are limited to the same database then avoid duplication by selecting different search terms to input into the alert search box. To do so, first check to see if your preferred database allows you to create an account with a unique login and password. Once you sign in check for an option called "Alerts" or "Search Alerts." Record your email address and add your search terms, for example, "grants" or "grant writing," into the search box and click the box for Alert. With some databases you also have the option to determine the frequency with which you receive alerts—your choices are daily, weekly, or monthly. Plan to discuss these articles and grant sources at your next library meeting.

FOUR STEPS OF WRITING GRANTS

There are four basic steps to any grant: rationale, research, revision, and evaluation.

1. Rationale

Your needs statement provides the rationale for the project; work together to describe the problem, offer some baseline data, and present your solutions. The teen librarian can research demographic information about the city from its resources while the school librarian collects the necessary information about the school and the district. Your paragraphs should explain why the project is needed, identify your partners, and describe how this project will benefit your library and your patrons. Tie your project to the mission statement of your agency and add your mission statement to the Appendix. The grant committee usually wants to know how many teens will benefit from the project. Project your passion! Promote your project as a means of transforming your library and the lives of your teens. Be sure this step includes a WOW factor; you want the grant committee to feel that they will be a part of something amazing!

Grant makers like to see projects that benefit large numbers of students. One measurement of poverty levels used by the federal government is based on family size and income level. If a large percentage of the children in your community qualify for free or reduced lunches in the schools (based on these guidelines), then you are dealing with a population that probably doesn't have much in the way of books in the home or computer and Internet access outside of school. This statistic is an invaluable piece of baseline data to include in your grant. Knowing this statistic can also help you to determine which, if any, federal grants you are eligible to receive since numerous federal grants are aimed at helping children in poverty. If you are in a school, include the appropriate state or national standards into your narrative and discuss how you will meet them. If you are in a public library, consider how to include students from a variety of schools, of different ages, and different districts. How can you reach beyond the teens who already visit your library?

Notes from the Field

Your needs must be reflected in your objectives and must be measured in your evaluation. Missy Lodge (2012), LSTA project coordinator for the State Library of Ohio, suggests that you think of the grant proposal as a circle. The needs you describe require that you create objectives that help you to meet the needs of your patrons. Objectives must be measurable so that you can evaluate whether your needs have been met and your goal has been achieved. A midgrant review of your objectives allows you to modify your activities, if needed, so that the next phase of your project can prove to be even more successful. The evaluation phase allows you to determine the overall success and impact of your project.

Measurable Objectives and Evaluation

Be sure to create concrete objectives and activities. They must be measurable, so that you can easily evaluate your success. In recent years I was introduced to the concept of phrasing goals using the acronym **SMART.** Numerous websites exist; however, they often differ in the wording that they use. SMART goals serve as the checklist that ensures that your goals and objectives can be evaluated (http://www.projectsmart.coud/smart-goals.html). Remember that if your objectives are vague it makes it difficult for you to quantify the impact that the grant has had on your library and your teens.

> S=Specific
> M=Measurable
> A=Attainable or Achievable
> R=Realistic or Relevant
> T=Timely or Time-based

To design your own SMART objectives, consider the examples below; note that all of them don't belong to the same grant application, but are used for clarification purposes.

Specific

"The Public Library will add three additional Teen Gaming Nights to the fall calendar." By specifying what is added to the schedule and how many special programs are added you make it easier to evaluate whether you have met this objective. Specify also which programs take place at each library to emphasize that this is a collaborative endeavor. Your proof of completion for the grant report can be a copy of the fall program guide or a link to the online page listing teen programs.

Measurable

"70% of sophomore Honors Biology students will correctly cite three scholarly articles on their Works Cited pages." You have identified the students and courses you will work with and the requirement that students must meet. Explain how both librarians work with students to determine what constitutes a scholarly article.

Attainable

"We will increase attendance at our Baby Sitting Clinics by 10% through the use of expanded publicity on the web and through local schools." Measurement will include past attendance numbers compared with current attendance at these clinics. Your grant report should include copies of flyers sent to the school, public service announcements read on school sites, local radio and cable outlets, and a screenshot of the website promotional link.

Realistic

"We expect to increase attendance by 10% in the CPR Workshop." Do not try to "right all wrongs" and fix all social ills in one grant. We often see grants that expect monumental gains in state or national test scores. Small annual gains are possible, 100% gains in one year are highly unlikely.

Time-Based

"The School Librarian and the Teen Librarian will team teach a unit on ACT test preparation to five junior College Level English classes using Learning Express Library." Use whichever database is available in your library; your measurement tool can be identifying the dates that presentations were made to these classes. Electronic or paper copies of the presentation can easily be included in the grant's final report.

2. Research: Creating a Budget

Budgets reflect the research step of writing a grant. Once you know what you want to achieve, you need to research the items that you need to make your project successful. Pose questions to your state, national, and international listservs for ideas and the names of reliable AND problem vendors. Ask lots of questions of colleagues, and of vendors. Contact public, and school, libraries of a similar size and budget to see what they might have already purchased. Their honest feedback about the models they chose and their satisfaction will prove invaluable. Request that vendors direct you to former customers so that you can determine how well vendors handled problems. Your budget narrative will explain what you need to purchase, which library will house and inventory the item, the amount that each library will contribute to the project, and will justify why each purchase is needed. Send out queries for bids, especially if you need equipment or software. Talk to your technology people about companies that are acceptable, so that you have no compatibility issues with existing equipment. It strengthens your appendices to include vendor bid sheets, they demonstrate that you have analyzed vendors and have determined which are best able to help you to meet your goals. Ask your statistics person to help you to create a budget that is clear, concise, and attractive. Categorize your expenditures into groupings such as equipment, supplies, speakers, contracts, and other. Justify your expenditures in your narrative. Let the grant committee know **why** you want a particular series of books, software, or equipment. Once items are ordered you will want to document your orders and maintain a phone log of calls to vendors.

3. Revision: Building a Support Team

Writing a grant shouldn't be a solitary experience, and the fact that you're collaborating means you already have one supporter! However, you need a team of supporters to help you to achieve your goals. These same people should help you later with the revision step of the grant writing process. Identify at least one person who is willing to read and critique your work. This will likely be your counterpart librarian, but sometimes you can find talented editors in teachers or other library staff members. Reach out to the person who is best suited to this task. We all know how it feels to repeatedly revise a report only to find an error later on. Often we are so close to the work that we know what we mean to say and miss the smallest errors. It helps if one of your proofreaders is a friend from outside the library world. They can help you to provide clarity to your work by searching for jargon, acronyms, and phrases that are common to our world, but that the average person (or grant reviewer) would not know. You may need a person for just one task, perhaps to check your grammar, or the math.

Your needs section will be strengthened by statistics and demographical information located in government documents available at public libraries or supplied by the staff marketing person, the principal's secretary, or guidance counselor in the school setting. Find coworkers with strong mathematical skills and/or expertise in creating spreadsheets to help you to create charts, budgets, and graphs for your reports. You may want this person to review your impact statements. If you have an in-house graphic expert you can also secure their assistance in creating publicity materials for your final report (see Figure 12.1).

4. Evaluation

The final segment of the circle is the evaluation of the project; luckily there are two of you to divide the work on this segment of the project. Your evaluation tools can be as unique as your project, but you need to include both quantitative and qualitative measures of the success of your grant. Surveys, "hits" on websites, class counts, a rise or fall in teen patron questions, attendance records, and spreadsheets of data can all serve as quantitative measures. Qualitative tools may include reflection pieces written by students, teachers, and the librarians involved. Open-ended responses to a question, artwork created by your teen patrons, self-evaluation pieces, anecdotal comments from colleagues, and, finally, quotes from the teens themselves are all forms of qualitative evidence that can be used to measure your success. Copies of these tools and your conclusions should be included in the Appendices segment of your final grant report.

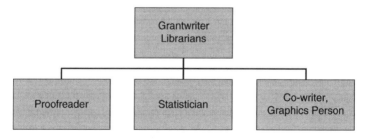

Figure 12.1: The Organizational Chart

PUBLICIZING YOUR GRANT

Include a Marketing or Publicity Plan in your grant. Plan a Family Night or Grand Opening complete with presentations and ribbon cuttings if you have opened a new lab, teen room, or other physical space. Most libraries announce the awarding of a grant on their website, in the local weekly newspaper and in signs around the building. Your communications director can help with press releases, and use his/her contacts to try to get the article in the nearest urban publications. Announcements at board meetings, city council and trustee meetings, and postings on city kiosks (physical or virtual) can ensure that others hear your news and know of your new-found partnerships.

Are you willing to work together to make short presentations at local meetings? Chambers of Commerce and service organizations welcome good news about their communities. If any of these groups contributed to your success or fundraising plea, then you **owe** them the courtesy of speaking, and thanking them publicly, at a meeting. Brainstorm with your support team about other creative ways to announce your good fortune to the community—all without spending a great deal of money. What visuals can you create to explain the impact of your project? Can you create a short YouTube video for posting? Do you publicize events through social media such as Facebook or Twitter? (See Figure 12.2 for other ideas.)

When computers were first added to the library we created a chart to show how students used them in the library. This was useful not just for the grant reports but also to quiet the naysayers who told us students would only use them for games and "fooling around."

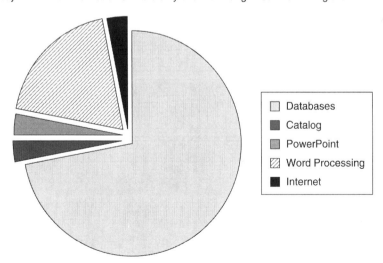

Figure 12.2: Evaluation Visual: Computer Use by Students

In Our Experience

Try to reach as many teens as possible by incorporating as many multiple intelligences learning styles as possible when planning your grant-funded event. Having teens learn through visual means, auditory means, and through hands-on activities (kinesthetic learning) can increase the number of students you reach and enhance the knowledge that all students gain. Collaborating with a history teacher, the school librarian, and the public librarian resulted in a Jazz Day experience for 125 sophomores, which included dance, music, art, lecture, and distance learning programs at Cherie's school. Rocky River Public Library houses the nationally known Cowan Pottery Museum, whose curator librarian brought pieces of pottery, and slides of their prized Jazz Bowl, for her talk. Funding from our educational foundation paid for a distance learning program on the art of the 1920s and swing dancers who provided lessons for small groups of students.

FINDING FOUNDATIONS GRANTS

If you are lucky enough to live in New York City, Atlanta, Cleveland (Ohio), San Francisco, or Washington, D.C., you have access to a wealth of resources at the local Foundation Center. In addition most states have multiple university, nonprofit, or public libraries that house cooperating collections of grant materials. Cooperating collections are also available in Washington, D.C., Puerto Rico, and the University of Toronto. Foundation Centers provide free workshops as well as intensive fee-based workshops. They can provide you with free *onsite* access to their database of nonprofit foundations and to librarians who will help you with your search. Tapping into the wealth of foundation monies is a wonderful source for any of the larger projects that you have in mind.

While some foundations that were historically very generous have cut back on giving, foundation center experts can help you to identify those that are a good fit for your library and your project. They will teach you how to search their resources and how to locate, and decipher, the financial statements for each funding source. Foundations can be private, corporate, or community based.

Private foundations are nonprofit agencies that are not governmental agencies. The largest groups of private foundations are independently run family foundations. For example, the Bill and Melinda Gates Foundation has given numerous grants to libraries.

Corporate foundations are funded through large publicly held companies such as the Ford Foundation; community-based foundations, such as the Cleveland Foundation, usually restrict their donations to their own geographic area.

If you wish to learn more about the grants a foundation makes, check out the Foundation Finder search box on the Foundation Center's opening page (http://foundationcenter.org/). Typing in a name, for example, Gates Foundation, generates a list of all foundations with Gates in the title. Selecting any of these brings you a page of contact information including the foundation's website, the types of grants they award, and financial data including the amount of money that was awarded in a particular year. It is also helpful to know the foundation's IRS exemption status. Some grants require that one of the grant-seeking partners be a nonprofit with a 501(c)(3), or equivalent, IRS tax designation. Not all nonprofits carry these designations; in fact most public schools and many libraries do not; so this is useful information to have when adding to, or eliminating, grants from your list of potential sources. You can also search the 990-PF Private Foundation tax forms, which provide further details on the amounts given out by each foundation.

Foundations practice what is known as "focused giving"; they make it easy to identify their mission and their grant cycle. They often post requests for proposal (RFP) on the Foundation Center's website, so that you know exactly what type of projects the foundation supports. For instance they may exhibit a partiality for arts organizations and cultural projects. They may provide a statement explaining that they do not fund capital improvement projects, such as furniture and computer equipment. Do not be discouraged by this, it is just as useful to know what they **WILL** fund as it is to know what they will **NOT** fund. This saves you time by eliminating those foundations that do not meet your needs.

Many foundations don't want you to start with an application; they are more interested in building a relationship with grant recipients! Most will provide information on their websites as to their preference for a query letter or a grant application. They may specify whether they accept grant applications on a monthly or quarterly basis, or will identify those specific months when they do accept applications. A helpful link to previous grant recipients allows you to determine the type of grants they typically fund.

Once you have determined that your project matches their mission and any geographic requirements, you should create an executive summary of your project. Determine what impact you expect to make on your teens, then make a phone call to the foundation to ask questions. Explain why you think your project would be a win-win situation for the foundation and for your library. Only after you have talked with them and know more about the foundation should you consider a query letter. Inform your administrators about the foundation you intend to approach; if it is local, there is a good possibility that someone on your staff already has a contact in the organization.

Communication is key! Funding organizations like to assist agencies that have used their money wisely on previous grants; they will likely view a future application favorably if you have been a good steward of their monies in the past. If you secure grant money, remember to send invitations to your contact at the foundation for special events and mention the grant source in ALL publications. Thank them publicly on websites, in newsletters, and in publications that go to the community. Remember to send copies of these publications to the foundation's office with a handwritten thank you note. Email alone is simply not enough.

INSTITUTE OF MUSEUM AND LIBRARY SERVICES AND LIBRARY SERVICES AND TECHNOLOGY ACT GRANTS

The Institute of Museum and Library Services (IMLS) provides libraries with grant funding administered through the State Library of each individual state. IMLS is the umbrella organization through which Library Services and Technology Act (LSTA) monies flow to the states. Checking the IMLS website allows you to click on the name of your state to see the money allocated. Each state has its own grant application procedure, so you need to check their website for details. Please note that many of these grants carry the expectation that libraries will partner with each other and with other agencies. This expectation is easily met when you collaborate; it also provides a rationale to present to your directors and administrators when you wish to work together. Unanswered questions should be directed to your state's LSTA project coordinator, who strives to make the process as user friendly as possible. IMLS also sponsors grants for staff development and is the sponsor of the Laura Bush 21st Century Librarian grants to educate and recruit librarians.

LETTERS OF SUPPORT AND APPENDICES

As foundations and federal grant makers face increasing requests for their money, they want to know that your project will include the participation of other agencies. They want to guarantee the usefulness of their cash and maximize the impact their money will have. It is not advisable to simply catalog a list of potential partners—you need to provide the grant maker with some assurance that this partnership truly exists. Letters of support from **each** agency are a must. It is important that these letters aren't form letters. (Grant reviewing teams often see multiple letters of support with identical text; these form letters don't carry the same weight as letters that show sincere interest from the person signing the letter.) Create an executive summary, a one-page synopsis of your project; email it to each partner for use in crafting their own letters of support. Meeting face-to-face with the person willing to write a letter of support is the best way to promote your project. Follow up with a phone call, and ask if the letter writer has any additional questions about the project.

The appendices section should contain vendor bid sheets, charts, graphs, and diagrams that support your application. Be sure to include only those items that are relevant to your grant. Don't pad the grant with extraneous materials—this makes grant reviewers cranky! Vendor bids are proof that you have given enough thought to the project to create a wish list of items, searched for vendors, and requested and received bids. Include documents, or the appropriate portion of them, detailing your mission statement, the long-range plans for your library, the strategic plan for your institution, and any relevant technology plans. Some federal grants require resumes from the people who will be coordinating the grant. Evaluation tools are also welcome additions here. A survey designed for your teens shows forethought and reflects well on your preparation skills, particularly if it aligns directly to your measurable objectives.

ANALYSIS OF THE UNSUCCESSFUL GRANT

Don't take it personally if your grant is not selected. If you are lucky, your rejection letter will detail some of the problems with the grant. You can then meet to review the letter and decide if you want to revise it and resubmit it to the same agency. NEVER throw out old grants. Much of the information about your institution will remain the same and can be used in future grants.

GRANT REPORTS

Grant reports must be prepared for the funding agency. The group providing the money needs to know whether your goals were met and if their money was wisely invested in your project. Be honest! Simply analyze what worked and what didn't. Not every grant runs perfectly. Detail the success but explain the stumbling blocks and the unexpected consequences along the way. For yourself and your libraries it is important to determine the impact that the grant had—both positive and negative. It may be that someone else will want to replicate your project; this information can be passed on to them from the grant-making source. Consider who else might benefit from the project and include that information in your report.

There are two major types of reports that you will be required to do—narrative and fiscal. The narrative report explains what you did while the fiscal report lists your purchase orders and details how the money was spent and when. Visual documentation can be made via digital cameras, cable TV reports, or web videos. Make sure that your visuals are easy to view and the content is relevant to your goals and objectives. Wherever possible include tables, charts, graphs, and pictures of teens interacting.

In Our Experience

Some unexpected results will be negative. We once secured a grant to improve computer access throughout the district, and required that students record their first name and the amount of time that they waited to gain access to a computer. While this presented little problem for high school students, we needed to adjust the demands for our special needs and younger students who had trouble calculating the time they waited for a computer to be free.

Regardless of the support that you have from your community, your administrative team, your trustees, and board members there are times when you need to seek additional funding. This often requires that you step outside your comfort zone, partner with another library, and search for a new way to augment your library's budget with another source of funding. Most often this requires that you tackle a new skill—learning to write a grant. Just keep your teens in mind and let the grant reviewer feel the passion you have for this extraordinary group.

REFERENCES

Anderson, Cynthia, and Kathi Knop. "Go Where the Grants Are." *Library Media Connection* 27, no. 1 (2008): 10–14.
Foundation Center. "Wisdom Exchange Project Outline: Proposal Writing Basics," http://www.yep.cohhio.org/pdf/Grantsmanship061208/FCblue.pdf (cited February 28, 2011).

Institute of Museum and Library Services. "Grants to States," http://www.imls .gov/programs/allotments.shtm (cited February 28, 2011).

Lodge, Missy. Email interview with Cherie Pandora, April 3, 2012, Columbus, OH.

Lodge, Missy. "Steps to Writing a Successful LSTA Mini-Grant." *OELMA News* (2011): 2–3.

Mezger, Roger. "Small print sidetracks grant request." *The Plain Dealer* (April 3, 2003), http://www.cleveland.com/westnile/index.ssf?/westnile/ more/1049365919137010.html (cited February 28, 2011).

Project Smart. Hughey, Duncan. "SMART goals," http://www.projectsmart .co.uk/smart-goals.html (cited February 28, 2011)

FURTHER READING

Geever, Jane C., and Patricia McNeill. *Guide to Proposal Writing.* New York: Foundation Center, 1993.

Golden, Susan L. *Secrets of Successful Grantsmanship: A Guerrilla Guide to Raising Money.* San Francisco, CA: Jossey-Bass Publishers, 1997.

13

◇ ◇ ◇

RESOURCE SHARING

Remember those meetings suggested in Chapter 1? Resource sharing is so much easier to accomplish if you see each other on a regular basis. Email is fine for some requests, but it cannot be compared with a face-to-face meeting. Most often the need for a change in direction comes through the strategic planning process in the public library, or from curricular changes in schools, or even a change in staff. For example, when a new business teacher is hired, often the materials they desire are beyond the scope of the school library budget. The thrifty and wise school librarian will turn to the public library for information on the subscription databases they offer to local business owners. Also in order is an in-person visit to review the materials housed at the public library that pertains to the curriculum of the business courses; these titles can be suggested to the new teacher with a sampling loaned to the school. What a fun way to unite public librarians, school librarians, and teachers in these disciplines! (Gorman 2009, 36).

When starting a new program at either the public library or the school library, be sure to contact your counterpart to determine how you can best support each other. While discussing upcoming events at your meetings, discuss materials that are needed; you may be able to provide some materials that are needed by the other library. Suggest topics for programs. Offer to promote the programs held at your sister library by posting flyers and posters on bulletin boards and in the teen areas of the public library; don't forget to note these events on the calendar segment of your website. If you are in a school setting, you can post flyers in your library, send email messages to faculty and staff, and add announcements to electronic bulletin boards and your website. School librarians can also try to bolster attendance at library functions by working with teachers and students promoting such events through word-of-mouth marketing. Do you have equipment, such as projectors or whiteboards that you can lend? Make a pledge to volunteer or attend at least one function held at your partner library each year.

In Our Experience

When planning a Freshman Mentoring Program for the high school, we knew we wanted a textbook that was a combination of workbook and inspirational reading. We contacted Rocky River Public Library (RRPL) teen and reference departments for suggestions. The committee was able to personally review each book with the comments from the public librarians to determine which text would best ease the transition of our youngest teens from their middle school years into the culture of the high school.

SHARING

How can schools repay this favor? By keeping teen librarians up-to-date on federal legislation that can cause increasing demands on their collection. The acronym STEM, standing for science, technology, mathematics, and engineering, has received a great deal of attention from school librarians, and administrations. STEM is the governmental response to poor international test scores especially in math and the sciences. Common Core national standards have been created to counter these deficiencies, in part by emphasizing the reading of nonfiction materials, and they have been adopted by 45 states. School librarians need to familiarize themselves with these standards and the resources that will help their math, science, and computer teachers to meet these new demands. It is also the duty of the school librarian to meet with teen and reference librarians to share this information and the demands that this will make on their collections. There has even been grant money made available for programs that encouraged teens to major in one of these underserved disciplines (Braun 2011, 60). As a result additional assignments and research projects were designed in these areas and librarians in both venues need to purchase up-to-date materials to meet the increased demand.

FIELD TRIPS

When you envision sharing resources or taking field trips to the public library, you might think solely of elementary students. This should not be the case; older students benefit from both as well. The common stumbling blocks of time away from the classroom and transportation costs can be circumvented in creative ways. If the public library is close, walking can take the place of bus transportation. If the district has an educational foundation or an active PTO/PTA, they are often willing to foot the bill for such worthwhile endeavors.

Time constraints imposed on subjects that have annual mandatory testing often make it impossible for students in the four core areas of English, history, math, and science classes to travel outside the school. Look instead to the classes that aren't yet tested, to art, music, health, and foreign languages for teens to involve in this field trip. If you want to initiate a program with one of the core area classes, then consider asking the teen or reference librarian at the public library to do the traveling and to visit the school, eliminating the time lost to and cost of transporting teens and chaperones.

In Our Experience

Jazz Day

When U.S. history teacher Sara Ziemnik approached Cherie about staging a nontraditional event so the entire sophomore class would get a feel for the era of the 1920s, we knew that we didn't want to do this through a series of lectures, because many teens learn best by doing (body-kinesthetic intelligence) rather than by sitting quietly and listening to a lecture. Instead, we wanted to create an interactive day using as many learning techniques as possible (TeacherVision, 2012). During our discussions, we envisioned a day of music (musical intelligence), dancing, and artistic (visual–spatial intelligence) presentations with a lot of history thrown in for good measure. After the initial planning sessions, Sara and Cherie wrote a grant application to the Rocky River Educational Foundation. Once granted, arrangements were made for an in-house field trip including a videoconference from the Cleveland Museum of Art; a presentation by a history professor from Cleveland State University; a talk by a RRPL librarian who spoke about special collections; with swing music provided by our own school jazz band. A schedule was drawn up so that all 125 sophomores could rotate through the presentations. Some of these events involved minimal cost. The librarian volunteered her time as a community service; the history professor received a small honorarium, and, of course, our jazz band played for free.

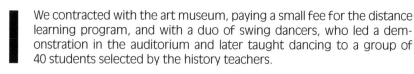

We contracted with the art museum, paying a small fee for the distance learning program, and with a duo of swing dancers, who led a demonstration in the auditorium and later taught dancing to a group of 40 students selected by the history teachers.

SPECIAL COLLECTIONS

School librarians should not feel limited to the usual curricular areas when considering joint ventures with the local public library. First, ask your teen librarian about special collections housed at the public library. You might find that they house diaries or journals from a prominent citizen or a special collection of maps, artwork, or realia donated by a community member. If this is not the case then use the resources of the library to investigate local collections.

Most towns have a historical society or an office that contains an archive of local history materials. These may include old maps, property evaluations, newspaper clippings, and other items from the earliest roots of your city. Historical societies are often looking for volunteers to write about their documents, artifacts, and work: why not take the newspaper staff to the society and have each student research and write an article about one artifact found there? Follow-up research can take place in both libraries.

Nonprofit organizations often need volunteers to create a simple website that they can easily maintain; why not take the Advanced Web Design class to the organization and have students create the website for them? Art galleries and music stores may welcome students in the performing arts if you let them know your curricular goal. Working creatively with a teacher allows you to plan an event that combines the efforts of both librarians, and creates a lasting impression on your students.

If field trips are no longer an option due to budget cuts then invite these organizations to send a speaker with some artifacts that they can share. Most museums, zoos, and hospital systems maintain speaker's bureaus, and are happy to send representatives, and artifacts, to schools, often without cost. Collaborate with your counterpart librarian to create bibliographies that contain materials housed at each library as a follow up to the visit.

In Our Experience

Art teacher Patty Tobin had the perfect idea for her Ceramics 2 class. She wanted her students to create "jazz bowls" based on the major piece in the Cowan Pottery Museum housed at RRPL. Curator Librarian Carol Jacobs introduced students to the history of this locally produced decorative pottery, and brought examples for students to examine. Students took a field trip to the library/museum to view the collection, followed by lunch in a restaurant known for its collection of Cowan Pottery. (Examples of the blue Cowan Pottery Jazz Bowl can be viewed at the following site: http://www.mfa.org/collections/object/punch-bowl-from-the-jazz-bowl-series-42177) Cherie attended the presentation, chaperoned the field trip, and concluded the lesson with an overview of the 1920s, jazz, and the Harlem Renaissance. Students designed and created their own jazz bowls, and wrote artist's statements to explain their designs. Jazz bowls were displayed in the school's library, main hall, and at the public library.

Notes from the Field

How about a contest that highlights resources in both print and nonprint format? We have all seen game show clones used as teaching tools and as test reviews. What about a game that allows students to **ask** the reference questions and forces the reference librarians to **answer** the questions? Manhattan Middle School students did just that in a game called "Stump the Librarian" (Schaffner 1995, 42). Reference librarians from New York Public Library carried numerous tomes from their branches to the school library where students competed to deliver a question that librarians could not answer in 10 minutes or less. Prizes and raffles followed and students had fun with reference tools!

TEAM TEACHING

Coteaching classes is another way to bring teen librarians into the school to show off their resources. This not only provides students with twice as many resources, but it introduces nonlibrary users to a friendly face, a name, and a reason to step into the local library. Coteaching with databases that the public library provides to students for free can be an eye opener for many students; it shows them the advantages that the public library provides, and reinforces the need to keep their library cards current. It often also surprises teachers to see what resources are available to them and to their students.

When starting a research unit in any subject, remind students ahead of time to bring their public library cards with them on research days. You might be surprised when students remark that they don't need the card as they have the number memorized! Start off by introducing students to print materials in the school library, and then progress to demonstrating the databases that they can remotely access from both libraries. Teens arriving with their classes are a "captive audience"; but they can be turned into regular users of the public library once they see all that is available. If your policy allows students to sign up for a library card without parental permission, have the teen librarian bring applications; students who notice that others are getting a head start by using their public library card may be enticed to sign up themselves (Scordato 2004, 33).

ACT and SAT Prep

School and public librarians can team teach a unit with high school juniors on the online support databases (e.g., Learning Express Library) and practice tests available to prepare students for the ACT and SAT college entrance exams.

In Our Experience

Although Cherie had done such a presentation many times before, former RRPL Teen Librarian Victoria Vogel came to the school and added a great deal of value to our presentation. She demonstrated the library's databases, took teens to helpful websites, and promoted the special test workshops and practice test session RRPL sponsors each May. Among the things she shared were websites from two universities that identified scholarship offers based solely on grade point average and ACT/SAT scores. This really helped students realize the importance of these exams! After the presentation, students moved to the RRHS school library where we guided them in setting up their own accounts using school library computers.

CURRICULUM CHANGES

Many schools update one curriculum area each year, science this year, foreign languages the next. Curriculum is rewritten to align with national, Common Core, and/or state standards. If money is available, new textbooks and support materials are adopted for the classroom. While the school library purchases materials to support the changes in curriculum, it would be helpful if this curriculum schedule was shared with the teen librarian. Changes in textbooks usually result in increased demands on the resources of the public library, as well as additional inquiries for information from students, parents, and teachers. Since many textbook companies now include materials on the Web, this may well increase the time that students need to spend on public library computers.

HOMESCHOOLED STUDENTS

If you are a public librarian, you also have a great opportunity to share information and resources with students who are not in high school full-time. Homeschooled students in particular need reliable sources of information and may need assistance during daytime hours (Anderson 2005, 66). How can school and public librarians work together to make sure that these students are assisted, and invited to take part in special programming?

Since schools keep records of the students who are homeschooled, the school librarian is in a good position to keep the teen librarian current on existing or newly homeschooled teens. If the school administration is reluctant to share this information outside of the school, join forces! Together the school and teen librarians should make a presentation to administrators regarding these often overlooked patrons. Focus on the positive impact sharing databases, resources, and passwords can have on both homeschooled students and their parents. Host this program at the public library, as some home school families prefer not to be involved with traditional schools for a variety of reasons. Besides using your database resources, print materials, and a place for social interaction, homeschooled teens may also need the information that you both provide to traditional school students on preparing for college entrance exams. Reach out to these students through contacts with the school and through homeschooler organizations such as the Home School Legal Defense Association (HSLDA 2012).

DUAL ENROLLMENT

Dual enrollment students are those who take BOTH high school and college classes in the same school year. These students go to college for part of the school day, and spend the rest of their day back on the high school campus. Their needs are different from that of the average high school student; since their time is limited on the college campus they are often reluctant to ask academic librarians for assistance with their coursework. School librarians can ease their anxiety by holding a group meeting early in the semester to offer them help with the transition. Be sure to include the teen or reference librarians from your local public library; allow time for these librarians to meet students, and to inform students of all the educational options that the public library offers in the evening and on the weekend. Many high schools provide these students with special library passes that allow unlimited access to the school library, for example, even when the library is full to capacity with scheduled classes (Anderson 2005, 67).

DROPOUTS

Students who have dropped out of high school generally require a different approach, but they do need the same level of care, and assistance as other teens. As candidates for the General Equivalency Diploma (GED), these teens will likely need your help locating a training class or need guidance on how to register for the training. If your public library offers GED workshops, or your schools offer night school classes, be sure that this information goes out to the community via different forms of media—Facebook, Twitter, newspapers, links on the website, and flyers at teen-friendly venues (Anderson 2005, 68).

MOCK ELECTIONS

Schools often hold mock elections during presidential election years as a culminating event to the study of the political process. Many public libraries sponsor candidate forums for local elections in their community rooms. How can you put these two endeavors together as a collaborative event? Start by approaching local political parties and nonpartisan groups such as the League of Women Voters for assistance. While government and history classes normally hold elections in the school library using computers a cooperative board of elections may be enticed to bring in voting machines to educate soon-to-be-voting YAs (Repp 2009, 16). Both libraries can showcase their resources and assist in planning displays, coordinating activities, and setting the ground rules. Do meet to set these ground rules, that is, the event is *not* intended for political speeches, but for helping teens to understand issues and the political processes.

Here's how it works. Students first need to come to the school library and register to vote. Volunteers (usually students and library staff from either library) collect the material and the teacher creates a list of those who can participate. (Since this is a Government class assignment, almost everyone registers.) Discussions, which can include mock debates or the requirement that students watch the televised debates, are held in the classrooms regarding the candidates if it is a presidential election year. Students should be encouraged to attend any related programs at the public library such as candidate's nights or informational programs sponsored by the League of Women Voters; often teachers will give extra credit for attendance at such events. Students will then cast their ballots online a few days prior to the actual election; and a tally will be sent back with data that include the name of the winning presidential candidate and the demographics, such as the number of males and the number of females who voted for each candidate. After the real election takes place, class discussions can center around the results of both elections—that of the students and general public (Pearson 2012).

EXAMS

Midterm and final exams present some of the most stressful times for teens. Wouldn't it be wonderful if libraries could work together to offer students a quiet place to study in the evenings and on weekends when the school library is closed to them? While school libraries create quiet study zones during final weeks, some public libraries have also sought to do so, as best they can without disrupting the rest of the library. Schedule your community room as a study room for group work, so that you can welcome students collaborating on group work, or those who have formed study groups. Move a staff member to the room to assist with research questions (Auxier 2010, 48–49). Keep your computer training room schedule open for these same days so that students can drop in to finish typing and print final papers.

Make sure your efforts are well advertised with teachers and students alike; if these resources aren't used, it becomes difficult to justify setting the time and space aside for student use. Using communal rooms can alleviate some of the overcrowding that might spill into your adult or reference areas. Remember, accommodating teens at this stressful time of year just might encourage more students to venture into the library for other events (Simpson and Duwel 2007, 71). Once you and your colleague start looking for ways to combine your effort, money, or materials to get the most out of a situation, you'll both find new levels of success.

REFERENCES

Anderson, Sheila B. *Extreme Teens: Library Services to Nontraditional Young Adults.* Westport, CT: Libraries Unlimited, 2005.

Auxier, Tiffany. "Hundreds of High School Students Study at the Library." In Smallwood, Carol, ed. *Librarians As Community Partners: An Outreach handbook*. Chicago, IL: ALA, 2010, 48–51.

Braun, Linda W. "The Lowdown on STEM." *American Libraries* 42, no. 9/10 (September/October 2011): 60.

Gorman, Michele. "Getting Graphic! Comics in the Curriculum: Math, Science, and History." *Library Media Connection* 28, no. 3 (November/December 2009): 36.

HSLDA (Home School Legal Defense Association). http://www.hslda.org/orgs/Default.aspx (cited September 29, 2012).

Pearson Foundation. "National Student Mock Election," http://www.national mockelection.org/curriculum/ (cited September 29, 2012).

Repp, Anne. "Thanks-a-Latte, Seniors: the Library Hosts an Election Day Event." *Library Media Connection* 28, no. 3 (November/December 2009): 16–17.

Schaffner, Judith. "Yo! I Stumped the Librarian!" *School Library Journal* 41, no. 8 (August 1995): 42.

Scordato, Julie. "A Tale of Two Libraries: School and Public Librarians Working Together." *Library Media Connection* 22, no. 7 (April/May 2004): 32–33.

Simpson, Martha Seif, and Lucretia I. Duwel. *Bringing Classes into the Public Library*. Jefferson, NC: McFarland, 2007.

TeacherVision. "Multiple Intelligences Chart," http://www.teachervision.fen.com/intelligence/teaching-methods/2204.html (cited May 1, 2012).

FURTHER READING

"AASL Standards for the 21st Century Learner," http://www.ala.org/aasl/guide linesandstandards/learningstandards/standards (cited May 2, 2012).

ALA. "Public Library Visits to Schools: Linda L. Homa," http://wikis.ala.org/read writeconnect/index.php/Public_Library_Visits_to_Schools (cited May 2, 2012).

Byrne, Richard. "Planning Common Core Lessons? Help Is Here." *School Library Journal* 59, no. 1 (2013): 22–28.

Dees, Dianne, Alisande Mayer, Heather Morin, and Elaine Willis. "Librarians as Leaders in Professional Learning Communities through Technology, Literacy, and Collaboration." *Library Media Connection* 29, no. 2 (October 2010): 10–13.

East Cleveland Public Library. "GED Flyer," http://www.ecpl.lib.oh.us/gedflyer.pdf (cited September 29, 2012).

Nesi, Olga. The Public Library Connection. *School Library Journal* 58, no. 12 (2012): 20.

Schaffner, Judith. "Yo! I Stumped the Librarian!" *School Library Journal* 41, no. 8 (August 1995): 42.

14

◇ ◇ ◇

PROFESSIONAL DEVELOPMENT

A great way to stay at the top of your profession is to attend conference presentations and sign up for workshops relevant to your job. From the grand possibilities inherent in attending ALA's Annual Conference to the uniquely local talent displayed through library consortiums, there is always something worthwhile being offered somewhere.

School and public librarians need to share their experiences. Before attending a conference review the list of sessions and vendors with your librarian partners. See if there are any questions that they would like you to ask, or any business cards that you can bring back for them. Put your conference notes to good use; discuss them with your partner after you return from a conference that specializes in your type of library. Share any resources, websites, and information gleaned from your sessions. If you've picked up a new skill be sure to teach it to your partner upon your return. Consider also that you and your partner can copresent at conferences, cowrite journal articles, and share your expertise with others.

WEBINARS

Be aware that professional journals, publishers, and database vendors offer a variety of webinars for librarians with topics that include the release of new nonfiction titles, awards for fiction, demonstrations on using databases more effectively, and how to creatively integrate the newest mobile device into your library. Many of these webinars are available free of charge, but require that you establish a free account in order to register; others may be fee based. Invite your counterpart to join you for free webinars that could benefit both of you. It's also worth noting that webinars are often archived for those who cannot attend at the announced time. Although you'll lose the ability to interact with the speaker and other participants, you can still hear the presentation and access materials posted online. Check to see if one of your resources offers webinars on Web 2.0 tools or another program of interest to you (Woodard 2011, 46). Webinars allow you to use such tools from the comfort of your own library saving you immense amounts of both time and cash (Bell 2011, 28).

STAYING CURRENT

Keeping current on the latest business tools and gaming software, gaining a better understanding of the ever-changing technology in libraries, and being aware of trends appealing to teens, are all important to your own professional development. This takes real time and commitment, but the rewards are great. Keeping up-to-date with business tools and technology makes it easier to speak with authority to coworkers, managers, and other agencies. Understanding pop culture and gaming helps you draw in the teens, as a result everyone around you will be in awe! If it feels overwhelming at first, don't worry. Once you learn how to incorporate these tools into your everyday working schedule, you'll discover which of these offerings is truly useful; you'll find these opportunities energizing. This chapter provides tips on how to make that change happen.

Professional development means more than meeting and greeting new friends or previewing and selecting electronic resources. It's also important to remain engaged and excited to try new things as a librarian working with teens. It can be discouraging to continually place new ideas, materials, and opportunities in front of teens, who may or may not appreciate your efforts. How do you manage your daily workflow, keep up with the trends in your field, and bring great energy to your next program? Learn something new for yourself! Have a conversation with your counterpart to discover what you might be able to teach each other or, better still, learn together. Have either of you ever wanted to explore the world of eReaders? Do it! Why not offer to become the in-house expert on some new tool that will improve your library, then take the time to share your experience with counterpart. You will be amazed at how often your own interests and skills will suddenly seem to solve unforeseen problems at work! Additionally, your feeling of satisfaction at work can help you feel happier at home, and that's a good thing too.

PROFESSIONAL ORGANIZATIONS

Search for professional groups to observe and join, from the obvious organizations like ALA's Young Adult Librarian Services Association (YALSA) to the less obvious, but just as useful, local groups like your Friends of the Library. In the spirit of collaboration, don't feel that you have to limit yourself to professional associations in your specialty. School librarians can benefit from joining associations oriented to public and academic librarians, while teen librarians are welcome to join associations aimed at their counterparts in schools such as the American Association of School Librarians (AASL). Both of you should consider attending your local Chamber of Commerce meetings, so you can meet and befriend local business owners in your area. Groups like the Chamber of Commerce and your public library's Friends of the Library are two excellent sources of potential programming ideas, outlets for teen volunteering, and additional financial support. Forming these networks is a great way to establish positive relationships for the future, especially if you live in a state that forces your library to return to the voters every few years for funding/operating monies. Spreading goodwill and establishing strong working relationships with a wide variety of adults in the community goes a long way, especially if any of your materials or services are called into question or challenged as inappropriate.

Joining the appropriate professional organizations and subscribing to newsletters aimed at topics that interest you can help you keep your skills current, even if you can't attend a conference. Be sure to sign up for the electronic email lists sponsored by professional library groups in your state and look for more unusual options such as an international list for the school library community, for example, LM_NET (http://lmnet .wordpress.com/) or a public library discussion list for YAs and children known as PUBYAC (http://pubyac.org/). To select the right organization and appropriate email lists to join, it's a good idea to consider what you hope to gain from these different opportunities. Are you only interested in learning what others in your position are trying or are you also interested in directly learning more about the challenges your counterpart might be facing? Be cautious about joining too many groups initially.

You can soon be overwhelmed by the quantity of emails coming in, and you'll feel obligated to respond to them all. Try checking out some list-serv archives to see if the discussions are really of interest to you. Talk to your counterpart to suggest that each of you join a group and trade tips back and forth between the two of you. Many professional organizations also maintain blogs or wikis to facilitate the discussion of problem areas; feel free to search their archives as a guest if you do not wish to register for an account. If you are looking for information on, say, a policy for hand-held devices, these resources can garner you a wealth of information from fellow practitioners in the field. If you use social media you can follow many of the experts and your favorite organizations through tools such as, Facebook, Twitter, and LinkedIn.

PERSONAL LEARNING NETWORKS

Personal Learning Networks, also known as PLNs, are electronic networks that function without the geographic limitations of most electronic lists. Most PLNs are used to electronically share concerns related to your field while allowing colleagues to respond to you with their suggestions. They represent a powerful tool for learning and keeping up on trends in your field (Perez 2012, 20). PLNs can include any number of social media formats and serve as both a force of support and a forum for gathering the best ideas from colleagues near and far. Creating your own network with your counterpart allows you to follow those librarians whose philosophies you share without traveling: it becomes another branch of your online community (Fredrick 2010, 38).

PROFESSIONAL LEARNING COMMUNITIES

Now common in many schools, PLCs can also be a useful means of collaborating with librarians from the public library. PLCs in the school setting rely on face-to-face (F2F) meetings between colleagues for the purpose of fulfilling one of the building's goals. In schools, that may mean creating a freshman mentoring program, or working together to revise the summer reading program with the English department. But now is your chance to think outside of the box and devise some new way to include the teen librarian from the public library. Since PLC group meetings are often held first thing in the morning, and students are excused from the first 90 minutes of the school day (Brown et al. 2011, 58), that means these meetings occur before the public library opens so the teen librarian may be able to attend without sacrificing time when patrons are in the library. Cherie's school building held PLC meetings every Wednesday morning from 7:45 to 8:45 A.M. Since the public library didn't open until 9 A.M. this was a time when the teen librarian could meet on a monthly basis to work on tasks such as staff development ideas for teachers, programming ideas for teens, or to refine procedures for starting a TAB (see also Chapters 3 and 10).

Don't limit your PLC to two librarians. Wouldn't you enjoy meeting on a quarterly basis with librarians from numerous area public and school libraries? Meeting in such a group allows you the time to discuss common problems—and their solutions—with colleagues who understand you and your patrons. Whether the common problem is patron behavior, budget cuts, personnel issues (no names allowed), or which databases best meet the needs of your teen patrons, these meetings can provide answers, support, and a great way to network. Yes, it does feel good to unburden yourself to an empathetic crowd, but make sure you keep the conversation productive. If someone is sharing a difficult situation, it should be to hear suggestions or ideas of what might help their colleague find a solution. Keep it a conversation, not a monologue, and you'll have a bigger, better collective brain as your reward.

In Our Experience

Cherie belonged to a group called West Shore Librarians that consisted of school librarians from 15 different high schools. They met informally twice a year and rotated the building where they met. It was informal and no minutes were needed. Their favorite activity was sharing time when they would bring and discuss books or journals or go online to demonstrate a favorite database or website. They also discussed their problems and had the wealth of wisdom of their fellow librarians to support them and suggest solutions to their dilemmas. Cherie's only regret now would be that they hadn't thought to ask teen librarians from public libraries to participate.

CONFERENCES

Conferences offer another way to increase your knowledge and connect with your colleagues. Don't ignore the conversations you have while waiting for a presenter to start, or the dialogues that occur over lunch. Think of these opportunities as networking if you'd like, and also as stolen moments! Even if you have only a few minutes, ask questions of those seated near you. If you're feeling brave or if the audience seems particularly open to frank discussion, you can try introducing sensitive topics into the conversation to hear how others handle them. Of course this is a much easier conversation to have in a small group. Have a list of questions to ask the other attendees on behalf of your colleague and attempt to gather a variety of answers. Be ready to exchange business cards, email addresses, or phone numbers, as you might just find a few new fabulous friends who want to share the best, and the worst, of their teen librarian experiences. Take good notes and go over them with your counterpart later to discuss the information you're bringing back. If you feel like the conference didn't cover a topic that concerns you and your colleague this is a sign you should begin working on your own collaborative presentation.

OTHER OPTIONS

A great deal can be gained through attending presentations, serving on panel discussions, or taking part in committee work that stretches your skills. All librarians can benefit from workshops in marketing, public relations, program analysis, and dealing with difficult people (both patrons and staff). Time management workshops are useful not only to help you to organize and prioritize your own tasks but help you to become a more efficient manager of time, resources, and staff. Watch for programs that concentrate on identity theft, privacy, and cyber security that can be used as you begin to work together on implementing new social media tools (see also Chapter 8). If both organizations are willing to send staff, the discussions later would be twice as productive and interesting. Workshops on evidence-based practice can help create measurable goals for collecting data and set a common understanding of how combined programs can be assessed (see also Chapter 15).

LEARN FROM YOUR LOCAL COLLEAGUES

Harking back to previous chapters, those monthly meetings with your counterpart at the neighboring library can be invaluable. If you're lucky, these may already be in place; if not, now is the time to start. This is where you will learn the strengths of your colleagues, their passions, and their specialties. You can also discuss topics such as new computer systems, programs, and databases added to either library. Once you've been working with them awhile, you should feel comfortable enough to share your weaknesses and ask for help. You may find that a weakness of yours is a strength of your counterpart, just another great reason for collaborating!

Professional development topics can be generated from either library. Teen librarians might want their colleagues to share what they know about how school assignments are communicated or how they use their technology, like whiteboards, differently than the public library. Keeping current with the concerns of your counterpart and working on joint solutions will improve both organizations. School librarians might want to start using the teacher in-service day to address professional development for the entire school library staff and invite the teen librarian, if possible. Use at least half of the day to learn and discuss a common concern, such as the use of spreadsheets.

Public libraries often provide wonderful free training on a variety of software and technology tools—word processing, presentation software, and digital enhancement of photos. They are often the first to offer special programs on newer technologies, such as eBooks, podcasting, and utilizing the functions of your MP3 players. Ask them to provide you with training schedules via booklet and email with links to the website. School librarians are also being asked to explore a whole different set of educational needs for students and teachers. Learning more from your colleague about the new tools, programs, and standards being adopted by the schools can help teen librarians to introduce similar ideas into the public library setting. If students are being required to use a technology that they don't understand, the school and public librarian should seize the opportunity to create a joint program for teens and their parents to attend.

In Our Experience

The public library technology trainers provided the school with a workbook for word processing programs. Cherie was the only staff able to attend their beginning 2007 workshop, but permission was granted for general distribution of the information to the entire school library staff. The booklet and advice from the public library technology trainers was most welcome as this was the only training that school librarians received about MS Office 2007.

PRESENTING

Are you looking for something beyond the normal, day-to-day challenge of working with teens? Consider presenting a program on a topic in which you feel confident in your knowledge. The more you learn through the years, with both successful and disappointing experiences behind you, it becomes your turn to mentor newer colleagues and to present at conferences. Don't shy away from sharing the pitfalls and those programs that weren't quite so successful, so that others can learn from your mistakes. Take time to explain how you think your successes can be recreated in other libraries and any changes you've made in the effort of achieving even greater success. Workshop organizers are always happy to have another volunteer; and you might just find out you enjoy sharing what you know! Understand that there are very few people who thrive on public speaking, but this is an obstacle that you can overcome. Remember you'll be presenting in front of a friendly audience, like-minded souls who also enjoy working with teenagers. Consider this a challenge you should try at least once in your professional life!

Of course, you don't have to present as a solo act, now that you're collaborating! Increased visibility can come to your library partnership by sharing presentations at local meetings and statewide conferences. There are many ways that you can proclaim your success stories, so that others can replicate your model. You can copresent with your friendly, neighborhood librarian, or you can create a panel discussion in which case each panelist has a short time to speak and you can riff off each other's comments just as if you were having a conversation over coffee. As money for attendance at conferences is reduced, the incentive of a reduced registration fee (usually reserved for the primary presenter) creates a powerful rationale for polishing up your success stories and analyzing your failures as a way to help other librarians.

In Our Experience

Once Cherie became a regular presenter at state conferences, her principal had little trouble approving her conference requests. In many cases the registration fee was waived or reduced saving the district money. He also felt that her efforts gave the district another positive tidbit to add to the community newsletter.

Once you take the plunge of becoming a presenter, there are just six small steps before you and your colleague can bask in the warm glow of success. (See Figure 14.1 for a simple outline that details the type of information usually requested when you make a proposal to speak at a conference.)

Name _____ Email address _____

Work Address _____

Work phone number _____ Home/Cell phone number _____

Intended Audience: Check all that apply ___K–3 ___4–6 ___7–8 ___9–12 ___Adults

Audio Visual Equipment needed: Check all that apply

      Note: You will need to borrow or supply your own laptop or device

___ Projector   ___Podium

___Screen or whiteboard   ___Microphone

Room configuration—choose only one

___Theater style (all chairs)

___Classroom style (tables and chairs)

___ Head table

Program Title (10 words or less) _____

Program Abstract (50–75 words) _____

Will there be additional speakers for this session? If so, please provide their contact information

Name _____ Email address _____

Work Address _____

Work phone number _____ Home/Cell phone number _____

Modified from the Call for Program Proposals created by Kate Brunswick for the Ohio Educational Library Media Association (OELMA). Used with permission. http://www.formstack.com/forms/oelma-cfp (cited March 29, 2012).

Figure 14.1: Presentation Checklist

Topics

Make sure that the topic you've chosen is one that you, and any copresenters, can talk about comfortably for 40–45 min. It should be something that you feel quite passionate about, something that inspires you to get up on the proverbial soapbox and share your thoughts with the world. Be timely, research any areas of weakness, and again, make sure you both feel as strongly as possible about your topic so endless repetition doesn't dim your enthusiasm. Choosing such a topic as the focus of a presentation or workshop helps quell performance anxiety. What can you present to your fellow librarians?

In Our Experience

Stacey confesses that she is a reluctant public speaker, at least until she starts sharing reading suggestions with colleagues. This is something she can, and will, talk about with great ease and confidence. Discussing any and all types of books has become a favorite topic for her to present. While she still suffers from some performance anxiety, her excitement about pairing books and readers helps her to overcome her butterflies.

Remember, your audience **wants** to hear what you have to say; they aren't coming to criticize. You and your colleague are certain to learn something new during the questions and answer period following your presentation, which means that the time spent preparing your talk will be time well-spent for both you and your audience.

Be sure to include information about those things that either of you have tried, but that didn't work out as planned. Did your plan fail? Then present those missteps so colleagues can learn from your experience and avoid your mistakes. Librarians are great believers in the phrase, "Don't reinvent the wheel." If someone has found a quicker, more efficient means of accomplishing a task, we want to know! What could be better than having someone tell us about a teen program that was wildly successful? And who wouldn't be grateful for the souls brave enough to share their stories about the policy change that fell flat, what they learned, and how they fixed it? We shouldn't all have to make the same mistakes! Warn us about the ones that you made and we will do likewise; then we are free to make new mistakes and learn from them in turn. Maybe we'll find that our communities are different enough that what didn't work for you might still work well for us. If so, then we can share the stories of how the project worked when schools and public libraries work together for the greatest results.

Focus

When planning your presentation, pick one particular focus and then break the talk down into smaller segments so that it doesn't feel over-whelming. Divide and conquer: divide the bigger portions between the two of you. If you start to consider how many books are published every year, how could you dream of sharing them all? Instead, focus on one theme, such as adult books with teen appeal or fantasy books that both boys and girls enjoy. If you choose to share fantasy books with dual gen-der interest, organize your titles into groups, for example, dragon books versus stories about magic, or stories that feature main characters that are male versus main characters that are female. Compare and contrast the titles and share the elements of the story that attracted your interest. It might be that you each read more of one genre than your copresenter dou-bling your knowledge base and proving again that two heads are better than one. Fashion your own booktalk style, and provide more depth and a teaser or cliffhanger not found on the book jacket (Figure 14.2 provides a sample timeline to help you plan your presentation).

Handouts

What handouts will be useful for your audience? Make sure that hand-outs have information people can add to, with a list for further research that can be accessed through bibliographic information, QR codes, or web links to follow after they return to their own libraries. Include rel-evant links to both libraries, favorite websites, blogs, wikis, and podcasts. Many conferences now require that you post your handouts online so attendees can refer to them after the conference is done. Don't be con-cerned if attendees grab your handout and leave for another session. Take it as a compliment! With conference budget cuts, we all have to cover sessions for our colleagues back home and are often faced with choosing between wonderful sessions that occur simultaneously. Finally, be sure that all handouts contain the logos, and names of both libraries, and both librarians.

Practice, Practice, Practice!

Practice your presentation aloud as often as you need to feel comfortable. Decide how you want to divide the spotlight, should it be one speaker at a time or more of a ongoing dialogue? Many speakers practice by standing

1. Most organizations that have regular workshops and conferences will have a schedule for submitting your program idea and description. Find your deadline and complete your paperwork.

2. Check with the coordinator if you are not contacted within two to three weeks of the submission deadline to ensure that your proposal was received. (If your program was not accepted, ask for more information so your next offer will be successful.)

Three Months before the Presentation:
3. Decide what handouts you'll need, if any, and begin to gather your materials. The more complex your tools, the more time you'll need to create or test out your presentation. Note any deadlines for posting handouts on the conference website.

4. Start to practice what you're going to say, both on paper and aloud. If you're already comfortable, find a practice audience.

Two Months before the Presentation:
5. If you haven't tried all the pieces put together, do that soon.

6. Check with organization's event coordinator to see if you can get a final count of attendees and room assignment and room size, if applicable.

7. If there is equipment you need available at the presentation venue, arrange for it with the coordinator now.

One Month before the Presentation:
8. This is the time to dot your i's and cross your t's. If you're missing materials, you need to get them now. If you haven't practiced out loud, you need to do that now. If you haven't checked in with the event coordinator, do that now.

One week to One day before the Presentation:
9. Recount any packets of materials being offered, and take 5–10 extra just in case. Double-check and pack up what you need to take with you. Make sure you know how to get to your event location. Find and take a phone number for the location and for the coordinator, just in case.

Day of the Presentation:
10. Test your laptop or tablet in the speaker's room or your assigned room.

   Relax! You're ready!

Figure 14.2: Presentation Timeline

From *Better Serving Teens through School Library–Public Library Collaborations* by Cherie P. Pandora and Stacey Hayman Santa Barbara, CA: Libraries Unlimited, Copyright © 2013.

in front of a mirror on their own or with their copresenter; others practice in front of colleagues to get the feel of a real audience and to relieve any jitters. Seek out friendly faces and ask them to listen to your program; let them know you'd like it to feel as real as possible with questions from the audience. Depending on the technology available, you might want to consider videotaping your program to better understand what you're doing right and where you might improve. If you have a tendency to talk "with your hands" use this mirror technique to ensure that your gestures are not distracting to the audience. One tip that will always be appreciated by attendees anywhere: slow down and speak up! As slowly and as loudly as you both talk, someone in the audience will wonder why you're talking so fast and so quietly. Be sure that you have someone in the back of the room do a sound check to be sure that you can be heard. Most conferences have podiums and microphones; don't be afraid to use the technology if you are soft-spoken by nature.

Evaluations

Remember that you can't and won't please everyone. Most conference organizers offer their presenters feedback from the evaluation forms they've collected from attendees. If you've written a solid description of the topic you intend to cover, and then speak on that topic, the people who come to hear you talk should leave satisfied. This is 100% true in theory, but the reality is that you will eventually find yourself reading comments indicating someone feels you didn't discuss your topic, or you didn't discuss your topic with authority, or that you discussed your topic too much. Create your own evaluation form and ask that it be completed immediately. Each of you should complete your own form noting audience responsiveness, questions asked, and the changes you would make when presenting this topic again. Discuss all the evaluations over coffee and make changes to your presentation as soon as you can before other duties demand your time and attention.

In Our Experience

Stacey and a fellow librarian were sharing titles with a group of attendees, who likely chose this program hoping to find books they could then share with their patrons; someone in the audience actually responded that we provided too many titles. Did that affect how Stacey felt about the presentation? No, she accepted it and moved on.

When you start presenting programs, don't let negative comments keep you from stepping in front of the crowd again. Take it with a grain of salt, make improvements where necessary, and go forward.

Have Fun!

Your audience will enjoy listening to you if you're enjoying yourself! And at the risk of repetition, remember that having a library friend and colleague by your side makes it much easier to prepare and easier to present.

REFERENCES

AASL (American Association of School Librarians). "Tweets," http://twitter.com/#!/AASL (cited April 1, 2012).

ALA (American Library Association). "ALA News," http://twitter.com/alanews (cited April 1, 2012).

Bell, Steven. "A Conference Wherever You Are." *Library Journal* 136, no. 16 (2011): 28–31.

Brown, Carol, Lana Dotson, and Elaine Yontz. "Professional Development for School Library Media Professionals." *TechTrends* 55, no. 4 (2011): 56–62.

Brunswick, Kate. Email interview with Cherie Pandora, March 29, 2012. Columbus, OH.

Church, Audrey P. "Definitely NOT Alone! Online Resources and Websites Help Keep School Librarians Connected." *Knowledge Quest* 40, no. 2 (2011): 36–39.

Fredrick, Kathy. "Resource Roundup for Your Personal Learning Network." *School Library Monthly* 27, no. 1 (2010): 38–39.

Lawrence, Kathy. Phone interview with Cherie Pandora. arch 12, 2012. Cleveland Heights, OH.

LM_NET. "Where School Librarians Connect," http://lmnet.wordpress.com/ (cited April 1, 2012).

Perez, Lisa. "Innovative Professional Development: Expanding Your Professional Learning Network." *Knowledge Quest* 40, no. 3 (2012): 20–22.

PUBYAC. "Our Mission," http://pubyac.org/ (cited April 1, 2012).

Woodard, Mary. "Supporting Solo at the District Level." *Knowledge Quest* 40, no. 2 (2011): 44–46.

FURTHER READING

Cox, Ernie. "Building a Future-Ready Personal Learning Network." *School Library Monthly* 27, no. 3 (2010): 34–35.

Harlan, Mary Ann. *Personal Learning Networks: Professional Development for the Isolated School Librarians.* Santa Barbara, CA: Libraries Unlimited, 2009.

15

$\diamond$ $\diamond$ $\diamond$

REPORTING YOUR SUCCESS

Why should you evaluate your programs, material purchases, and collaborative work? First and foremost, you need to see the impact that they have on your patrons. Showing the results of your hard work and measuring the success of existing programs is always a good way to secure additional funding, whether you are requesting monies from the General Operating Fund, from a grant source, or from one of your support groups. To convince your manager or principal that what you do matters, you need the data to back that up (Jones 2009, 13). In addition to showing the data for each project your reports need to emphasize the value of your collaborative work. Explain why you decided to work together, what you accomplished, and how this work benefited both libraries. Include a timeline of your meetings as well to illustrate that time is needed to create quality projects.

Then create a newsletter or brochure using word processing or desktop publishing software that already exists on your computers; there is no need to purchase additional programs. Photographs of your teens working together on joint endeavors are a necessary element of this communication tool. This visual report should include anecdotes and quotes from teens as well as the statistical data that you've collected. Such a visual record will prove useful not just to report your successes but also for promotional use with grant funders and businesses that you approach for funding for your next project.

Plan evaluation meetings after each event to debrief and decide if you need to create two separate reports, one for each library, or if you can create one model that will suffice for both sets of administrators. If only one library director requires a specific format then tailor your report to this format; it is possible that this one report format will be sufficient saving time for both of you.

Schools use the phrase data-driven decision-making to describe decisions made on the basis of hard data. The idea is to create goals, and in a school setting to link the goals to national and state content standards. You then decide how to record your data, collect it, and plan how to best present it to your stakeholders. This entire process is called "evidence-based practice" (Todd 2011, 18).

MEETING GOALS

Evaluating your progress forces you to measure if you have met the goals that you've set for yourself. Both types of libraries serve many bosses including boards, directors, superintendents, headmasters, student patrons, parents, and community members. How can you prove your effectiveness to them in a way that will substantiate the anecdotal evidence you've collected? Tie all projects back to the mission statements and goals of each library. Whenever possible school librarians will need to show connections to the standards of the American Association of School Librarians (AASL) "Standards for the 21st-Century Learner" (http://www.ala.org/aasl/guidelinesandstandards/learningstan dards/standards) and to state and national teaching standards such as the Common Core Standards. Teen librarians need to show how projects meet YALSA Competencies for Librarians Serving Youth: Youth Adults Deserve the Best (http://www.ala.org/yalsa/guidelines/yacompeten cies2010). You need to generate reports that support your requests for funding and provide data that your public relations departments can include in their annual reports to the community. Such concrete data keep the teen department visible to the eyes of managers and makes everyone aware of the ways in which our public–school library partnership benefits the community.

There are many types of record-keeping and evaluative tools that you can use to accomplish these goals. In this chapter, you'll review some of the simple ways that can be used to analyze successes and to pinpoint weaknesses without spending hours collecting the needed information. As you record your data and visual record you may want to use an online file sharing program such as Google Docs to easily share data with your partner. Such programs allow you to share information no matter which word processing programs you use. Another option is to save and share information on servers such as Drop Box that allow users to save information "in the cloud" and to limit access to colleagues working on your project.

When you first begin your partnership, analyze your libraries to determine the strengths and weaknesses of each program. School librarians might want to encourage their public library counterparts to think of this as the equivalent of a pretest, a way to assess your starting point or baseline. You can then build on your respective strengths to support both programs. One of the ways to begin your conversations with your library counterpart is to ask yourself these four questions about your libraries.

1. What are the strengths of your program?
2. What are your personal strengths? What are the strengths of your staff?
3. Conversely, what are the weaknesses of your library program?
4. What are your personal weaknesses? What are the weaknesses of your staff?

SWOT ANALYSIS

If you want a more in-depth look, you can use the visual critiquing tool called the SWOT analysis. If you haven't already used this tool, SWOT stands for **Strengths, Weaknesses, Objectives,** and **Threats** and can be used with anyone: staff, patrons, or managers to analyze your program (http://www.mindtools.com/pages/article/worksheets/SWOTAnaly sisWorksheet.pdf). Although first used as a tool in business, it has been used to critique school library programs as well as public libraries. In Figure 15.1, this business model is adapted to better fit library needs. The worksheet is divided into four quadrants, each labeled with one of the terms listed above. Strengths and weaknesses are self-explanatory but opportunities and threats may warrant a little more explanation.

The **opportunities** quadrant allows you to review your weaknesses and to search for ways to overcome them (Jones 2009, 11–12). First identify those services, programs, and resources that you wish to expand. Sometimes this can be done without additional costs—by rearranging staff

Strengths: What are your current assets?	**Weaknesses:** What you need to improve?
Objectives: Review your weaknesses and search for ways to overcome them.	**Threats:** Roadblocks that you must recognize so you can determine a way to work around them. Remove Improve

Figure 15.1: SWOT Analysis for Libraries

Source: Adapted from MindTools. "SWOT Analysis Worksheet," http://www.mindtools.com/pages/article/worksheets/SWOTAnalysisWorksheet.pdf

hours to fit your busiest times, for example. Brainstorm ways to reach those students who aren't normally visible in the library—perhaps those who are homeschooled or those who are without transportation. Reaching out to community agencies such as Boys and Girls Clubs, the YMCA, and YWCA, if they are active forces in your town, then they may welcome a new group of teens into your library (ibid., 11).

Threats, on the other hand, are those roadblocks that you must recognize so you can determine a way to work around them. They are not always related to money, but may relate to personnel issues, space limitations, and other factors. Like weaknesses, threats give you a starting point from which you can turn negatives into strengths (ibid., 11). They provide you with a list for further study. Divide this list into two parts—those items that are beyond your control, and those that you can remove or improve through some form of advocacy. Use this information to create an action plan that counteracts these weaknesses and perceived threats.

Analyze your own libraries first by gathering input from your library staff and comparing it to your own analysis. Have your counterpart use the same tool to analyze your library while you do likewise. This will give you a good picture of your libraries, both the strengths that staff would like you to keep, as well as those policies that merit review. Pat yourself on the back for the items that should be maintained. Don't take the list of weakness personally; it provides you with data that allows you to improve your workplace for the betterment of the community. Now you can plan joint activities that take advantage of your strengths and those of your partner librarian. You have listed the obstacles that need to be addressed and can work together to overcome these barriers.

Use this tool as well with school administrators, public library directors, parents, and teen patrons/students to gain their thoughts and ideas. Revise the four SWOT analysis questions to reflect your needs before turning your questions into an online survey that can be posted on the front of your website, then use the results to further refine your programs. Be sure to include this data in your annual report and community newsletters (see Figure 15.2).

EVALUATION

How do you currently evaluate your YA programs and the materials that you purchase for them? What information do you need to measure your success? What data must you collect to satisfy your managers that your collaborations are worthwhile? Share this data with your partner librarian and look for additional ways to measure your success. Perhaps

Why do you like to visit the library?

Which librarian helps you the most?

Which departments do you visit the most?

What services do we need to improve?

What materials would you like us to purchase for your use?

What class would you like to see us offer in the training lab?

What equipment would you like to have available for your use?

Have you ever used our community room for a meeting? If not, did you know that this room can be reserved for free?

Have you used our training lab to learn, or refine, a computer skill? If so, which class did you take?

Figure 15.2: Sample Survey Questions

From *Better Serving Teens through School Library–Public Library Collaborations* by Cherie P. Pandora and Stacey Hayman Santa Barbara, CA: Libraries Unlimited, Copyright © 2013.

you can compare hits on the literacy databases from each library after you have completed a team teaching unit. Do you sample the number of students who visit the library each afternoon, evening, and weekend? If you are in a school do you measure your collaboration attempts by the number of classes that walk through your door for instruction from the school or the teen librarian? Your dilemma—how do you easily evaluate all that you do without making the task time-consuming and cumbersome? Don't let this overwhelm you; there are simple solutions to this problem.

FORMS OF EVALUATION
Quantitative

First, keep in mind that there are two main forms of evaluation—quantitative and qualitative. Both are needed to truly measure the success of a project. (See Chapter 12 for additional ideas on analyzing and evaluating your program.) **Quantitative** measures are those that people normally turn to when asked to measure the success of a project. The simplest and most often used are number-gathering, recording the number of sessions and the number of participants in each program or training session. Resist the urge to stop there! You need to make the statistics meaningful for your reader and in the words of library philosopher Ranganathan, you need to "save the time of the reader." Evaluation surveys should be short, five questions or less, and can be done on paper or using a free online survey tool, such as SurveyMonkey (http://www.surveymonkey.com). Use your post-program surveys to decide if there is enough interest to offer the same, or an expanded, program again. These surveys will help you to decide if such a program is a good use of staff time (Levin 2012).

When gathering quantitative data, it is especially helpful to clearly show either growth (e.g., increased attendance at the term paper clinics) or a decline (e.g., fewer disciplinary problems among middle school students). Using spreadsheets for your data allows you to create charts, pie graphs, bar graphs, and other illustrations that are easy to read at a glance and which make your point clearer to your audience. Visuals are often welcome additions to community bulletins, newsletters, and your marketing manager or communications person can add them to the website. For example, if you team teach ACT test prep to junior English classes you can include a line graph that shows the increasing number of classes that you reach each year, see Figure 15.3.

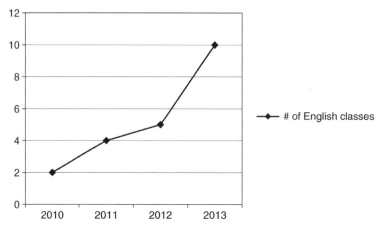

Figure 15.3: Online ACT Prep

Tracking attendance at YA programs in the public library should include a running count of YA attendees during all special services provided for them. Keep track of the number of projects you work on with your school librarian, and the number of contacts made at each middle school and high school, and with homeschooled students, include presentations made with teachers and booktalks with the English teachers as well (Walter 1995, 4). Divide the number of contacts you've made by the number of schools in your area (include secondary schools, both private and public and vocational schools) to reach the number of contacts per school (ibid., 75). One example can be seen in Figure 15.4.

Another means of analyzing statistics is to divide the total number of teens attending your programs by the teen population in the communities you serve. This can be done via census data or by determining the total number of students in the secondary schools in your area (Tuccillo 2010, 229). If you use teen volunteers in your collaborative programs, be sure one of you tracks the hours and shares with the other; you will want to note the cumulative number of hours that your teen volunteers have given to the library. Refer back to Figure 10.2 in Chapter 10, the "Service Hours Form" template used for your TAB.

Quantitative measures can also include documenting your programming expenses and contacts (Honnold 2003, 179). If you keep a programming log (such as the one found in Figure 3.1), you have all the information needed to write a paragraph for your reports *and* you can easily recreate successful programs the following year. While most libraries keep general

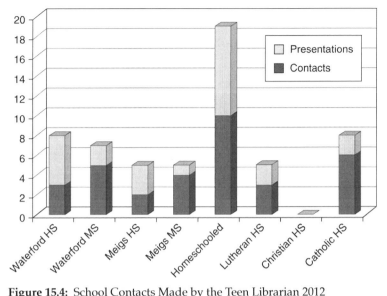

Figure 15.4: School Contacts Made by the Teen Librarian 2012

circulation statistics, any jump in circulation related to the topic of a teen program should be noted and celebrated!

Qualitative

You should always include **qualitative** measures in your evaluation report as well. Qualitative measures include anecdotes about programs as well as quotations from teen participants, workshop leaders, observers, staff members, or parents. Ensure that the voice of your patrons is evident in your reports by including open-ended questions on your post-program surveys. Such questions allow your teens to reflect about their experiences. Include comments, in the student's own words, as well as quotes from parents, administrators, board members, and members of the community; they serve a very important purpose, one that is difficult to measure with objective data. They supply the authentic voice of your patrons and are powerful tools when added to community newsletters and reports. After all, how many times have you seen a lengthy report and simply skimmed it? With so little time for professional reading, people want to glean the most important information in the least amount of time. They read the executive summary, the captions under photos, the sidebars, and any quotes that have been isolated in boxes using prominent fonts.

Take advantage of the quotes you've gathered (and received written permission to use)—they are formidable marketing tools (Harland 2011, 36). Sprinkle positive quotes about your services, programs, and materials throughout any publication and on the library website. Department heads and managers can use them for award applications and may include positive statements in performance evaluations (Levin 2012). An easy way to obtain feedback is to ask teens to complete short reflection papers after every program or activity (see Figure 15.5). You will need their, or their guardian's (if they are under 18) written permission to publish the papers, so it's a good idea to include a blank permission form with this assignment.

You can also survey teens verbally, and take notes on their comments. Reflection questions should be short and open ended, so the responses aren't skewed. By asking students "Which games took too long to play?" and "What would you change about the program that just ended?" you will receive honest feedback on your progress, and hopefully, also some ideas for improvement. It's best to ask these questions in group settings, so that teens will see that you are interested in their honest answers. Leaving a written survey unattended in a teen area will show you that teens have a sense of humor, as some will provide you with silly or unrealistic answers.

Responses can also be gathered through interviews and focus group discussions with library users (Walter 1995, 4). Review your list of preteens and teens who volunteer in either library helping with summer reading games, working on programs, even those who shelve materials. Ask their opinions! Chances are, teens feel comfortable with your teen staff and will give you an honest answer. Your book discussion groups, TAB, anime club, and Tuesday night gamers are potential sources of information that can help you to assess your programs and resources. Ask them how to best gain comments from other teens (Tuccillo 2010, 230). Be sure that you gauge the emotion of your teens at the end of each program; record your own thoughts and ask random teens for their opinions. Did they have fun? Were they glad that they came to the program? (Honnold 2003, 181).

REPORT TIPS

Don't be afraid to show your unexpected results, failures, and missteps along with your successes. Sometimes you risk trying something new, and it simply doesn't work for your population. Your managers and patrons need to realize the challenges you face, whether they are the result of insufficient budgets, decreased staffing, or aging materials and

Date: _____

Please circle the designation that best describes you as a student.

Middle School   High School   Homeschooled

1. Which program did you attend?
   Term Paper Clinic   Anime   Graphic Novels

2. Which time did you attend? (Please circle only one answer)
   Afternoon or Evening

3. What did you like best about the program? (25 words or less)

4. What needs to be improved?

5. What other programs would you like to see?

6. Would you be willing to host or help with such a program?

Figure 15.5: One-Minute Teen Reflection

From *Better Serving Teens through School Library–Public Library Collaborations* by Cherie P. Pandora and Stacey Hayman Santa Barbara, CA: Libraries Unlimited, Copyright © 2013.

technologies. The problems that you encounter remind you to team up to search for creative solutions; they actually help you improve and make your library stronger for the effort. After you analyze your successes and failures, consider them as learning experiences. Consider writing articles for professional journals or making presentations at library conferences (Harland 2011, 36).

If you don't have a standard report format to follow in your library, you can create a very short, single-page form that includes both quantitative and qualitative information. Since it is brief, this can be used to alert managers and principals to your progress, and your challenges, during the course of the year. Complete this one-page form after every collaborative project so that you don't forget any details; if your manager prefers, send it quarterly. Remember, you want your communication with them to be ongoing, not just a single event at the end of the fiscal year. Although taken from Massachusetts Institute of Technology's Global Education and Career Development site "Find a Job/Internship," the hiring and interviewing technique process, named STAR, may serve you well as a reporting tool (see Figure 15.6).

Be sure to also use an evaluation tool that considers the process of collaboration, not just the outcome (O'Dell 2002, 152). In your narrative reflect on any roadblocks that you encountered, from either library, discuss how you worked around them, and how much of an impact you felt you had on your YAs. If you need to work on the dynamics of the partnership, this is the time to say so. Remember, not every evaluation needs to be written and communicated to others. This partnership evaluation can be something that you do to tweak the working relationship you have with each other; if so, then you need not send this information elsewhere.

Public librarians, don't forget to gain feedback from the teachers, as well as from the teens. This will help you forge stronger relationships with individual teachers who can help you fill subject-specific programs at a later date. While the school librarian must judge the impact on student learning as part of the evaluation process, both of you need to ascertain if your current collections meet the needs of students and the teachers. If the project is one that the teacher plans to assign annually, knowing this will have an impact on the purchasing, or rearranging, of materials to support the curriculum.

Don't forget to record your own thoughts and reflections. Consider recording them in a portable collaboration journal and then meeting with your library partner for coffee to debrief and determine what you will retain and what you will change next year (Honnold 2003, 180). Keeping a journal of your joint activities allows you to review past experiences,

S—Situation—Describe the situation: it can be a problem to be solved or a situation that you resolved in a favorable manner. Use whatever numbers you can find, for example, students turned away as there weren't adequate numbers of computers or inadequate copies of a best seller. Add any comments from students that will help your case. If you keep a journal of reference questions that cannot be answered, you can add any appropriate questions here.

T—Task—What have/had you chosen to do about this situation? Is there a task force that was formed? Are you meeting with your counterpart from your sister library? Are there other agencies that can help you?

A—Action—This step gets down to the personal level, namely, what action did <u>you</u> take to promote the program, resolve the problem, or benefit your teen patrons?

R—Results—Your results, both the immediate and the long-term should be placed in terms that are measurable. Twenty students attended Game Night at the last Tuesday night doubling our attendance from the previous week.

Figure 15.6: STAR Reporting Form

Source: Adapted from Massachusetts Institute of Technology's Global Education and Career Development. "Find a Job/Internship," http://gecd.mit.edu/jobs/find/apply/interview (cited April 25, 2012).

note your successes and difficulties, record changes you would make if you repeat the program, and record ideas for future collaborations as well. Having all of these ideas, both past and future, in one place makes it easy to take it to meetings, brainstorm programs with colleagues, and reflect back on your many successful endeavors.

REFERENCES

AASL (American Association of School Librarians). "Standards for the 21st-Century Learner," http://www.ala.org/aasl/guidelinesandstandards/learningstandards/standards (cited January 12, 2013).

Harland, Pamela. *The Learning Commons: Seven Simple Steps to Transforming your Library.* Santa Barbara, CA: Libraries Unlimited, 2011.

Harland, Pamela. "Toward a Learning Commons." *School Library Monthly* 28, no. 1 (September/October 2011): 34–36.

Honnold, RoseMary. *101+ Teen Programs that work.* New York: Neal-Schuman Publishers, 2003.

Jones, Ella. *Start to Finish YA Programs: Hip-Hop Symposiums, Summer Reading Programs, Virtual Tours, Poetry Slams, Teen Advisory Boards, Term Paper Clinics, and More!* New York: Neal Schuman Publishers, 2009.

Levin, Nancy. Phone interview by Cherie Pandora. January 13, 2012. Cleveland Heights, OH.

Massachusetts Institute of Technology (MIT), Global Education and Career Development. "Find a Job/Internship," http://gecd.mit.edu/jobs/find/apply/interview (cited October 10, 2012).

MindTools. "SWOT Analysis Worksheet," http://www.mindtools.com/pages/article/worksheets/SWOTAnalysisWorksheet.pdf (cited April 24, 2012).

O'Dell, Katie. *Library Materials and Services for Teen Girls.* Greenwood Village, CO: Libraries Unlimited, 2002.

Todd, Ross. "A Question of Evidence." *Knowledge Quest* 37, no. 2 (November/December 2008): 16–21.

Tuccillo, Diane P. *Teen-Centered Library Service: Putting Youth Participation into Practice.* Santa Barbara, CA: ABC-CLIO, 2010.

Walter, Virginia A. *Output Measures and More: Planning and Evaluating Public Library Services for Young Adults.* Chicago, IL: ALA, 1995.

YALSA (Young Adult Library Services Association). "Competencies for Librarians Serving Youth: Youth Adults Deserve the Best," http://www.ala.org/yalsa/guidelines/yacompetencies2010 (cited January 12, 2013).

FURTHER READING

Jones, Patrick. *New Directions for Library Service to Young Adults.* Chicago, IL: ALA, 2002.

Martin, Ann M. "Data-Driven Leadership." *School Library Monthly* 28, no. 2 (November 2011): 31–33.

Mulvihill, Amanda. "Ask a Librarian." *Computers in Libraries* 31, no. 9 (November 2011): 40.

Nichols, Mary Anne. *Merchandising Library Materials to Young Adults.* Greenwood Village, CO: Libraries Unlimited, 2002.

Shoemaker, Joel. "Evaluating Customer Service." In Jones, Patrick and Joel Shoemaker, eds. *Do It Right! Best Practices for Serving Young Adults in School and Public Libraries.* New York: Neal-Schuman, 2001.

Appendix A

READING CALENDAR
MONTH-BY-MONTH

These time-specific events were gathered using a favorite reference book (*Chase's Calendar of Events*), YALSA's website, and some old-fashioned scouting via a search engine. The ideas and suggestions outside of the quotation marks have been added to aid in kick-starting the inspiration of the end user—you and your teens!

JANUARY

NCTE Orbis Pictus Award for Outstanding Nonfiction for Children, http://www.ncte.org/awards/orbispictus?source=gs

Orbis Pictus Award for Outstanding Nonfiction for Children is given each year to non-fiction books deemed exceptionally well-written. The winning title, and up to five honor books, are announced in January. This is an excellent chance to explore the field of narrative nonfiction. Allow teens to find a variety of titles for multiple age ranges and ask them to come to a consensus on what their final list would be. Create a display for the winning title and honor books, an annotated list, or both, for sharing with teens not directly involved.

Quick Picks for Reluctant Young Adult Readers, http:// www.ala.org/yalsa/booklists/quickpicks

Teens from 12 to 18, who don't generally enjoy pleasure reading, should be more than able to find something of interest on the Quick Picks list. The list is created during ALA's Midwinter Meeting. Using an official nomination form, found on the YALSA website, all interested parties are invited to suggest a book they think would appeal to a reluctant reader. This has the potential to be a good group or individual project, with the librarian acting as coordinator. Books could be discussed, and nominated, all year long.

Youth Media Awards, http:// www .ilovelibraries.org/articles/featuredstories/ newberycaldecottawards

Awarded each year by the ALA, books and other media materials are recognized for being outstanding within their category. The Newbery Award, Alex Award, and Michael L. Printz Award, are just three of the many awards and quality reading lists revealed at the ALA's Midwinter Meeting where these winning titles are announced. After looking at all the types of awards possible, your teens may be inspired to make their own list for an existing award or suggest a whole new award, and go on to define the parameters of their newly created award.

Newbery Award, http:// www.ala.org/alsc/ awardsgrants/bookmedia/newberymedal/ newberymedal

The Newbery Medal's namesake was an 18th-century British bookseller John Newbery. The Association for Library Service to Children (ALSC) selects an author it feels has made a distinguished contribution to children's literature in America each January. You may want to use the winner and the honor titles for a book group discussion; of those titles recognized, did the right book win?

Alex Award, http:// www.ala.org/yalsa/ booklists/alex

Ten adult books with appeal to teens from 12 to 18 are selected for the Alex Awards during ALA's Midwinter Meeting. For your most voracious readers, even this could be a challenge, who can read all 10 books first? What titles might teens suggest for this top 10 list?

Margaret A. Edwards Award, http://www.ala.org/yalsa/edwards

Established in 1988, The Margaret A. Edwards Award is awarded by YALSA to honor an author for their notable contributions to teen literature. An author likely to win this award will have multiple books to their credit. Would your teens like to consider other authors they would like to see win this award? Or maybe they would like the chance to rank the award winning author's titles from most to least favorite?

Michael L. Printz Award, http://www.ala.org/yalsa/printz

Based solely on what is deemed "literary merit," the Michael L. Printz Award is given during each year to one book written for teens. Another opportunity to judge the work of adult readers involved, as they did with the Newbery Award. Did the right book win? Why do the teens think this one book was selected above all others? If they were nominating a title, based on literary merit, what would it be? The Printz Award committee also selects four honor books, and your teens might want to do the same. The librarian can create a ballot of nominated titles for voting on by interested teens.

(Laura Ingalls) Wilder Award, http://www.ala.org/alsc/awardsgrants/bookmedia/wildermedal

This award is presented by the ALSC to an author or illustrator whose books, published in the United States, have made a lasting impact on children's literature. Get your teens thinking about what books they've read while growing up and which they'd be likely to reread or recommend to a younger friend. Part of the challenge will be to find someone who's responsible for multiple titles, at least one of which has been available for the past 10 years. Once the group has a short list of nominees, allow the teens to present the books of their top choices to younger readers who will also be voting to select the winner.

FEBRUARY

Children's Authors and Illustrators Week (first week in February), http://www .childrensauthorsnetwork.com/caiw.htm

In one of the shortest, and sometimes least energetic, months of the year, ask your teens to write and illustrate their own simple, or complex, story. Sharing these books with peers or younger students can be empowering for creative or shy teens.

Library Lovers' Month, http://www.librarysupport .net/librarylovers/

All through the month teens should be encouraged to celebrate all kinds of libraries: school, public, and private libraries. Get your support groups involved with the teens by asking them to share what they do and see if there is a chance for collaboration. Your teens might appreciate this chance to promote the library services they most enjoy, including the reading of books, graphic novels, magazines, or newspapers found in libraries.

MARCH

Read Across America Day (March 2), http://www .readacrossamerica.org/

The same day as Dr. Seuss' birthday, readers of all ages are encouraged to show their love of the written word. What teen can't quote some part of a Dr. Seuss book from childhood? But now they can also quote Stephanie Meyer and Rick Riordan. Consider celebrating the day with a read-in, where teens take turns reading in a public area for a scheduled amount of time. Or encourage a finding of favorite quotes, from past or present books, to put on display.

Read Me Week, http://www.bookem-kids.org/ readmeweek.htm

Spend an entire week sharing and showing teens how reading is important to their future success. Find local organizations who might be interested in sponsoring or guiding your TAB who in turn will get involved guiding younger readers. Adults helping teens helping children love to read can inspire us all!

Children's Book Week, http://www
.bookweekonline.com/for-teens

Teens are invited to start voting online for the Teen Choice Book Awards in mid-March. They can choose their favorite books and authors from a short list. The winners in the different age groups and an Author of the Year are announced during Children's Book Week. What a great chance for teens to feel the satisfaction of voting for something they feel strongly about, to feel like they've made a difference. Encourage teens to read all the nominated titles before voting, as they will want to do in any election they participate in.

APRIL

Literacy Education Advocacy Month, http://www
.ncte.org/action/advocacyday

This may be aimed more for the adults in the crowd but after you speak out, why not comb the ideas suggested by The National Council of Teachers of English for what can be tailored to the teen crowd? Ask your TAB to share its experiences from the other side of the desk on a blog or with parents at a PTA meeting.

National Library Week (second week of April),
http://www.ala.org/conferencesevents/
celebrationweeks/natlibraryweek

Meant to be a seven-day celebration, patrons of all ages are asked to consider the variety of ways and means their local library has enhanced their lives. You can approach this as a week to celebrate the wide variety of reading opportunities provided by your library or you can use the specific events: Teens' Top Ten and/or Support Teen Literature Day, detailed below.

Teens' Top Ten, http://www.ala.org/yalsa/
teenstopten

The Teens' Top Ten list is created from a list of nominated books by selected teen book groups in schools and public libraries across the country. The list of nominated titles is announced on Support Teen Literature Day and teens, age 12–18, everywhere are encouraged to vote online for their favorites in August and September. Winners are revealed during

Teen Read Week in October. This can be a big or small project. If you start in April, your teens can come up with their own long list of titles they would like to see on an official top ten list. They can challenge each other's choices, defend their own, and vote for a winner in the Fall. Or wait for the short list announced on Support Teen Literature Day and ask the teens to read the entire list over the next few months to be ready for online voting.

Support Teen Literature Day, http:// www .atyourlibrary.org/libraries/support- teen-literature-your-library

YALSA has designated the Thursday of National Library Week as Support Teen Literature Day. Be on the lookout for the Teens' Top Ten nominations and create a display of the titles you already have. Consider any missing titles for purchase. You may also want to post the list on your website or blog for teens who can't make it into the library right away.

Reading Is Fun Week (fourth week in April)

This event may have started to encourage children that reading can be fun, but the focus has widened to include adults celebrating their love of reading as well. Be seen reading, try a new genre of books, and model good reading behavior to those around you. Teens can be asked to think of titles that were suggested to them, and they wound-up loving. Or is there a book they've read in one sitting? What is the one book they would specifically suggest to someone else in their group, including you, that might make you think "Reading is Fun?"

MAY

Get Caught Reading Month, http:// www .getcaughtreading.org/

The Get Caught Reading (GCR) organization wants everyone to remember how much fun it can be to spend some real quality time reading. GCR offers free posters, online videos, and a newsletter to help promote this event. Use the free materials provided to get teens thinking. Prepare yourself with fun reading giveaways. As you go through the day, be watching for teens voluntarily reading and feel free to reward them generously.

Choose Privacy Week, http://www .privacyrevolution.org/

Spend time discussing what it means to have the legal right to search for information on any topic, in print or online. Share the ALA Bill of Rights with your teens. Now turn the discussion over to the teens. Do your teens want to learn without fear of what they are investigating being exposed or questioned? This is a great chance to have your teens become advocates for their own future, have them write to local, statewide, or nationwide leaders to express their thoughts on keeping reading choices private.

JUNE

National Spelling Bee, http://www.spellingbee .com/

The Scripps National Spelling Bee has declared their purpose as helping students become better spellers, add words to their vocabulary, and improve their usage of the English language. A good vocabulary can help teens enjoy reading even more. Why not celebrate the National Spelling Bee by sharing a new word every day? Ask teens to think of interesting ways to find and use new words to peak the curiosity of other patrons.

Anne Frank: Birth Anniversary (June 12)

Born in Frankfurt, Germany, in 1929, Anne Frank is known for the diary she kept while in hiding from the Nazi government. Only 15 at the time of her death, her writings live on to give us all an unique perspective on life. Get your teens thinking about keeping a diary of their own. Help them think of the future, and how they'll feel, reading how they felt as a teen, after becoming adults.

JULY

Clerihew Day (July 10)

A four-line verse that can be autobiographical or biographical but will always start with the subject's name and will always be humorous. This style of poetry was invented by a gentleman named Edmund Clerihew Bentley. Challenge teens to write their own biographical poem, a poem about someone else, or a fictional character. (All accepted forms of Clerihew.)

Paperback Books Anniversary (July 30)

The first paperback, as we know them today, was introduced by the publishing company Penguin. Easy to transport, paperbacks are popular reading, especially with the teen crowd. Why not encourage your teens to head outside with a paperback? Maybe even an assigned summer reading selection? Your TAB might want to group titles together, based on genre or storyline, for other teens to grab and go.

AUGUST

National Scrabble Championship (August 11–15)

The North American Scrabble Players Association organizes the national championship games for avid players. There are levels of competition offered, and smaller tournaments for beginners, but there's plenty to learn from this game and from the people who play competitively. Teens might want to start a tournament to challenge each other, building up to the national level.

SEPTEMBER

International Literacy Day (September 8), http://www.reading.org/General/Conferences/InternationalLiteracyDay.aspx

Even though this event is only given one day on the calendar, teens should be encouraged to think globally, as well as locally, when it comes to the importance of reading. According to the International Reading Association "more than 780 million of the world's adults (nearly two-thirds of whom are women) do not know how to read or write, and between 94 and 115 million children lack access to education." Teens might not realize how lucky they are to have access to so much in the way of recreational and educational materials. Consider having teens raise funds or donate a favorite book for students who are in need. Encourage the teens to send a note explaining their choice.

Banned Books Week (last week of September), http://www.bannedbooksweek.org/

This week is a time to start conversations with adults and teens about what it means to have free and open access to all kinds of materials. It's also the time to discuss when and why books have been challenged or banned in the United States, which can become a fairly surprising exercise. A week that already receives so much attention is easier to build upon, with free materials, media attention, and familiarity amongst all ages. Displays of controversial titles, lists of challenged books with information about why they've been challenged, or asking teens to discuss a challenged book as a group, are all worthwhile ideas.

OCTOBER
Dictionary Day (October 16)

Honoring Noah Webster, creator of the beloved Webster's Dictionary, celebrate the day by expanding your own vocabulary with the dictionary at hand. Can you use that word in a sentence? You might, if you knew what the word meant. Ask teens to find obscure words in the dictionary and create sentences for other students to understand proper usage. Words can be used in display or as blog posting.

The National Day on Writing, http://www.ncte.org/dayonwriting/about

The National Council of Teachers of English (NCTE) would like to draw everyone's attention to how important writing is in all the stages of a person's life. The NCTE has chosen October 20th as the National Day on Writing to provide a specific date to focus on this issue. You can honor their efforts by handing teens a writing challenge. Have your teens tried their hand at reviewing titles yet? This is an excellent time to show teens how they can share their opinions on what they're reading with a well-written book review. Provide guidelines and a place for teens to publish their work.

Teens' Top Ten, http://www.ala.org/yalsa/teenstopten

Nominated titles were announced on Support Teen Literature Day in April, online voting was available during August and September, with the list finally being revealed during Teen Read Week. Post the list that was announced in April and get your teens talking about the books they liked, or disliked. Link to voting on your website or blog and get the kids voting!

Teen Read Week, http://www.ala.org/yalsa/teenreading/trw/trw2011/home

Join librarians in libraries all across the world when you celebrate Teen Read Week with original programming that highlights the joy of pleasure reading. Draw teens in when you show them the variety of free materials they can find on your shelves, just waiting to be discovered. This week can be a bonanza of fun! What can't be done to celebrate teens who read? Displays, giveaways, lists of award winning books, get your TAB to start thinking about how they might like to reward or challenge their class-mates to celebrate reading during these seven days. (Look for free materi-als on YALSA's website.)

NOVEMBER

National Authors' Day (November 1) http://www.answers.com/topic/national-authors-day#ixzz1pyYfzrzn

Started by the General Federation of Women's Club in 1929 and placed on a list of special days to observe by the U.S. Department of Commerce, this day is meant to celebrate American authors and their works. Have teens select one author for the group to celebrate. Research your author, make a collage of important moments in their life, and let the teens come up with ways to share what they've found. This would be a great time to see if the (living) author chosen would respond to direct questions by your teens.

National Novel Writing Month, http://www.nanowrimo.org/

A challenge set forth for all ages, to write an entire novel in one month. This NaNoWrMo organization provides a great deal of assistance to budding writers, and every teen who has any interest writing should be encouraged to sign up. Make it easier for your teens by providing a time, place, and equipment, if you can.

DECEMBER

Melvil Dewey: Birth Anniversary (December 10)

In 1851, in Adams Center, New York, Melvil Dewey was born. Maybe the most famous American librarian of all time, Mr. Dewey designed the

Dewey Decimal Classification system that is still used today. This can be a fabulous segue into the world of nonfiction and how to search by subject. How about a quiz to see if the teens can guess what book would belong with which number range?

And if you still find yourself with a month of the year coming up, and you're looking for something else to try, you can always go to the search engine of your choice, use the terms "author birthday" and the month in question. The result list should provide at least one author you and your teens would like to celebrate through displays, reading group guides, a blog posting, or discussion.

Appendix B

LISTING OF STATE AND PROVINCIAL LIBRARY ASSOCIATIONS

PUBLIC LIBRARY STATE ORGANIZATIONS

Each state has its own method of funding and so some states are better funded than others but they all provide some organization for librarians, old and new, to connect and share ideas. It may be as simple as joining the state organization to get a directory of members and start contacting other teen librarians on your own, or you might have the opportunity to join a teen-specific division of the larger group.

Alabama Library Association
http://allanet.org/displaycommon.cfm?an=1&subarticlenbr=10

Alaska
http://www.akla.org/site-index.html

Arizona
http://azla.org/displaycommon.cfm?an=1&subarticlenbr=138

Arkansas
http://arlib.org/sitemap/

California
http://www.cla-net.org/displaycommon.cfm?an=1&subarticlenbr=2

Colorado
http://www.cal-webs.org/Associations.html

Connecticut
http://ctlibraryassociation.org/about.php

Delaware
http://www2.lib.udel.edu/dla/divisions/index.htm

Florida
http://www.flalib.org/membership.php

Georgia
http://gla.georgialibraries.org/divisions.htm

Hawaii
http://hla.chaminade.edu/about/sections.html

Idaho
http://www.idaholibraries.org/groups

Illinois
http://www.ila.org/forums/library-forums

Indiana
http://www.ilfonline.org/units/ilf-divisions/

Iowa
http://www.iowalibraryassociation.org/

Kansas
http://kslibassoc.org/home/sectionsroundtables/

Kentucky
http://www.kylibasn.org/sections951.cfm

Louisiana
http://www.llaonline.org/sig/

Maine
http://mainelibraries.org/departments/youthservices

Maryland
http://www.mdlib.org/divisions/tig/default.asp

Massachusetts
http://mla.memberlodge.org/yss

Michigan
http://www.mla.lib.mi.us/groups

Minnesota
http://mnlibraryassociation.org/committees-subunits/children-
   and-young-people-s-section/

Mississippi
http://www.misslib.org/index.php/organization/web-site-index/

Missouri
http://molib.org/

Montana
http://www.mtlib.org/

Nebraska
http://www.nebraskalibraries.org/SCYP/scypHome.html

Nevada
http://www.nevadalibraries.org/organization/sections.html

New Hampshire
http://www.nashualibrary.org/YALS/

New Jersey
http://njla.pbworks.com/w/page/12189972/Young-Adult-Services

New Mexico
http://nmla.org/resource-links/

New York
http://www.nyla.org/

North Carolina
http://www.nclaonline.org/yss

North Dakota
http://www.ndla.info/

Ohio
http://www.olc.org/YoungAdult.asp

Oklahoma
http://ola.oklibs.org/organization/Divisions/

Oregon
http://www.olaweb.org/mc/page.do?sitePageId=61034

Pennsylvania
http://palibraries.org/

Rhode Island
http://www.rilibraries.org/

South Carolina
http://www.scla.org/content/youth-services-section

South Dakota
http://sdstatelibrary.com/

Tennessee
http://www.tnla.org/displaycommon.cfm?an=1&subarti
   clenbr=77

Texas
http://www.txla.org/TLA-groups

Utah
http://www.ula.org/content/young-adult-round-table

Vermont
http://www.vermontlibraries.org/sections

Virginia
http://www.vla.org/?page_id=2329

Washington
http://cayas.wla.org/

West Virginia
http://wvla.org/divisions/divisions.html

Wisconsin
http://www.wla.lib.wi.us/yss/

Wyoming
http://www.wyla.org/groups/

CANADIAN LIBRARY ASSOCIATION

This central agency provides a long list of every association in
   Canada.
http://www.cla.ca/AM/Template.cfm?Section=List_of_
   Library_Associations&Template=/CM/HTMLDisplay
   .cfm&ContentID=4697

Canadian Association of Public Libraries
http://www.cla.ca/AM/Template.cfm?Section=CAPL2

Canadian Association for School Libraries
http://www.cla.ca/AM/Template.cfm?Section=CASL2

BY PROVINCE AND TERRITORY

Alberta
Library Association of Alberta (LAA)
http://www.laa.ca/default.aspx

British Columbia
British Columbia Library Association (BCLA)
http://www.bcla.bc.ca/

Manitoba
Manitoba Library Association (MLA)
http://www.mla.mb.ca/

New Brunswick
Association of Professional Librarians of New Brunswick (APLNB)
http://www.abpnb-aplnb.ca/english/index.php

Newfoundland & Labrador
Newfoundland and Labrador Library Association (NLA)
http://staff.library.mun.ca/nlla/

Northwest Territories
Northwest Territories Library Association
http://www.nwtla.nt.ca/membership.html

Nova Scotia
Nova Scotia Library Association (NSLA)
http://nsla.ns.ca/

Nunavut
Nunavut Library Association
http://www.nunavutlibraryassociation.ca/

Ontario
Ontario Library Association (OLA)
http://www.accessola.org/ola_prod/OLAWEB

Prince Edward Island
Prince Edward Island Professional Librarians Association (PEIPLA)
http://peipla.wordpress.com/

Quebec
Quebec Library Association (QLA)
http://www.abqla.qc.ca/

Saskatchewan
Saskatchewan Library Association (SLA)
http://www.lib.sk.ca/

Yukon
Yukon Library Association
http://yukonpubliclawlibrary.pbworks.com/w/page/8370504/
   FrontPage

SCHOOL LIBRARY STATE ORGANIZATIONS

American Association of School Librarians
http://aasl.ala.org/essentiallinks/index.php?title=Professional_
   Development

The AASL has made a State-by-State list available for school
   librarians to make connections with others in similar positions,
   and for the wise public librarian to find their counterparts.

Alabama School Library Association
http://www.alaima.org/

Alaska Association of School Librarians
http://www.akasl.org/

(Arizona) Teacher Librarian Division of Arizona Library Association
http://www.azla.affiniscape.com/

Arkansas Association of Instructional Media
http://aaim.k12.ar.us/

Arkansas Association of School Librarians
http://arlib.org/organization/aasl/index.php

California School Library Association
http://www.csla.net/

Colorado Association of School Libraries (formerly Colorado
   Educational Media Association)
http://cal-webs.org/CASL_.html

Connecticut Association of School Librarians
http://www.ctcasl.com/

Delaware Library Association
http://www2.lib.udel.edu/dla/

Florida Association for Media in Education (FAME)
http://www.floridamedia.org/

Georgia Association for Instructional Technology, Inc
http://www.gait-inc.org/

Georgia Library Media Association, Inc.
http://www.glma-inc.org/

School Library Media Division of the Georgia Library Association
http://gla.georgialibraries.org/div_media.htm

Hawaii Association of School Librarians
http://hasl.ws

Illinois School Library Media Association
http://www.islma.org/

Indiana—Association of Indiana School Library Educators
http://www.ilfonline.org/units/aisle

Iowa Association of School Librarians
http://www.iasl-ia.org/

Kansas Association of School Librarians
http://kasl.typepad.com/kasl/

Kansas Association for Educational Communications and Technology
http://kaect.org/

Kentucky School Media Association
http://www.kysma.org/

Louisiana Association of School Librarians
http://llaonline.org/sig/lasl/

Maine Association of School Libraries
http://www.maslibraries.org/

Maryland Association of School Librarians
http://www.maslmd.org

Massachusetts School Library Media Association
http://www.maschoolibraries.org/

Michigan Association for Media in Education
http://www.mimame.org/

Minnesota Educational Media Organization
http://memotech.ning.com/

Missouri Association of School Librarians
http://www.maslonline.org/

Nebraska Educational Media Association
http://www.schoollibrariesrock.org/

New England School Library Media Association (NESLA)
http://neschoolibraries.org/

New Hampshire School Library Media Association
http://nhslma.org/

New Jersey Association of School Librarians
http://www.njasl.org/

(New York) Section of School Librarians of New York Library
   Association
http://www.nyla.org/page/slms-school-library-media-
   section-301.html

North Carolina Association School Library Media Association
http://www.ncslma.org/

North Carolina Association of School Librarians
http://www.nclaonline.org/ncasl

Ohio Educational Library Media Association
http://www.oelma.org/

Oklahoma School Librarians Division
http://ola.oklibs.org/organization/Divisions/oksl.htm

Oregon Association of School Libraries
https://oasl.memberclicks.net/

Pennsylvania Association for Educational Communications and
   Technology
http://www.paect.org/

Pennsylvania School Librarians' Association
http://www.psla.org/

School Librarians of Rhode Island
http://www.slri.info/

South Carolina Association of School Librarians
http://www.scasl.net/

Tennessee Association of School Librarians
http://www.tasltn.org/

Texas Association of School Librarians
http://www.txla.org/groups/TASL

Utah Educational Library Media Association
http://www.uelma.org/

Vermont School Library Association
https://sites.google.com/site/vermontschoollibraries/

Virginia Association of School Librarians
http://www.vemaonline.org/

Washington Library Media Association
http://www.wlma.org/

Wisconsin Educational Media Association
http://www.wemaonline.org/

Wisconsin Educational Media & Technology Association
http://www.wemtaonline.org/

(Wyoming) Teacher-Librarians Interest Group of Wyoming Library
   Association
https://sites.google.com/site/wlateacherlibrarians/

BIBLIOGRAPHY

"826 Valencia Annual Report, 2010–2011," http://826valencia.org/our-programs/publishing/#tabs-173–0-0 (cited March 27, 2012).

AASL (American Association of School Librarians). "Standards for the 21st Century Learner," http://www.ala.org/aasl/guidelinesandstandards/learningstandards/standards (cited May 2, 2012).

AASL (American Association of School Librarians). "Tweets," http://twitter.com/#!/AASL (cited April 1, 2012).

AASL/ALSC/YALSA. "School/Public Library Cooperation," http://wikis.ala.org/readwriteconnect/index.php/AASL/ALSC/YALSA_School/Public_Library_Cooperation (cited May 2, 2012).

ALA (American Library Association). "ALA News," http://twitter.com/alanews (cited April 1, 2012).

ALA (American Library Association). "Michael L. Printz Award Winners," http://www.ala.org/ala/mgrps/divs/yalsa/booklistsawards/printzaward/Printz.cfm

ALA (American Library Association). "Programming Librarian," http://www.programminglibrarian.org/library/programs.html (cited February 29, 2012).

ALA (American Library Association). "Public Library Visits to Schools: Linda L. Homa," http://wikis.ala.org/readwriteconnect/index.php/Public_Library_Visits_to_Schools.

ALA (American Library Association). "School/Public Library Partnerships Bibliography," http://wikis.ala.org/readwriteconnect/index.php/School/Public_Library_Partnerships_Bibliography (cited May 18, 2011).

ALAN (Assembly on Literature for Adolescents). http://www.alan-ya.org/2010/08/alans-picks-july-2010-6/

ALAN (Assembly on Literature for Adolescents). "ALAN Awards," http://community.alan-ya.org/ALANYA/ALAN/ALANAwards/ (cited February 29, 2012).

ALSC (Association for Library Service to Children). "School/public Library Cooperative Programs," http://www.ala.org/ala/mgrps/divs/alsc/externalrelationships/coopacts/schoolplcoopprogs.cfm (cited May 18, 2011).

Adams, Suellen S. "Marketing the Homework Center Digitally." *Young Adult Library Services* 8, no. 2 (2010): 11–12.

"Activities: History as Story," http://www2.ed.gov/pubs/parents/History/Story.html (cited May 18, 2011).

Agosto, Denise E., and Sandra Hughes-Hassell. *Urban Teens in the Library: Research and Practice.* Chicago, IL: ALA, 2010.

Alessio, Amy J., and Kimberly A. Patton. *A Year of Programs for Teens 2.* Chicago, IL: ALA, 2011.

Anderson, Cynthia, and Kathi Knop. "Go Where the Grants Are." *Library Media Connection* 27, no. 1 (2008): 10–14.

Anderson, Sheila B. *Extreme Teens: Library Services to Nontraditional Young Adults.* Westport, CT: Libraries Unlimited, 2005.

Aptowicz, Cristin O'Keefe. *Words in Your Face: A Guided Tour Through Twenty Years of the New York City Poetry Slam.* New York: Soft Skull, 2008.

Asher, Jay. "Th1rteen R3asons Why." http://www.thirteenreasonswhy.com/ (cited May 18, 2011).

Auxier, Tiffany. "Hundreds of High School Students Study at the Library." In Smallwood, Carol, ed. *Librarians As Community Partners: An Outreach Handbook.* Chicago, IL: ALA, 2010, 48–51.

"Award-winning Poet Visits Rocky River High School." *Westlife* (March 5, 2008): 14B.

Bell, Steven. "A Conference Wherever You Are." *Library Journal* 136, no. 16 (2011): 28–31.

Benedum, Sheila, and Cathy Schultis. "Building Strong Partnership between School & Public Libraries." PowerPoint presentation. 2001. Modified December 5, 2005.

Benedum, Sheila, and Cathy Schultis. "Parents as Partners: Homework Help @ Home." PowerPoint Presentation to the West Shore Librarian's group, 2001. Modified August 17, 2009.

Berry III, John N. "Transformed by Teamwork." *Library Journal* 137, no. 2 (2012): 20–23.

Braun, Linda W. "The Lowdown on STEM." *American Libraries* 42, no. 9/10 (September/October 2011): 60.

Brown, Carol. "America's Most Wanted: Teachers Who Collaborate." *Teacher Librarian* 32, no. 1 (October 2004): 13–19.

Brown, Carol, Lana Dotson, and Elaine Yontz. "Professional Development for School Library Media Professionals." *TechTrends* 55, no. 4 (2011): 56–62.

Brown, Margaret. "Teen Advisory Board (TAB)." In Tuccillo, Diane P., ed. *Library Teen Advisory Groups.* Lanham, MD: VOYA Guides, Scarecrow Press, 2005, 139–40.

Brozo, William G. *To be a Boy, to be a Reader: Engaging Teen and Preteen Boys in Active Literacy*. Newark, DE: International Reading Association, 2010.

Brunswick, Kate. Email interview by Cherie Pandora, 2012, Columbus, OH.

Byrne, Richard. "Planning Common Core Lessons? Help Is Here." *School Library Journal* 59, no. 1 (2013): 22–28.

Catalano, Lee, Catherine Carroll, Kiva Liljequist, and Susan Smallsreed. "It's as Simple as a Phone Call." *OLA (Oregon Library Association) Quarterly* 15, no. 4 (2010): 4–7.

Chapman, Jan. "The Care and Feeding of a TAB." In Tuccillo, Diane P., ed. *Library Teen Advisory Groups*. Lanham, MD: VOYA Guides, Scarecrow Press, 2005, 152–53.

Chilcote, Lee. "Lake Erie Ink Inks Deal for Coventry School." *Freshwater* (September 1, 2011). http://www.freshwatercleveland.com/devnews/lakeerieink 090111.aspx (cited March 15, 2012).

Chudnov, Daniel. "Show Me the Budget." *Computers in Libraries* 31, no. 3 (September 2008): 28–29.

Church, Audrey P. "Definitely NOT Alone! Online Resources and Websites Help Keep School Librarians Connected." *Knowledge Quest* 40, no. 2 (2011): 36–39.

"Club Penguin," http://www.clubpenguin.com/ (cited April 15, 2012).

"College Board Resume Writing," http://www.collegeboard.com/student/plan/ high-school/36957.html (cited April 15, 2012).

Collett, Amy. "Practical Tips to Help the Collaborative Process Work More Effectively in the School Library Media Program." *Library Media Connection* 26, no. 4 (2008): 20.

Colpi, Emily. Phone interview by Cherie Pandora. July 29, 2012. Mariemont, OH.

Cox, Marge. "10 Tips for budgeting." *Library Media Connection* 26, no. 4 (January 2008): 24–25.

Cuffe-Perez, Mary. "Story Quilt." *American Libraries* 39, no. 3 (2008): 50–52.

Cuyahoga County Public Library. "Free Homework Centers," http://www .cuyahogalibrary.org/HomeworkCenters.aspx (cited March 27, 2012).

Dees, Dianne, Alisande Mayer, Heather Morin, and Elaine Willis. "Librarians as Leaders in Professional Learning Communities through Technology, Literacy, and Collaboration." *Library Media Connection* 29, no. 2 (October 2010): 10–13.

DelGuidice, Margaux. "Are You Overlooking a Valuable Resource? A Practical Guide to Collaborating with Your Greatest Ally: The Public Library." *Library Media Connection* 27, no. 6 (May/June 2009): 38–39.

"Disney," http://www.disney.go.com/games/ (cited April 15, 2012).

Dominican University. "The Dominican Study: Public Library Summer Reading Programs Close the Reading Gap," http://www.dom.edu/newsroom/ press/2010/august/article_0001.html

Dowd, Nancy, Mary Evangeliste, and Jonathan Silberman. *Bite-Sized Marketing: Realistic Solutions for the Overworked Librarian*. Chicago, IL: ALA, 2010.

"Drug Abuse Resistance Education. D.A.R.E.," http://www.dare.com/home/ default.asp (cited May 18, 2011).

EdTech Teacher Inc. "Best of History Web Sites," http://www.besthistorysites .net/ (cited April 15, 2012).

Farkas, Meredith. *Social Software in Libraries: Building Collaboration, Communication, and Community Online.* Medford, NJ: Information Today, 2007.

Fletcher, Adam. "Ladder of Youth Voice," http://www.freechild.org/ladder.htm (cited March 21, 2012).

Flowers, Sarah. *Young Adults Deserve the Best: YALSA's Competencies in Action.* Chicago, IL: ALA, 2011.

Foundation Center. "Wisdom Exchange Project Outline: Proposal Writing Basics," http://www.yep.cohhio.org/pdf/Grantsmanship061208/FCblue.pdf (cited February 28, 2011).

Fredrick, Kathy. "Musings about Moodle Continued." *School Library Monthly* 27, no. 4 (2011): 40–41.

Fredrick, Kathy. Personal interview with Cherie Pandora. March 21, 2012. Shaker Heights, OH.Fredrick, Kathy. "Resource Roundup for Your Personal Learning Network." *School Library Monthly* 27, no. 1 (2010): 38–39.

"Free Yahoo Games," http://games.yahoo.com/free-games (cited April 15, 2012).

Fresno County Public Library. "Read Watch Listen," http://www.fresnolibrary.org/teen/hc/schools/html (cited February 27, 2012).

Gallaway, Beth. *Game On! Gaming at the Library.* New York: Neal-Schuman Publishers, 2009.

Geever, Jane C., and Patricia McNeill. *Guide to Proposal Writing.* New York: Foundation Center, 1993.

Georges, Fitzgerald. "Information Literacy, Collaboration, and 'Killer Apps': New Challenges for Media Specialists." *Library Media Connection* 23, no. 2 (2004): 34–35.

Gilton, Donna L. "Information Literacy as a Department Store: Applications for Public Teen Librarians." *Young Adult Library Services* 6, no. 2 (Winter 2008): 39–44.

Glazner, Gary Mex, ed. *Poetry Slam: The Competitive Art of Performance Poetry.* San Francisco, CA: Manic D. Press, 2000, 11–21.

Godwin, Peter, and Jo Parker, ed. *Information Literacy Meets Library 2.0.* London: Facet Publishing, 2008.

Golden, Susan L. *Secrets of Successful Grantsmanship: A Guerrilla Guide to Raising Money.* San Francisco, CA: Jossey-Bass Publishers, 1997.

Gorman, Michele. "Getting Graphic! Comics in the Curriculum: Math, Science, and History." *Library Media Connection* 28, no. 3 (November/December 2009): 36.

Gorman, Michael. "The Indispensability of School Libraries (and School Librarians)." President's Message. *American Libraries* 36, no. 9 (October 2005): 5.

Gorman, Michael. *Our Singular Strengths: Meditations for Librarians.* Chicago, IL: ALA, 1998.

Gray, Elana, and Catherine E. Wilkins. *Investigating Opportunities for School-Public Library Cooperation Involving Boards of Education, Public Library Boards.* Mississauga, ON: Peel Board of Education, 1997.

Hand, Dorcas. "Adolescent Literacies: Reading, Thinking, Writing." *Knowledge Quest* 35, no. 1 (September/October 2006): 40–43 (cited May18, 2011).

Hakala-Ausperk, Catherine. *Be a Great Boss: One Year to Success.* Chicago, IL: ALA, 2011.

Hamilton, Buffy J. "Pivots for Change: Libraries and Librarians." *Library Media Connection* 28, no. 6 (2010): 54–56.

Hampton Bays Public Library. HBay Teen Services. "Blog," http://hbayya.blog spot.com/ (cited February 29, 2012).

Hart, Roger A. *Children's Participation: From Tokenism to Citizenship.* Florence: UNICEF, 1992, 8.

Heeger, Paula Brehm. "A Tie for Third Place." *School Library Journal* 52, no. 7 (2006): 27.

Hellmich, Nanci. "Social Media Websites Can Help and Harm Kids." *USA Today* (March 28, 2011). http://www.usatoday.com/yourlife/parenting-family/2011–03–28-pediatrics28_ST_N.htm?csp = 34 (cited April 15, 2012).

Henrico County Public Library. "Teen Stuff. Quick Picks," http://www.henricolibrary.org/teens/b&a_quickpicks.html (cited May 18, 2011).

Holtslander, Linda. "Loudoun County Public Library: Try Poetry 2010." *Virginia Libraries* 57, no. 2 (2011): 5–12.

"Home School Legal Defense Association (HSLDA)," http://www.hslda.org/orgs/Default.aspx (cited September 29, 2012).

Honnold, RoseMary. *101+ Teen Programs that work.* New York: Neal-Schuman Publishers, 2003.

Honnold, RoseMary. *Get Connected: Tech Programs for Teens.* New York: Neal-Schuman Publishers, 2007.

Honnold, RoseMary. "See YA Around: Library Programming for Teens," http://www.cplrmh.com/ (cited February 29, 2012).

Institute of Museum and Library Services. "Grants to States," http://www.imls.gov/programs/allotments.shtm (cited February 28, 2011).

"IPL2: Information You Can Trust," http://www.ipl.org/ (cited April 15, 2012).

IPL2, Internet Public Library. "Clubs and Organizations (Programming Ideas)," http://www.ipl.org/IPLBrowse/GetSubject?vid=10&cid=2&tid=2630&parent=0 (cited February 29, 2012).

IXL. "Sixth Grade Math Practice," http://www.ixl.com/math/grade-6 (cited March 27, 2012).

Jasany, Nancy. Email interview with Cherie Pandora, April 3, 2012, Cleveland, OH.

Jones, Ella W. *Start to Finish Young Adult Programs: Hip-Hop Symposiums, Summer Reading Programs Virtual Tours, Poetry Slams, Teen Advisory Boards, Term Paper Clinics and More.* New York: Neal-Schuman Publishers, 2009.

Jones, Patrick, Michele Gorman, and Tricia Suellentrop. *Connecting Young Adults and Libraries: A How-to-Do-It Manual.* 4th ed. New York: Neal-Schuman Publishers, 2009.

Jones, Patrick, Joel Shoemaker, and Mary K. Chelton. *Do It Right! Best Practices for Serving Young Adults in School and Public Libraries.* New York: Neal-Schuman Publishers, 2001.

Jones, Patrick, Joel Shoemaker, and Mary K. Chelton. *New Directions for Library Service to Young Adults.* Chicago, IL: ALA, 2002.

Karabush, Cynthia, and Pam Pleviak. "Talk Me Off the Ledge: Surviving Solo Librarianship." *Knowledge Quest* 40, no. 2 (2011): 48–53.

Katz, Jeff. "A Common Purpose: Public/School Library Cooperation and Collaboration." *Public Libraries* 48, no. 3 (2009): 28–31.

Keeter, Scott, and Paul Taylor. "The Millennials." PEW Research Center. http://pewresearch.org/pubs/1437/millennials-profile (cited February 22, 2012).

Kenney, Brian. "Imagine This." *School Library Journal* 51, no. 12 (2005): 53–55.

Kniffel, Leonard. "From Cradle to Grave: A Lifetime in Libraries." *American Libraries* (September 2005): 33, http://search.ebscohost.com/login

.aspx?direct=true&AuthType=cookie,ip,uid,url&db=aph&AN=18140636& site=ehost-live&scope=site (cited May 24, 2013).

Krashen, Stephen D. *The Power of Reading: Insights from the Research*. Westport, CT: Libraries Unlimited, 2004.

Kunzel, Bonnie, and Constance Hardesty. *The Teen-Centered Book Club: Readers into Leaders*. Westport, CT: Libraries Unlimited, 2006.

LM_NET. "Where School Librarians Connect," http://lmnet.wordpress.com/ (cited April 1, 2012).

Lake Erie Link. "A Writing Space for Youth," http://lakeerieink.org/ (cited March 15, 2012).

Lawrence, Kathy. Phone interview by Cherie Pandora, March 12, 2012. Cleveland Heights, OH.

Lenhart, Amanda. "PEW Internet and American Life Project: Teens, Smartphones and Texting," http://pewinternet.org/topics/Teens.aspx (cited April 15, 2012).

Lenhart, Amanda, M. Madden, A. Smith, K. Purcell, K. Zickuhr, and L. Rainie. "PEW Internet and American Life Project: Teens, Kindness and Cruelty on Social Network Sites," http://www.pewinternet.org/Reports/2011/Teens-and-social-media.aspx (cited April 15, 2012).

Levin, Nancy. Phone interview by Cherie Pandora, January 13, 2012. Cleveland, OH.

Library of Congress (for all ages). http://www.loc.gov/families/ (cited April 15, 2012).

Lichman, George. Interview with Stacey Hayman. March 17, 2012. Rocky River, OH.

Lodge, Missy. Email interview with Cherie Pandora, April 3, 2012, Columbus, OH.

Lodge, Missy. "Steps to Writing a Successful LSTA Mini-Grant." *OELMA News* (2011): 2–3.

Lodge, Sally. "Spotlighting YA." *Publishers Weekly* 258, no. 40 (2011): 24.

"Louder Than a Bomb," http://www.louderthanabombfilm.com (cited March 15, 2012).

MacDonald, Cynthia. "Public Libraries + School Libraries = Smart Partnerships." *CSLA Journal* 30, no. 2 (Spring 2007): 11–12. http://search.ebscohost.com/ login.aspx?direct=true&AuthType=cookie,ip,uid,url&db=aph&AN=24894 248&site=ehost-live&scope=site (cited May 24, 2013).

Massachusetts Institute of Technology (MIT), Global Education and Career Development. "Find a Job/Internship," http://gecd.mit.edu/jobs/find/apply/ interview (cited April 25, 2012).

"The Math Forum," http://mathforum.org/dr.math/ (cited April 15, 2012).

McNally, Joanna. Personal interview with Cherie Pandora, February 9, 2012. Cleveland, OH.Mercier, Jean M. "Cooperation Between School Library Media Centers and Public Libraries." Master's Thesis. Mankato State University, 1991.

Messner, Kate. "Kate's Book Blog. Authors Who Skype with Classes and Book Clubs," http://kmessner.livejournal.com/106020.html (cited February 22, 2012).

Messner, Kate. "Met Any Good Authors Lately?" *School Library Journal* 55, no. 8 (2009): 36–38. http://www.schoollibraryjournal.com/article/CA6673572 .html (cited February 22, 2012).

Meyers, Elaine, and Virginia A. Walter. "Talk to Teens: They're Still Listening." *American Libraries* 42, no. 9/10 (September/October 2011): 37–39.

Mezger, Roger. "Small print sidetracks grant request." *The Plain Dealer* (April 3, 2003). http://www.cleveland.com/westnile/index.ssf?/westnile/more/10 49365919137010.html (cited February 28, 2011).

Mikhail, Dunya. *The War Works Hard.* New York: New Directions Publishing Corp., 2005.

MindTools. "SWOT Analysis Worksheet," http://www.mindtools.com/pages/article/worksheets/SWOTAnalysisWorksheet.pdf (cited April 24, 2012).

Mitchell, Connie. "Schools Can Have Advisory Groups, Too! Writers and Readers Advisory Panel (WRAP). "In Tuccillo, Diane P., ed. *Library Teen Advisory Groups.* Lanham, MD: VOYA Guides, Scarecrow Press, 2005, 133.

Mulder, Natalie. "Encouraging Community Service in the Public Library." *Young Adult Library Services* 10, no. 1 (2011): 25–27.

Multnomah County Library. "Bucket of Books," http://www.multcolib.org/schoolcorps/bucket.html (cited February 27, 2012).

Mulvihill, Amanda. "Ask a Librarian." *Computers in Libraries* 31, no. 9 (2011): 40.

Murvosh, Marta. "Partners in Success." *School Library Journal* 59, no. 1 (2013): 22–28.

NASA (for grades 5–8). http://www.nasa.gov/audience/forstudents/5–8/fea tures/homework-topics-index.html (cited April 15, 2012).

NASA (for grades 5–8). http://www.nasa.gov/audience/forstudents/5–8/multi media/funandgames_archive_1.html (cited April 15, 2012).

NASA (for grades 9–12). http://www.nasa.gov/audience/forstudents/9–12/A-Z/index.html (cited April 15, 2012).

NATI (National Association of Teen Institutes). "Teen Institute," http://www.tee ninstitute.org/NEW%20SITE/site/ (cited February 22, 2012).

National Suicide Prevention Lifeline. "With Help Comes Hope," http://www.sui cidepreventionlifeline.org/ (cited February 22, 2012).

Nesi, Olga. The Public Library Connection. *School Library Journal* 58, no. 12 (2012): 20.

New York Times Best Sellers. http://www.nytimes.com/pages/books/best seller/

Nichols, C. Allen, ed. *Thinking Outside the Book: Alternatives for Today's Teen Library Collections.* Westport, CT: Libraries Unlimited, 2004.

Nichols, Mary Anne. *Merchandising Library Materials to Young Adults.* Westport, CT: Libraries Unlimited, 2002.

Nowak, Kristine. "Serving Teens in the Public Library." *Kentucky Libraries* 75, no. 3 (2011): 611.

O'Dell, Katie. *Library Materials and Services for Teen Girls.* Westport, CT: Libraries Unlimited, 2002, 101–19.

Office of Juvenile Justice and Delinquency Prevention. "Appendix A: National Child Protection Act of 1993," http://www.ojjdp.gov/pubs/guidelines/appen-a.html (cited March 27, 2012).

Oliver, Jo. "A Practical Partnership: Library, Museum and Family History Society Cooperation in Camden NSW." *Aplis* 24, no. 4 (2011): 167–71.

OneLook Dictionary, http://onelook.com (cited April 15, 2012).

Ontl, Margaret. "Noted Young Adult Literature Author visits Hudson High School." *Hudson Star-Observer* (April 15, 2011). http://www.hudsonstarob server.com/event/article/id/42623/ (cited February 22, 2012).

Ott, Valerie A. *Teen Programs With Punch.* Westport, CT: Libraries Unlimited, 2006.

Owens, Theresa, and Jackie Dunn. "Super Projects for Super Teens!" *VOYA* 34, no. 4 (2011): 340.

PEW Research Center. "Trend Data for Teens: Teen Gadget Ownership," http://www.pewinternet.org/Static-Pages/Trend-Data-for-Teens/Teen-Gadget-Ownership.aspx (cited April 15, 2012).

Parkes, Dave, and Geoff Walton, ed. *Web 2.0 and Libraries: Impacts, Technologies and Trends.* Oxford: Chandos Publishing, 2010.

Payne, Mary Ann. *Grant Writing DeMystified: Hard Stuff Made Easy.* Dubuque, IA: McGraw-Hill, 2011.

Pearson Foundation. "National Student Mock Election," http://www.national mockelection.org/curriculum/ (cited September 29, 2012).

Perez, Lisa. "Innovative Professional Development: Expanding Your Professional Learning Network." *Knowledge Quest* 40, no. 3 (2012): 20–22.

Pierce, Jennifer Burek. *Sex, Brains, and Video Games: A Librarian's Guide to Teens in the Twenty-first Century.* Chicago, IL: ALA, 2008, 50–59.

Poetry Alive. "PoetryAlive! Assembly Show Syllabus," http://poetryalive.com/services/shows/current_shows.html (cited March 15, 2012).

Pogo.com (You are not required to register, but must be 18 if you want to create an account). http://www.pogo.com/ (cited April 15, 2012).

Project for Public Spaces. "Ray Oldenburg," http://www.pps.org/articles/rolden burg/ (cited March 15, 2012).

Project Smart. Hughey, Duncan. "SMART Goals," http://www.projectsmart.co.uk/smart-goals.html (cited February 28, 2011).

The Public Library of Cincinnati and Hamilton County. "Teenspace. Books and Reading," http://teenspace.cincinnatilibrary.org/books/ (cited February 22, 2012).

PUBYAC (Public Librarians Serving Young Adults and Children). "Our Mission," http://pubyac.org/ (cited April 1, 2012).

Quinn, Anne. "School and Public Library Collaboration in Washington Court House, State Library of Ohio." *The News.* November 2010.

"Read Across America: An NEA Project," http://www.readacrossamerica.org/ (cited March 15, 2012).

Repp, Anne. "Thanks-a-Latte, Seniors: the Library Hosts an Election Day Event." *Library Media Connection* 28, no. 3 (November/December 2009): 16–17.

Riddle, Carmen. Phone interview with Cherie Pandora. March 28, 2012. Marysville, OH.

Ritzo, Christopher, Chaebong Nam, and Bertram (Chip) Bruce. "Building a Strong Web: Connecting Information Spaces in Schools and Communities." *Library Trends* 58, no. 1 (2009): 82–94.

Rondeau, Vicki. "Community Partnerships = A+." *CSLA Journal* 30, no. 2 (Spring 2007): 15–16. http://web.ebscohost.com/ehost/detail?sid=57144ab9-a4f3-4040-8df1-fed3200a7df1%40sessionmgr10&vid=1&hid=27&bdata=JkF1d GhUeXBlPWNvb2tpZSxpcCx1aWQsdXJsJnNpdGU9ZWhvc3QtbGl2ZSZ zY29wZT1zaXRl#db=aph&AN=24894249 (cited May 24, 2013).

Rosen, Larry D. with Mark Carrier and Nancy Cheever. *Rewired: Understanding the iGeneration and the Way They Learn.* New York: Palgrave Macmillan, 2010.

Rowland, Martha. "Partnerships Mean Active Participation." *CSLA Journal* 30, no. 2 (Spring 2007): 4. http://web.ebscohost.com/ehost/detail?sid=d0a9cd 97-d325-444a-946e-0ab821c8944a%40sessionmgr12&vid=1&hid=27&bdata= JkF1dGhUeXBlPWNvb2tpZSxpcCx1aWQsdXJssJnNpdGU9ZWhvc3QtbGl2 ZSZzY29wZT1zaXRl#db=aph&AN=24894246 (cited May 24, 2013).

Rutherford, Dawn. "Building Strong Community Partnerships: Sno-Isle Libraries and the Teen project." *Young Adult Library Services* 9, no. 1 (2010): 23–25.

Schaffner, Judith. "Yo! I Stumped the Librarian!" *School Library Journal* 41, no. 8 (August 1995): 42.

Scholastic. "The Stacks," http://www.scholastic.com/kids/stacks/games/ (cited April 15, 2012).

Scordato, Julie. "A Tale of Two Libraries: School and Public Librarians Working Together." *Library Media Connection* 22, no. 7 (April/May 2004): 32–33.

Scott, W. Clayton. "Slamming Arkansas Schools!" *Teaching Artist Journal* 8, no. 2 (2010): 88–95.

Search Institute. "40 Developmental Assets for Adolescents (ages 12–18)," http:// www.search-institute.org/system/files/40AssetsList.pdf (cited May 18, 2011).

Shaffner, Judith. "Yo! I Stumped the Librarian!" *School Library Journal* 41, no. 8 (1995): 42.

Shoemaker, Joel. "Evaluating Customer Service." In Jones, Patrick, and Joel Shoe-maker, eds. *Do It Right! Best Practices for Serving Young Adults in School and Public Libraries.* New York: Neal-Schuman, 2001.

Simpson, Martha Seif, and Lucretia I. Duwel. *Bringing Classes into the Public Library.* Jefferson, NC: McFarland, 2007.

Siu-Runyan, Yvonne. "Public and School Libraries in Decline: When We Need Them." *The Council Chronicle, The National Council of Teachers of English* 21, no. 1 (2011): 28–29.

Smallwood, Carol, ed. *The Frugal Librarian: Thriving in Tough Economic Times.* Chicago, IL: ALA, 2011.

Smallwood, Carol, ed. *Librarians as Community Partners: An Outreach Handbook.* Chicago, IL: ALA, 2010.

Smith, Bob. Phone interview with Cherie Pandora. March 26, 2012, Medina, OH.

Somers-Willett, Susan B. A. *The Cultural Politics of Slam Poetry: Race, Identity, and the Performance of Popular Verse in America.* Ann Arbor, MI: University of Michigan Press, 2009, 141–51.

Squires, Tasha. *Library Partnerships: Making Connections Between School And Public Libraries.* Medford, NJ: Information Today, Inc., 2009.

Students Against Destructive Decisions. "Welcome to SADD," http://www.sadd .org/ (cited February 22, 2012).

Story Quilt: Poems of a Place. Galway, NY: Galway Public Library, 2007.

Streen, Milena. Phone interview with Cherie Pandora. July 27, 2011. Cleveland, OH.

Suellentrop, Tricia. "Get out of the Library!" *School Library Journal* 52, no. 9 (September 2006): 39.

Taracuk, Krista, and Heidi Fletcher. "Building Partnerships." *Ohio Media Spectrum* 61, no. 1 (Spring 2009): 36–42.

TeacherVision. "Multiple Intelligences Chart," http://www.teachervision.fen.com/ intelligence/teaching-methods/2204.html (cited May 1, 2012).

Todd, Ross. "A Question of Evidence." *Knowledge Quest* 37, no. 2 (November/December 2008): 16–21.

Tuccillo, Diane P. *Library Teen Advisory Groups.* Lanham, MD: VOYA Guides, Scarecrow Press, 2005.

Tuccillo, Diane P. *Teen-Centered Library Service: Putting Youth Participation into Practice.* Santa Barbara, CA: ABC-CLIO, 2010.

U.S. Census Bureau. "American Factfinder," http://factfinder2.census.gov/faces/nav/jsf/pages/index.xhtml (cited April 15, 2012).

U.S. Government. IRS. "Exemption Requirements IRS 501 (c)(3) Organizations," http://www.irs.gov/charities/charitable/article/0,,id=96099,00.html (cited February 22, 2012).

VOYA (Voice of Youth Advocates). "Best Non-fiction Books for Teens," http://us.macmillan.com/MacmillanSite/categories/Childrens/ProfessionalJournalBestBookAwards/VOYAsNonfictionHonorList (cited February 22, 2012).

VOYA (Voice of Youth Advocates). "Best Science Fiction, Fantasy and Horror List," http://us.macmillan.com/MacmillanSite/categories/Childrens/ProfessionalJournalBestBookAwards/VOYAsBestScienceFictionFantasyand Horror (cited February 22, 2012).

VOYA (Voice of Youth Advocates). "NonFiction Honor List 2010," http://www.voya.com/wp-content/uploads/2011/06/nonfiction_honorlist.pdf (cited February 29, 2012).

VOYA (Voice of Youth Advocates). "Top Shelf Fiction for Middle School Readers 2010," http://www.voya.com/wp-content/uploads/2011/06/top_shelf_fiction.pdf (cited February 29, 2012).

Vaillancourt, Renée. *Bare Bones Young Adult Services: Tips for Public Library Generalists.* Chicago, IL: ALA, 2000.

Valenza, Joyce Kasman. "The Virtual Library." *Educational Leadership* 63, no. 3 (2005): 54–59.

Vittek, Robyn E. "The People in Your Neighborhood: Using Local Collaboration to Advocate for Teen Patrons." *Young Adult Library Services* 9, no. 1 (2010): 13–14.

Walter, Virginia A. *Output Measure and More: Planning and Evaluating Public Library Services for Young Adults.* Chicago, IL: ALA, 1995.

Weber, Ann. "NextGen: Best Tool for 21st Century School Librarians." *Library Media Connection* 26, no 4, (2008): 54–55.

Wepking, Mary. "From Communication to Cooperation to Collaboration: School and Public Librarians as Partners for Student Success." *Library Media Connection* 28, no. 3 (2009): 24–26.

Western Reserve Academy. "Summer Reading," http://www.wra.net/page.cfm?p = 618 (cited February 29, 2012).

Whalen, Tomi. "Teenagers and a Space of Their Own." Review of Taney, Kimberly Bolan. *Teen Spaces: The Step-by-Step Library Makeover.* Chicago, IL: ALA, 2003.

Wilson, Stu. "Saint Paul's Strategic Plan." *Library Journal* 130, no. 1 (2005): 34–37.

Woodard, Mary. "Supporting Solo at the District Level." *Knowledge Quest* 40, no. 2 (2011): 44–46.

YALSA (Young Adult Library Services Association). "Best Books for Young Adults," http://www.ala.org/ala/mgrps/divs/yalsa/booklistsawards/bestbooksya/bbyahome.cfm (cited February 29, 2012).

YALSA (Young Adult Library Services Association). "The Michael L. Printz Award for Excellence in Young Adult Literature," http://www.ala.org/ala/mgrps/divs/yalsa/booklistsawards/printzaward/Printz.cfm (cited February 29, 2012).

YALSA (Young Adult Library Services Association). Professional Development Center. Professional Development Topics. "School and Public Library Cooperation," http://www.ala.org/ala/mgrps/divs/yalsa/profdev/schoolpublic.cfm (cited May 18, 2011).

YALSA (Young Adult Library Services Association). "YALSA Award for Excellence in Nonfiction for Young Adults," http://www.ala.org/yalsa/nonfiction/ (cited February 22, 2012).

YALSA (Young Adult Library Services Association). "YALSA's Teens' Top Ten," http://www.ala.org/ala/mgrps/divs/yalsa/teenreading/teenstopten/teenstopten.cfm (cited February 22, 2012).

Young, Robyn R. "Eight Easy Steps to Maintain and Increase the Library Media Center Budget." *Library Media Connection* 26, no. 4 (January 2008): 26–27.

Zalusky, Steve. "Winners of the 2011 John Cotton Dana Library Public Relations Awards," http://americanlibrariesmagazine.org/news/ala/winners-2011-john-cotton-dana-library-public-relations-awards (cited March 15, 2012).

INDEX

ABOUT THE AUTHORS

CHERIE P. PANDORA, MLS, Ed. Spec., is an instructor at Bryant and Stratton College, Akron, Ohio, where she teaches a beginning research class. She was a teacher and school librarian for 35 years teaching first in Parma, Ohio, and later serving as the high school librarian and library coordinator at Rocky River High School, Rocky River, Ohio. Since retiring from school librarianship in 2010 she has worked as a library consultant and writer. Her published works for the *Ohio Media Spectrum* include "Using TRAILS for Data-Driven Decision-Making" (Spring 2011), "STEM: How Libraries Provide STEM Information" (Spring 2009), and "Grantwriting Made Easy" (Winter 2002). She is a frequent presenter at state conferences on subjects that include the Transition from High School to College Level Research, creating a Master Teacher portfolio, and forging collaborations between teachers and librarians and between school librarians and academic librarians. Pandora holds an educational specialist degree in Staff and Personnel from Cleveland State University, Cleveland, Ohio, an MLS degree from Kent State University, Kent, Ohio, and a BS in education from Miami University in Oxford, Ohio.

STACEY HAYMAN, MLS, a former YA librarian, has been working at Rocky River Public Library for over 15 years but still finds herself surprised by what each day brings. Although she's no longer directly responsible for the teens, Stacey continues to enjoy their unique and irrepressible energy. She gladly shares her experience and time to help provide a positive experience for teen patrons at her library. Being accepted as a reviewer for *Voice of Youth Advocates* (*VOYA*) and *Library Journal,* in 2006 and 2007, respectively, made the avid reader in Stacey quite happy. Contributing content to Reader's Advisor Online database gave Stacey another outlet for connecting the right books with the right readers. Selected as Committee Chair for VOYA's Nonfiction Honor List for the years 2008 and 2009, this experience was more than an exciting challenge, it was also a great opportunity to strengthen community relationships. In 2011, she started a regularly appearing online column for VOYA magazine featuring author interviews entitled "Wouldn't You Like to Know. . ." Appointed to the Notable Books Council in 2013, Stacey is eager to see what the next chapter will bring.